MW00904349

Dietary patterns of low overall quality are the single leading p
mortality and chronic morbidity in the modern world. No nutrient can remedy
that. Changing dietary patterns so they routinely promote rather than undermine
health means changing food choices, meal selection, daily routines, and the skill
sets – especially **cooking** – on which they rely. The emergence of "culinary
medicine" where once only biochemistry prevailed is testimony to this shift in
problem, solution, and the primacy of the actionable and pragmatic. **This textbook**
- with a focus on cultivating a discrete set of skills to be practiced, and paid forward
through teaching- **takes its place among the important and promising advances in
the vanguard of public health nutrition**. If the potential of diet – to add years to
lives, life to years and help sustain the vitality of our planet – is to be fulfilled it will
owe much to the widespread uptake of the crucial lessons found in the Culinary
Medicine Textbook.

David Katz MD, MPH, FACPM, FACP, FACLM

**Kuddos to Dr Deb for getting both chefs and nutrition scientists to the table to
create a masterpiece**. The Culinary Medicine Textbook lists the essential
culinary skills that are required to be able to eat and ENJOY a healthy diet. Anyone
can learn how to cook; it takes practice and a sense of humor to learn from
mistakes. Deliciously eat your way towards health.

Chef Cat Cora

My dad understood that all life begins in the soil and that healthy soil leads to
healthy plants, which leads to healthy people and a healthy planet; it is the only
way we can literally save ourselves from ourselves! Dr. Deb truly understands this
and has put together an incredible work combining nutrition science and the
culinary arts by bringing together chefs with nutrition scientists. **Both are pioneers
in their own righ**t – helping people to eat healthy plants.

Farmer Lee, author of *The Chef's Garden*.

The Culinary Medicine Textbook: A Modular Approach to Culinary Literacy

Part 3
The Diets

Deborah Kennedy PhD,

With Julia Hilbrands MS, MPH, RD,

Laura Thomas MED, RD, LD, FAND, Catrina Hidalgo Schick BS, Denise Potter RDN, CSP, CDCES, Lisa Vanatta MS, RDN, CSP, Gita Patel, MS, RDN, LD, CLT, Jasna Robinson-Wright, MSc, RD, CDE, CIEC

Content and expertise provided by a dozen chefs and over 40 nutrition experts

Copyright© 2021 by Culinary Rehab LLC

All rights reserved. No part of this publication may be reproduced, stored in a retrieval system, or transmitted in any manner or in any form, electronic, mechanical, photocopying, recording, scanning, or otherwise except as permitted under Section 107 or 108 of the 1976 United States Copyright Act, without the prior written permission from a representative of Culinary Rehab LLC. Requests for permission can be emailed to CulinaryRehab@gmail.com or by calling 203-430-4899.

Limit of Liability/ Disclaimer of Warranty: While Culinary Rehab LLC, the authors, chefs and contributors have used their best efforts in preparing this work/book, they make no representations or warranties with respect to the accuracy or completeness of the content of this work/book.

Notice: This book is not a medical manual and in no way should take the place of medical treatment. **It is always best to check with your healthcare provider before embarking on a health and wellness plan**, especially if you are on any medications or currently have any disease or illness. Culinary Rehab LLC, the authors, chef or contributors disclaim liability for any medical outcomes that may occur as a result of following guidance in this book.

Culinary Rehab© is a copyright owned by Deborah Kennedy

5% of the proceeds goes to support the True Health Initiative
https://www.truehealthinitiative.org/

THE CHEF PANEL

Chef Lyndon Virkler

Chef Russel Michel

Chef Scott Giambastiani

Chef Cyndie Story

Chef Erika Holland-Toll

Chef Kate Waters

Chef Debbie Kennedy

Chef Ron Desantis

Chef Janet Crandall

Chef Kelsey Johnson

Table Of Contents

THE DASH DIET

By Laura Thomas MED, RD, LD, FAND {DASH DIET INTRO}

Forty six percent of adults in the United Sates have high blood pressure (hypertension) as defined by a blood pressure of 130/80 mm Hg or greater by the American Heart Association, the American College of Cardiology, and nine other expert associations (Whelton et al., 2018). A person with high blood pressure has double the risk of cardiovascular complications than does someone with normal blood pressure, and these complications include heart attack, stroke, heart failure, vision loss, kidney disease and sexual dysfunction. Because of the risk of numerous health complications, it is recommended that lifestyle interventions be started in those diagnosed with hypertension to prevent damage to the arteries and susceptible organs. Diet and exercise are on top of the list of effective interventions, as is decreasing stress and limiting alcohol consumption.

NUTRIENTS THAT AFFECT BLOOD PRESSURE

Sodium may be the mineral one thinks of first when thinking about hypertension, **however other minerals – calcium, magnesium, and potassium – also play critical roles in blood pressure regulation**. Epidemiologic studies support that dietary patterns rich in these minerals as well as in dietary fiber are associated with lower blood pressure (Sacks et al., 1995). Food sources of these nutrients include dairy products (calcium and protein), fruits (potassium, magnesium, and fiber), vegetables (potassium, magnesium, and fiber), nuts, seeds and legumes (magnesium, protein, and fiber) and whole grains (magnesium).

SECTION 1: DEFINING THE DASH DIET

Dietary Approaches to Stop Hypertension, also known as the **DASH diet** or DASH eating style, is an eating pattern that was created through research (L. J. Appel et al., 1997) by the National Institute of Health (NIH) over twenty years ago. The goal of the DASH diet is to lower hypertension in adults. Today, it is a **recognized treatment for hypertension, heart disease, and kidney disease** and is approved by 11 leading health organizations, including the National Heart, Lung, and Blood Institute, the American Heart Association, the Dietary Guidelines for Americans and the National Kidney Foundation (Whelton et al., 2018).

The DASH diet is a total food-based approach that focuses on nutrients associated with lower blood pressure – calcium, potassium, magnesium and dietary fiber. The core foods in the original DASH diet were fruits, vegetables, low fat dairy products, nuts, beans and seeds. It is important to note that the **focus and evidence supporting the DASH diet is on food-based delivery of nutrients, not on supplementation**. In fact, studies of individual mineral supplementation have not consistently produce lower blood pressure (Sacks et al., 1995).

Updates to the original DASH diet in response to maintaining a healthful weight included replacing refined grains with whole grains, limiting sodium to 2,300 mg/day, adding more lean sources of protein and/or heart healthful fats. Other important elements of the DASH diet include limiting the intake of alcohol (limited to two drinks per day), caffeine (limited to three caffeinated drinks per day), trans fat and saturated fat.

Table 1: DASH Eating Plan: Servings for a 2,000 Calorie Level Eating Plan

	Vegetable	4 to 5/day – serving size: ½ cup fresh or cooked, except 1 cup leafy greens
	Fruit	4 to 5/day – serving size: ½ cup fruit or juice, 1 medium piece fresh or ¼ cup dried
	Grain	6 to 8/day, at least half whole grain – serving size: ½ cup cooked cereal, pasta, rice or 1 oz dry cereal or 1 slice (1 oz) bread or bun
	Dairy	2 to 3/ day. Non-fat or low fat – serving size 1 cup milk/yogurt; 1½ ounce cheese
	Protein	Nuts, seeds, dried beans and peas: 4 to 5/week – Serving Size ½ cup beans, 1½ ounces nuts, 2 Tbsp seeds or nut butters Meats, poultry, fish, and eggs: 6 oz or less/day – serving size is total cooked weight; 1 egg = 1 oz
	Fats/Oils	2 to 3/day – serving size: 1 tsp oil or soft margarine, 2 Tbsp salad dressing
	Sweets	No more than 5 small servings/week – such as 1 T sugar or Jelly, small cookie, ½ cup sherbet
	Sodium	No more than 2,300 mg/day (1 tsp salt) 1,500 mg/day if desired – combined from naturally occurring in food and added in processing, preparation and at table

Data from National Heart, Lung, and Blood Institute, including serving sizes.

Servings per day for the DASH eating plan for other caloric levels.

SECTION 2: RESEARCH SUPPORTING THE DASH DIET

The National Heart, Lung, and Blood Institute ran four trials looking at the health benefits of the DASH diet versus the standard American diet (SAD) or various versions of the DASH diet. Below is a summary of those four trials which showed a reduction in blood pressure and LDL cholesterol when a DASH diet was followed. Adding sodium restrictions improved the positive effects on blood pressure, as did replacing 10% of carbohydrates with unsaturated fat or protein and adding a lifestyle component.

THE ORIGINAL STUDY ON BLOOD PRESSURE REDUCTIONS WITH DASH

Epidemiological studies provided evidence of lower blood pressure among individuals consuming a diet rich in vegetables, fruits, and dairy products. The original multicenter, randomized controlled feeding study to test the efficacy of an entire dietary pattern in lowering blood pressure occurred in 1997 (L. J. Appel et al., 1997). While previous studies had focused on the  relationship between single nutrients and blood pressure, this landmark study documented the combined effects of various nutrients found together in foods. The study was designed to **combine foods rich in calcium, potassium, magnesium and dietary fiber** while simultaneously **lowering foods with nutrients known to negatively influence blood pressure or cardiovascular health, such as saturated fat, total fat, cholesterol and sodium.**

The three specific diets (all of which provided 3,000 mg sodium per day) that were studied in the original randomized study included:
- The control diet (typical American diet) – low in calcium, magnesium, and potassium
- The control diet plus additional fruits and vegetables – higher in potassium and magnesium
- The combination diet – higher in calcium, magnesium, and potassium – which later become known as DASH that emphasized fruits, vegetables, and low-fat dairy products, whole grains, legumes, lean meats and nuts with limits on saturated and total fats

Reductions in blood pressure with the DASH diet occurred **within two weeks of initiating the diet** and were maintained for the following six weeks of the diet study and were similar to first line blood pressure medication (L. J. Appel et al., 1997). Subjects that were hypertensive demonstrated an even greater reduction in blood pressure as compared to those with prehypertension. Blood pressure reductions occurred while the participants maintained their pre-study weights and alcohol intakes (less than two alcoholic beverages daily). Both weight loss and reduced alcohol intake are lifestyle factors that could reduce blood pressure even further than dietary changes alone.

Subjects in the original DASH study represented a cross-section of the American population. Half of the subjects (49%) were women, 60% were black, and 37% were from households with incomes of less than $30,000 per year. All study participants — men, women, and members and nonmembers of minority groups — experienced similar reductions in blood pressure. Thus, it was postulated that the results are broadly applicable to the adult U.S. population.

DASH SODIUM STUDY

A second DASH study, published in 2001 (Sacks et al., 2001), examined the effect of various sodium levels on blood pressure by comparing the typical American diet as the control, to the DASH diet. This research study produced two compelling results. First, the trial verified the effectiveness of the DASH diet in lowering blood pressure. Second, the research confirmed the **positive influence of sodium restriction on blood pressure.**

This multicenter, randomized controlled feeding study mimicked the original DASH trial in terms of participant recruitment. Participants in the DASH sodium study had blood pressures that exceeded 120/80 mm Hg at the time of recruitment. Again, the study criteria relied on widely available foods to create meal patterns. The various sodium level diets are listed below and they were taste tested for palatability.

Sodium restriction significantly lowered both systolic and diastolic blood pressure for both the control diet and the DASH diet, and with each reduction in sodium level, blood pressure decreased even more (Sacks et al., 2001). The control diet required a greater sodium restriction to achieve results and does not meet other nutrient recommendations for optimal health.

The DASH diet produced statistically significant lower blood pressures at each sodium level compared to the control diet, and the sodium restriction added to the overall effectiveness of the DASH diet. The takeaway message is that for the **most effective blood pressure lowering results, combine the DASH diet with sodium restrictions**.

Graph 1: Three Sodium Levels Targets for DASH Sodium and Control Diets with Blood Pressures

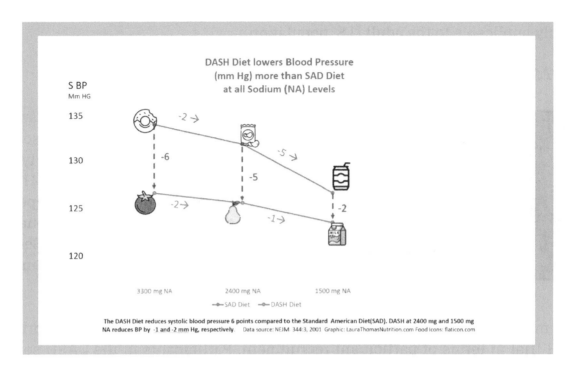

THE OMNIHEART TRIAL (ALTERED MACRONUTRIENTS)

The *OmniHeart Trial* (Lawrence J. Appel et al., 2005) **evaluated changes in the macronutrient distribution of the DASH diet**, which was, by design, carbohydrate rich at 55% of total calories. The original DASH diet provided 18% of total calories from protein and 27% of total calories from fat. Researchers modified the DASH diet by replacing 10% of total daily carbohydrate with either protein or unsaturated fat. The test diets (DASH, DASH + protein, DASH + fat), which were provided to participants, retained all food groups of the DASH diet with modifications in servings or food choices within groups to accommodate for the macronutrient changes. Sodium levels were 2,300 mg for all diets.

Blood pressure and lipid levels were measured to assess the effectiveness of the macronutrient changes. All diets lowered blood pressure in all subjects and both the protein and unsaturated fat diets significantly lowered blood pressure compared to the carbohydrate diet. **The protein diet significantly reduced LDL cholesterol compared with the two other diets. The unsaturated fat increased HDL cholesterol compared to the two other diets**. Both the protein and unsaturated fat diets significantly lowered triglycerides, total cholesterol, and non-HDL cholesterol levels compared to the carbohydrate diet. The researchers calculated that based on the Framingham risk equation, 10-year cardiovascular risk was 16.1% to 21% lower for all study diets when compared to baseline. The **protein and unsaturated fat diets produced greater risk reduction**.

The *OmniHeart Trial* provides evidence that modifying the DASH diet by replacing 10% of carbohydrates with unsaturated fat or protein produces:
1. Enhanced blood pressure reductions
2. Positive changes to blood lipids, which further reduces cardiovascular disease risk

THE PREMIER CLINICAL TRIAL (ADDED LIFESTYLE FACTORS)

The original DASH and DASH sodium trials controlled for weight loss, a known factor that reduces blood pressure. The *PREMIER* clinical trial (Lawrence J. Appel et al., 2003) **studied the combination of established lifestyle factors** (lose weight if overweight, reduce sodium intake, increase physical activity and reduce alcohol intake if alcohol is consumed) **and the DASH diet employed simultaneously**. The *PREMIER* study was the first to have free living research subjects follow the DASH diet independently, without all foods provided by the research trial.

Subjects were randomized into an "Advice Only" group, which received advice to adopt the established lifestyle factors; an "Established Group" which received behavioral intervention to adopt the lifestyle factors; and "Established plus DASH," which received behavioral intervention to adopt the lifestyle factors and the DASH eating style. The Advice Only group received a 30-minute advice session upon randomization to the control group. Both behavioral interventions consisted of group sessions that were held during the 18-month trial (weekly for the first eight weeks, biweekly for the remainder of the first six months, and monthly until a year). The sodium level advised for the intervention groups was 2,300 mg daily, similar to the intermediate sodium level of the *DASH Sodium Trial* (Lin et al., 2007).

Study results found that both intervention groups lost weight, improved fitness, reduced both systolic and diastolic blood pressure and reduced sodium intake as compared to the advice only group. The DASH intervention group increased intake of DASH foods: Dairy products, fruits and vegetables. **This study documents the potential health benefits of a behavior change intervention combined with the DASH diet**.

DASH REDUCES RISK OF OTHER CHRONIC DISEASES

The blood pressure lowering results of the DASH eating style are well-documented in randomized controlled trials (Gay et al., 2016; Saneei et al., 2014). The DASH diet lowers blood pressure to a degree similar to that of many blood pressure lowering medications. Research also demonstrates that the DASH eating style may be protective against other chronic diseases as well. The original DASH Study found that the DASH eating style significantly reduced total, LDL, and HDL blood cholesterol levels when compared to the typical American control diet (Obarzanek et al., 2001). These reductions were in tandem with stable weight maintenance among study participants during each diet phase of the study.

Cardiovascular Disease

A 2019 umbrella review of systematic reviews and meta-analyses of the DASH diet and cardio-metabolic outcomes (Chiavaroli et al., 2019), which included 11 prospective cohort studies from the United States (n=7), Sweden (n=2), China (n=1) and Italy (n=1), assessed the DASH diet and incidence of cardiovascular disease. **Consuming the DASH diet significantly reduced the incidence of cardiovascular disease**. A 2015 meta-analysis (Siervo et al., 2015) found that the decreases in systolic and diastolic blood pressures coupled with decreases in total and LDL blood cholesterol levels would predict **a 13% decrease in the 10-year Framingham risk score for cardiovascular disease.**

Coronary Heart Disease

The DASH Eating Style has multiple studies that support its role as a cardiovascular protective measure, and if fully adopted, it could produce significant reductions in cardiovascular disease. The original DASH study researchers cited a potential 15% reduction in the incidence of coronary heart disease with a population-wide shift in lower blood pressure (L. J. Appel et al., 1997).

The 2019 Chiavaroli et al publication included a systematic review and meta-analysis of three prospective cohort studies (all U.S.-based) ranging from 14.6-year to 24-year timespans (Chiavaroli et al., 2019). Middle-aged or elderly women who consumed diets similar to the DASH diet had a significantly reduced risk of coronary heart disease. Higher DASH scores were correlated with lower relative risks of coronary heart disease.

Serum Homocysteine – A Cardiovascular Disease Risk Factor

Elevated levels of serum homocysteine, a breakdown product of certain amino acids, is associated with increased risk of atherosclerotic cardiovascular disease and kidney disease. An unexpected outcome of the original DASH trial was **lower serum homocysteine levels produced by the DASH diet as compared to the control or fruit and vegetable diet** (Appel Lawrence J. et al., 2000). The DASH diet provided increased levels of dietary folate (from fruits, vegetables, and perhaps dairy products) and vitamin B_{12} (from dairy products, meat, poultry, fish and eggs); these two B vitamins are associated with lower serum homocysteine levels. The researchers noted that dietary folate intake had a major influence on fasting serum homocysteine levels and vitamin B_{12} may have had a lesser effect.

Stroke

The incidence of stroke is closely tied to high blood pressure as high blood pressure is a major risk factor for stroke. Therefore, the blood pressure lowering effect of the DASH diet logically reduces the risk of stroke. The original DASH study researchers (L. J. Appel et al., 1997) cited **a potential 27% reduction in the incidence of stroke with a population wide shift in lower blood pressure**.

Dietary data and ischemic stroke incidence from two prospective cohort studies of the DASH diet and stroke risk affirm this finding (Larsson et al., 2016). A modified DASH diet adherence score was used; the score excluded sodium because the food frequency questionnaire used in the studies omitted both salt in cooking and at-table use, thus preventing accurate sodium estimation. This study of middle-aged and older Swedish adults found that **adherence to the DASH** 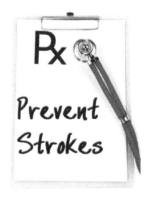 **diet was inversely associated with incidence of ischemic stroke**. A similar trend was found between DASH and intracerebral hemorrhage; however, the results were not statistically significant. This study also found the inverse relationship was stronger among study participants who were "never smokers."

A 2019 publication by Chiavaroli et al included a systematic review and meta-analysis of three prospective cohort studies (two U.S.-based, one from Italy) ranging from 7.9-year to 24-year timespans. **The DASH dietary pattern**

scores were correlated with significantly reduced incidence of stroke (Chiavaroli et al., 2019). Similarly, a 2018 meta-analysis of 12 prospective cohort studies (Feng et al., 2018) found higher adherence to the DASH diet was associated with lower risk of stroke, with benefits higher among Asian cohorts as compared to Western cohorts. The dose-response meta-analysis found that for every four-point increase in the DASH diet adherence score (an eight-point to 40-point range) reduced stroke risk by 4%. This study found **a DASH benefit for both ischemic and hemorrhagic stroke**.

Cancer

Food frequency questionnaires from the *Nurses' Health Study* (NHS) and *Health Professionals Follow-up Study* (HPFS) were scored for adherence to the Alternate Mediterranean Diet (aMED) and the DASH diet (Fung et al., 2010). In both female (NHS) and male (HPFS) cohorts, **a higher DASH score was associated with a lower risk of colorectal cancer and rectal cancer**. No significant association was found between the aMED and colorectal, colon, or rectal cancers. A major difference between the aMED and the DASH diet is the prominence of dairy products in DASH. The researchers cited a meta-analysis that found an association between dairy product consumption and lower risk of colon cancer as a possible explanation for the some of the differences observed between the two diets.

Canadian researchers noted a similar lower risk of colorectal cancer particularly among Canadians males with a high DASH adherence score (Jones-McLean et al., 2015). For males, a significant trend towards decreased risk of colorectal cancer occurred as DASH scores increased. Among women, the trend of increasing DASH scores with lower risk of colon cancer, rectal cancer, or both cancers combined was not significant.

An updated systematic review on diet quality indexes, including DASH, found positive correlations to health (Schwingshackl et al., 2018). **Along with DASH, high dietary scores on the Healthy Eating Index (HEI) and Alternate Healthy Eating Index (AHEI) were associated with a significant reduction in of risk of cancer (15%), in addition to all-cause mortality (22%), risk of cardiovascular disease (22%), risk of type 2 diabetes (18%), and neurodegenerative disease (15%).** High quality diets were inversely associated with overall mortality and cancer mortality in cancer survivors.

Diabetes

Hypertension is a common comorbidity of diabetes. According to the American Diabetes Association, two of three individuals with diabetes take medication to treat high blood pressure (ADA).

A 2019 study of the *DASH diet and Cardiometabolic Outcomes* (Chiavaroli et al., 2019) found that among five prospective cohort studies that evaluated the DASH diet and incidence of diabetes, the DASH diet was associated with significant reduction in diabetes. These results affirm the 2013 meta-analysis (Shirani et al., 2013) that found the DASH diet may lead to an improvement in insulin sensitivity, independent of weight loss.

A review article (Hinderliter et al., 2011) examined the independent and combined effects of the DASH diet in combination with weight loss and exercise on blood pressure and insulin sensitivity. These reviewers cited the blood pressure lowering effect of the DASH diet among overweight subjects. When the DASH diet was combined with a holistic lifestyle change including exercise and weight loss, improvements in insulin sensitivity were observed.

A *DASH Diet for Diabetes* was studied among 11 adolescents with type 1 diabetes enrolled in a feeding study (Peairs et al., 2017). The diet was modified from the original DASH protocol to provide increased amounts of mono- and polyunsaturated fats to offset decreases in carbohydrate. The results indicate a DASH diet approach may be beneficial in helping adolescents be more compliant with the American Diabetes Association recommendations and improve glucose control. Moreover, the modified diet may be cardio-protective in adolescents with type 1 diabetes.

As noted previously, an updated large meta-analysis (Schwingshackl et al., 2015) found **an 18% reduced risk of type 2 diabetes with a high DASH score**, along with high scores for both the Healthy Eating Index (HEI) and Alternate Healthy Eating Index (AHEI).

Gestational diabetes mellitus can lead to health complications for both mother and child. Studies have reported reduced risk of gestational diabetes with pre-pregnancy adherence to a healthy eating pattern such as DASH (Tobias et al., 2012), less total gestational weight gain with a technology-enhanced DASH diet and lifestyle intervention (Van Horn et al., 2018), and improved pregnancy outcomes in women with gestational diabetes treated with the DASH diet for four weeks (Asemi et al., 2014).

The Academy of Nutrition and Dietetics *Evidenced-Based Gestational Diabetes Practice Guideline* states: "Dietary patterns based on the DASH diet (that contained higher amounts of carbohydrate and dietary fiber, and less sucrose, total fat, dietary cholesterol and less sodium), when compared with a control diet, were effective in improving both fetal and maternal outcomes in women with gestational diabetes who did not require insulin at the time of diagnosis. Improvements were found in glucose tolerance, glycosylated hemoglobin levels, insulin resistance, need for insulin, lipid profile, systolic blood pressure and biomarkers of oxidative stress. There was also a lower incidence of cesarean-section deliveries. Infant birth weights, head circumferences, ponderal indexes and the incidence of macrosomia (heavier than average birth weight) were lower in infants whose mothers consumed the DASH diet" (Duarte-Gardea et al., 2018).

Gastrointestinal Disorders
The DASH eating style is compatible with current dietary recommendations for gastrointestinal health (Diet-and-the-Gut-English-2018.Pdf, 2018). The eating style includes abundant amounts of fruits, vegetables, legumes, nuts and seeds – all important sources of prebiotic fibers – and the inclusion of yogurt and other fermented dairy foods, which provides live probiotics cultures. Individuals with intolerance to lactose can select lactose-free dairy products and yogurt with live active cultures. Intolerances to fructose, sucrose, or other dietary carbohydrate may require medical nutrition therapy services of a registered dietitian/nutritionist or other qualified health professional.

Gout

Gout is a common type of inflammatory arthritis caused by hyperuricemia. A 2016 ancillary analysis of the DASH sodium data from one of the four research sites (Juraschek et al., 2016) found that the DASH diet substantially lowered serum uric acid levels among people with hyperuricemia as compared to the control diet (typical American or Western diet). Medium and high sodium intakes with the DASH diet lowered serum uric acid more than lower sodium intakes. The differences between the medium and high sodium DASH diets were not significantly different.

A prospective cohort study (Rai et al., 2017) applied a DASH dietary pattern score for foods emphasized or minimized in the DASH diet to the dietary components of the food frequency questionnaire used in the *Health Professionals Follow-up Study*. The researchers found the **DASH diet is associated with a lower risk of gout** and suggest this nonpharmacological approach as a preventive dietary measure that may appeal to individuals at risk of developing gout. The DASH diet is associated with a dose-response reduced risk of gout. Three out of four individuals with gout also have hypertension, thus the dietary style could address both conditions. The data analysis found the typical Western diet is independently associated with a higher risk of gout.

Kidney Disease

DASH is recommended for the prevention and treatment of blood pressure induced kidney disease and the prevention of kidney stones by the National Kidney Foundation. For those who have chronic kidney disease, they should check with their kidney doctor and a dietitian who specializes in kidney disease before beginning the DASH diet; for those who have severe kidney disease and/or on dialysis, the DASH diet is **not** recommended.

A prospective analysis of the *Atherosclerosis Risk in Communities* (ARIC) study explored the potential for the DASH eating style as a prevention measure for kidney disease (Rebholz et al., 2016). This study, published in 2016, employed two different DASH diet scores, one based on the foods emphasized or minimized in the DASH diet and a second nutrient-based approach. The nutrient-based score assigned values for low intakes of saturated fat, total fat, cholesterol and sodium and high intakes of protein, fiber, magnesium, calcium and potassium. In each scoring system, a higher score indicates the subject's dietary pattern more closely resembles the DASH eating style.

Subjects with the lowest adherence to a DASH diet were **16% more likely to develop kidney disease** than subjects with the highest DASH diet score. When food components of the diet scores were evaluated, higher intakes of nuts, legumes, and dairy products were associated with a lower risk of kidney disease, while higher intakes of red meat and processed meats were associated with higher risk. When nutrient scores were reviewed, higher intakes of magnesium and calcium were statistically significantly associated with a reduced risk of kidney disease. Conversely, higher risk of kidney disease was associated with higher dietary protein intake.

The researchers concluded, "...**consumption of a DASH-style diet was associated with a lower risk of kidney disease**, independent of demographic characteristics, caloric intake, socioeconomic status, lifestyle factors, comorbid conditions, anti-hypertensive medication use and baseline kidney function in this general population sample of African American and Caucasian men and women. The DASH diet, designed for blood pressure reduction and now widely recommended for reducing the risk of cardiovascular disease and other chronic diseases, may also protect against kidney disease" (Rebholz et al., 2016).

Neurodegenerative Diseases
The DASH eating style is associated with reduced risk of hypertension, cardiovascular disease, and diabetes, conditions that may increase cognitive decline. Researchers have used dietary adherence scores to assess the relationship between diet quality and cognitive decline.

Baseline food frequency questionnaires from the *Memory and Aging Project* were scored for adherence to DASH or the Mediterranean diet (Tangney et al., 2014). Comparisons were made to results of cognitive assessments conducted in annual neurologic examinations. In this population, **greater adherence scores for DASH and the Mediterranean dietary patterns were associated with slower rates of mental decline**. The association was stronger at higher dietary scores for both diets in this study of 826 older people (average age 81.5 years ± 7.1 years).

A similar finding was reported among the 3,381 participants in the *Cache County Study on Memory, Health and Aging* (Wengreen et al., 2013). **Higher DASH and Mediterranean diet scores were associated with higher cognitive function scores at baseline and over time** (11 years).

Reduced risk of Alzheimer's disease was also correlated with the highest adherence to the DASH diet, Mediterranean diet, and MIND diet (a hybrid of the DASH and Mediterranean diets) (Morris et al., 2015). The MIND diet at moderate adherence may also decrease risk of Alzheimer disease.

The updated systematic review and meta-analysis study by Schwingschakl et al found high dietary scores on DASH, Healthy Eating Index (HEI), and Alternate Healthy Eating Index (AHEI) were associated with a significant reduction (16%) of neurodegenerative diseases. The updated review included 34 new research studies; the previous published results did not find this degenerative risk reduction relationship for any of the diet quality measures (Schwingshackl & Hoffmann, 2015). The evolving research on DASH (and other high-quality diets) continues to build the case for benefits beyond lowering blood pressure.

The role of elevated serum homocysteine levels as a risk factor for dementia is detailed in a 2018 international consensus statement on the topic (Smith et al., 2018). The lower serum homocysteine levels reported from the first DASH trial data (L. J. Appel et al., 1997) are an interesting observation as to another potential benefit from the DASH eating style.

Osteoporosis/Osteopenia

The International Osteoporosis Foundation (Nutrition IOF) highlights several nutrients and a healthful diet for the prevention and management of osteoporosis and related musculoskeletal disorders. Ranked highest on their recommendations are the nutrients dietary calcium and vitamin D. Additionally, a variety of other foods, vitamins, and minerals are recognized as important to overall bone health, including adequate dietary protein from desirable sources including fish, whole grains, nuts and seeds.

The **DASH eating style provides substantial amounts of nutrients associated with positive bone health**: higher calcium, potassium, magnesium, vitamins

C and K, beta carotene and fiber with moderate protein and lower sodium intakes. Analysis of the *DASH Sodium study* found the DASH diet significantly reduced bone turnover (Lin et al., 2003), which if sustained may improve bone health. The researchers noted that the DASH diet and sodium reduction may have complementary beneficial effects on bone.

As noted previously, the DASH diet produced lower serum homocysteine levels (Appel Lawrence J. et al., 2000). IOF notes that higher levels of serum homocysteine may be linked to lower bone density and higher risk of hip fracture in the elderly. Ongoing research is exploring the role of diet and B vitamins as a means to reduce fracture risk.

Weight Loss

The original DASH and *DASH sodium trials* controlled for weight loss, a known factor that reduces blood pressure. The *PREMIER clinical trial* (Lawrence J. Appel et al., 2003) studied the combination of established lifestyle factors (lose weight if overweight, reduce sodium intake, increase physical activity and reduce alcohol intake if alcohol is consumed) and the DASH diet employed simultaneously. The *PREMIER study* was the first to have free living research subjects follow the DASH diet independently, without all foods provided by the research trial. Subjects were randomized into an "Advice Only" group which received advice to adopt the established lifestyle factors; an "Established Group" which received behavioral intervention to adopt the lifestyle factors; and "Established plus DASH," which received behavioral intervention to adopt the lifestyle factors and the DASH eating style. Both the "Established" and "Established plus DASH" groups lost significant amounts of weight, 4.9 kg and 5.8 kg average, respectively at six months.

Researchers for the *PREMIER trial* (Lin et al., 2007) found that free living individuals incorporated more DASH foods into their diets when **treatment incorporated a behavioral lifestyle invention**. Group sessions were held during the 18-month trial (first weekly for eight weeks, biweekly for the remainder of the first six months, and monthly until a year). Intake of DASH foods significantly increased, however levels in this free-living population did not reach those of the DASH clinical feeding trials. The study also found weight loss and lower blood pressures resulted with DASH as compared to the control of 30 minutes of advice.

SECTION 3: IS THE DASH DIET FOR EVERYONE?

The DASH eating style has been recommended as a healthy eating pattern for all Americans for the last two decades. The DASH diet was included in the 2000 Dietary Guidelines for Americans (DGA 2000) and has continued to be a foundation of dietary guidance for Americans over the age of two ever since (2015-2020 Dietary Guidelines | Health.Gov; Hennessey, 2010; U.S. Department of Health and Human Services and U.S. Department of Agriculture, 2005). The National Heart, Lung, and Blood Institute (NHLBI) adopted DASH as the optimal nonpharmacological means for prevention and treatment of hypertension and lowering blood cholesterol. NHLBI provides extensive resources promoting the DASH eating style (NHLBI website).

The American College of Cardiologists and the American Heart Association are among 11 leading health organizations (Whelton et al., 2018) that recommend the DASH eating style to reduce, manage, and treat hypertension. Moreover, **the DASH diet has ranked #1 or #2 for overall healthful dietary pattern by *U.S. News and World Reports* since 2010**. The publication convenes a panel of medical and nutrition experts to evaluate popular diets in the media and/or diets/eating styles with peer-reviewed research annually for the list. (*US News & World Reports*).

CHILDREN

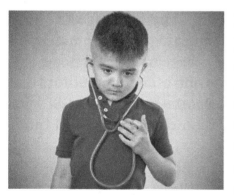

In 2011, the American Academy of Pediatrics published a summary report of an *Expert Panel on Integrated Guidelines for Cardiovascular Health and Risk Reduction in Children and Adolescents* ("Expert Panel on Integrated Guidelines for Cardiovascular Health and Risk Reduction in Children and Adolescents," 2011), which noted dietary approaches such as DASH, which have been shown to be effective in adults, are a promising approach for improving nutrition and reducing risk of cardiovascular disease in children. The 2017 *Clinical Practice Guidelines for Screening and Management of High Blood Pressure in Children and Adolescents* cites **the absence of a DASH-like diet as a risk factor for hypertension children and youths** (Flynn et al., 2017). Recent updates to the meal pattern for the Child and Adult Care Food Program (CACFP) of the United States Department of Agriculture (USDA CACFP Standards for Meals and Snacks) encourage fruits, vegetables, whole grains, low fat dairy products and lean meat/protein choices as developmentally appropriate beginning around six months when solid foods are introduced to the older infant's diet through the preschool years.

PREGNANCY AND LACTATION

The DASH diet is consistent with dietary recommendations during pregnancy and lactation (2015-2020 Dietary Guidelines | Health.Gov; Hennessey, 2010; U.S. Department of Health and Human Services and U.S. Department of Agriculture, 2005). Data is mixed regarding the DASH diet and hypertension disorders of pregnancy (HDP). *Project Viva* data — a longitudinal study looking into the effects of a mother's diet on her child's health — did not find a protective effect between adherence to the DASH diet early in pregnancy and reduced risk of HDP (Fulay et al., 2018). In contrast, Arvizu et al found that adherence to a DASH diet prior to pregnancy significantly lessened the likelihood of developing preeclampsia (Arvizu M, 2019). Compher et al also found that adherence to a DASH diet prior to the third trimester was associated with reduced risk of HDP (Compher C, Elovitz M, Parry S, Chittams J, Griffith C, 2018). In this study, the group with the lowest adherence to a DASH diet experienced the highest risk of HDP. The DASH diet is recommended by the Academy of Nutrition and Dietetics in their Evidence-based Practice Guideline for Gestational Diabetes (Duarte-Gardea et al., 2018).

ATHLETES

Athletes may benefit from the abundant level of antioxidants in the DASH diet (Elkington et al., 2015; Pingitore et al., 2015). **The DASH eating style is recommended as a nonpharmacological approach to treat high blood pressure in athletes of all competitive levels** (Dixit S, DiFiori J, 2020). Elite athletes and other competitors can access the services of board Certified Specialist in Sports Dietetics (CSSD) for personal guidance on appropriate sodium, micronutrition distribution and other nutrition concerns of human performance.

SENIORS

Older Americans are at risk of many chronic diseases that **multiple studies have found the DASH eating style confers protection against high blood pressure, stroke, heart disease, type 2 diabetes, osteoporosis and cognitive degenerative diseases**. The research summaries featured in this chapter address the multiple studies and findings supporting the DASH diet for older Americans.

ALLERGIES

Individuals with allergies to cow's milk should consult a registered dietitian/nutritionist (RD/RDN) to modify the DASH diet to meet specific needs. Because dairy products are a component of the DASH diet, results may vary for those individuals unable to follow the complete protocol. Individuals with sensitivity to lactose can incorporate lactose-free milk, yogurt, and cheese into their diet.

CONTRAINDICATIONS FOR THE DASH DIET

No potential health concerns with the DASH diet are reported in the scientific literature for the general healthy population, including those at risk for chronic disease. It is however contraindicated for all medical conditions that restrict any of the dietary components provided by the diet, like those undergoing kidney dialysis treatments who have to watch their potassium intake (National Kidney Foundation).

SECTION 4: MODIFICATIONS TO THE DASH DIET

REPLACE 10% OF CARBOHYDRATES WITH FAT OR PROTEIN

There are several different iterations of the DASH diet that have been shown to lower blood pressure and improve blood lipid levels. The *OmniHeart* study (Lawrence J. Appel et al., 2005) discussed previously evaluated the DASH diet and two variations **that substitute 10% of the calories from carbohydrate with either protein or unsaturated fat**. Both the higher protein and higher unsaturated fat DASH variations lowered blood pressure and improved lipid levels compared to the standard DASH diet.

USE FULL-FAT DAIRY PRODUCTS

A 2016 study evaluated the **use of full-fat dairy products in place of low-fat dairy foods and a lower carbohydrate (from sugar) diet** on blood pressure and blood lipids (Chiu et al., 2016). The higher fat DASH diet lowered blood pressure similar to the traditional DASH diet and lowered plasma triglycerides and very low density lipoproteins (VLDL) without significantly increasing low density lipoprotein (LDL) levels.

Table 2: Summary of DASH Modifications

Study/Researchers	Modification	Result
OmniHeart	Increase % of protein to 25%	Lowered BP, improved lipids
OmniHeart	Increase % of fat, primarily from unsaturated to 37%	Lowered BP, improved lipids
Chiu et al	Full fat dairy products and lower carbohydrate diet	Lowered BP, lowered triglycerides and VLDL without significant increase in LDL levels

SECTION 5: PALATABILITY AND ADHERENCE TO THE DASH DIET

A concern with any diet change is whether an individual can adhere to the dietary changes long-term. This holds true with the DASH diet as well. Study after study, many of which were described above, has found that health benefits increase as DASH diet adherence scores increase, whether that is adherence to the DASH diet protocol, or extrapolating a DASH score from the FFQs in another study (*Nurse's*

Health Study). One attribute of the DASH diet that contributes to high adherence scores is that **it doesn't require perfection to achieve positive health outcomes**, even modest adherence scores show a benefit. Additionally, DASH is a flavorful eating style that allows for a wide array of food consumption.

Another encouraging message is that study participants indicated **liking the DASH diet more than the control diet**, which was the typical American diet at various sodium concentrations (Karanja et al., 2007). A post hoc survey reported participants were more willing to continue following the DASH diet than the control diet, attesting to DASH's palatability.

Participants in the *ENCORE study* (Epstein et al., 2012) reported greater intake of DASH foods post-treatment, a positive observation for sustained dietary change. In this study, greater adherence to the DASH diet was associated with greater blood pressure reductions. Ethnicity predicted adherence, with African Americans less adherent to DASH compared to whites. This finding prompted researchers to call for culturally sensitive dietary strategies to improve adherence.

SECTION 6: CULINARY COMPETENCIES

In addition to following the culinary competencies for Fruit, Vegetables, Grains, Dairy, Fats & Oils, Protein and Sodium, individuals who wish to follow a DASH diet will do well if they can:

1. Describe the DASH Diet, including food groups included and amounts recommended
2. List the health benefits and risks of following the DASH Diet
3. List the minerals that positively affect blood pressure and the food sources of them
4. Model consumption of the DASH diet
5. Consume optimal servings (two to three) of low fat dairy foods
6. Design a weekly menu that aligns with the DASH diet
7. Identify foods low in sodium for purchase
8. Select herbs and spices to flavor food instead of relying on salt

SECTION 7: AT THE STORE

Follow shopping tips in the following chapters for Fruit, Vegetables, Grains, Dairy, Fats & Oils, Protein and Sodium. In addition, focus on foods high in calcium, potassium and magnesium.

Table 3: DASH Friendly Foods High in Calcium, Magnesium, and Potassium

FOOD GROUP	CALCIUM	MAGNESIUM	POTASSIUM
MILK/DAIRY	Milk, yogurt, cheese, and fortified soy beverage	Milk, yogurt	Milk, yogurt
FRUIT	Dried figs, oranges, fortified juices	Bananas, dried apricots, raisins, kiwi, prunes, watermelon	Dried apricots, prunes, raisins, orange juice, bananas, nectarines, cantaloupe
VEGETABLE	Kale, broccoli, Chinese cabbage, collard greens, broccoli rabe	Spinach, chard, broccoli, avocado, artichoke, squash, potato with skin	Acorn squash, artichoke, potatoes, spinach, tomatoes, broccoli, Brussels sprouts, pumpkin, zucchini, winter squash, parsnip
PROTEIN	Canned sardines and salmon, fortified tofu	Peanut butter, peanuts, almonds, cashews, baked	Lentils, kidney beans, soybeans, tree nuts

		beans, soy products, lentils, hummus, pumpkin seeds, Halibut, pollack, tuna, crabmeat, salmon, bluefish
GRAINS	Fortified cereal, bread, oatmeal	Brown rice, whole wheat bread, oatmeal, wheat germ, 100% bran, bran flakes, shredded wheat cereal, fortified cereal
OTHER		Cocoa, molasses

SECTION 8: IN THE KITCHEN

When following the DASH diet, it is important to focus on serving the core DASH diet foods: eight to 10 servings of fruit and vegetables, two to three servings of low-fat or non-fat dairy and a variety of protein (with a concentration on plant proteins – nuts, beans, and seeds – in addition to fish, lean meat, and poultry), while limiting sodium to 2,300 mg a day (L. J. Appel et al., 1997). The best way to do this is to prepare foods at home where there is more control over the sodium content of foods and dishes.

Plan a week's worth of dinners by focusing on the protein source. Below is just one example, and options are endless:

- 2 nights of fish
- 1 night of meat
- 1 night of poultry
- 3 nights of vegetable sources of protein: legumes, nuts, and seeds

Knowing how to expand and enhance flavor without using too much salt, sugar, and saturated fat is the key to cooking a delicious meal on the DASH Diet. Review the Kitchen sections in the following chapters for tips and tricks on how to do this well: Fruit, Vegetables, Grains, Dairy, Fats & Oils, Protein, Sodium and Herbs and Spices.

For a modular approach, start with any of the core food chapters for fruits, vegetables, dairy or protein in the form of nuts, seeds and beans. Once the client has mastered the culinary competencies of one chapter, move on to the next. The National Heart, Lung, and Blood Institute (NHLBI) promotes making small attainable changes rather than trying to take on too much at once (DASH Eating Plan at NHLBI).

SECTION 9: TIPS FOR ADOPTING THE DASH DIET

1. Start where you are

DASH is a lifestyle shift, not a short-term diet change. It is best to make incremental changes based on one's confidence, ability, and desire. Review the client's current eating habits and compare it to the DASH eating style to see where flavorful DASH foods can be added. While the name is DASH, slow and steady wins the healthful lifestyle race. Start by making one change at a time focusing on the core DASH foods. That may be adding more vegetables or nuts, seeds, and legumes. Once the client has made sufficient change in one area, add on another one. Make sure you ask them which area they want to focus on and which area they feel most confident in changing.

2. Give time to acclimate

Individuals can get used to consuming less sodium in their diet. Train their taste buds to adjust to a lower sodium content by making incremental changes to recipes and by purchasing lower sodium food. If changes are made gradually, an individual might not even notice a difference in the saltiness of their food.

3. Drink plenty of water (fluid)

The DASH eating style provides a lot of fiber through fruits, vegetables, and whole grains. Fiber needs to be consumed with fluid to work properly in the body and to avoid gastrointestinal upset or constipation. As DASH limits the amount of sugar sweetened beverages, look to water to fulfill hydration needs. Try flavoring it with slices of citrus, cucumber, or berries, if desired.

4. Get cooking!

The DASH eating style is a flavorful diet pattern that allows for *MORE* – more vegetables, whole grains, fruits, low-fat dairy foods and lean protein options. Preparing food at home rather than relying on restaurant fare is a client-centered way to take control of flavorful eating – many ethnic style dishes emphasize vegetables and whole grains with smaller amounts of animal proteins. Home cooks can select products with less added sodium and boost flavor with herbs and spices.

5. Drain, rinse, and repeat

Canned legumes are a convenient shelf-stable ingredient. Many are available in lower sodium options. Here is a culinary tip to reduce the sodium level of regular canned vegetables, especially black beans and other legumes: drain the liquid and rinse the beans with cold running water in a colander. This removes up to 40% of the sodium added in processing to regular canned beans. Try this on other canned vegetables, too, if the fresh or frozen version is not available ("Essentials of Nutrition for Chefs," 2011).

6. Focus on taste

Each person has unique taste experiences based on individual genetics. Some people taste the bitterness in vegetables more than others [www.laurathomasnutrition.com/BitterTaste]. Simple culinary techniques can help improve the taste of bitter foods, such as leafy greens. Refer to the various chapters on how to make delicious vegetables, fruit, grains, dairy and proteins.

An Experiment in Taste [www.laurathomasnutrition.com/SaltTaste]: You will need a potato chip and ground pepper. Break the chip into two pieces. The assumption is that the same chip will have the same amount of salt. Taste one piece of the chip, paying attention to how much salty flavor you perceive. Next, sprinkle pepper on the remaining potato chip. Place the chip on the tongue so that the pepper touches the tongue before the chip. Use a tipping action but take care not to inhale or the pepper may cause a coughing reaction. Pay attention to the perception of salt for the pepper-coated chip.

The taste experience of pepper suppresses the perception of salt for most people. Peppercorn potato chips have more sodium per chip than plain potato chips. The pepper flavor components affect the perception of salt. Manufacturers add more salt to peppercorn potato chips to increase the perception of salt's flavor. This activity illustrates why reading the Nutrition Facts label is useful in making a choice between two foods. A person might expect the sodium content of all types of potato chips to be similar but they are not.

7. Understand food labels

FDA Food Facts: Sodium in Your Diet is a great handout for learning how to select food lower in sodium. Try this taste activity [www.laurathomasnutrition.com/SaltTaste] and see how to compare labels of similar products can help you find the right choice.

8. Use the dilution solution

For the occasional meal when a commercial frozen dinner or mix is prepared, use a DASH dietary staple to "dilute" the sodium per serving. Add fresh or frozen vegetables to the prepared meal — it adds extra nutrients while saving money. What was a meal for two can be transformed into a meal for four. Add some extra liquid (water) into the sauce for the skillet dinner to help coat the veggie-rich version.

9. Plan plant-based snacks

An easy and delicious way to increase fruit and vegetable intake to DASH levels is to swap packaged snacks for fruits and vegetables. Stock up on packs of dried fruit and nuts, shelf-stable single serve cups of fruit canned in juice or water, and 100% vegetable juices (many are available in lower sodium versions) for keeping handy in desk drawers and snack shelves. When refrigeration is available, rely on single-serve, low-sugar yogurt, fresh fruit, and vegetables. For more ideas on adding fruits and vegetables to the diet, check out Have a Plant: Fruit and Veggies for Better Health.

SECTION 10: AT THE TABLE

Below is an example of a day of eating on the DASH diet with recommended amounts of vegetables, fruits, dairy products and whole grains, lean meats, legumes, nuts and limited sweets and added fats:

BREAKFAST

Oatmeal prepared with fat free milk (½ cup uncooked oats and 1 cup milk)
Blueberries (1/2 cup)

SNACK

Apple and Cheese Stick (1 medium piece fruit and 1 ounce natural cheese)

LUNCH

Leafy greens or chopped romaine lettuce (2 cups) topped with:
- Avocado Beet Citrus Salad (1 cup) and
- Flaked fish, tuna or salmon (1 ready to eat pouch) or
- ¼ cup Glazed White Beans (drained and rinsed)
Served with a whole grain Soft Breadstick (2 ounce)

SNACK

Celery sticks, baby carrots, cherry tomatoes, and garlic hummus (¼ cup each, 1 cup total)

DINNER [www.laurathomasnutrition.com/StirFry]

Stir-fry vegetables - Red and yellow peppers, onions, broccoli, (¼ cup each, 1 cup total) served with:
- Diced chicken (3 ounces cooked) in
- Pineapple-teriyaki ginger sauce over Brown Rice (1 cup)
- Milk (1 cup fat free or low fat)

Banana Slices (1/2 cup or 1 medium) with
- Vanilla Greek Yogurt (5.3 ounce cup)
  [for more yogurt ideas see
  https://www.laurathomasnutrition.com/YogurtIdeas]

For more DASH recipes and meal planning tips, check:
www.laurathomasnutrition.com/DASHRecipes
How to turn 1 chicken into 3 meals

SECTION 11: RESOURCES

WEBSITES AND BOOKS

NHLBI How to Gradually Make the Move to a DASH Diet
NHLBI DASH Eating Plan
NHLBI Tips to Reduce Salt and Sodium
NHLBI Over 100 Heart Healthy Recipes
Oregon Dairy Council DASH Eating Plan
DASH Diet Mediterranean Solution

EXAMPLES OF COOKBOOKS

The Everything DASH Diet Cookbook by Christy Ellingsworth and Murdoc Khaleghi
The DASH Diet Action Plan by Maria Heller, MS, RD
The Everyday DASH Diet Cookbook by Maria Heller, MS, RD
The DASH Diet Younger You by Maria Heller, MS, RD
MIND Diet Plan & Cookbook by Julie Andrews, MS, RDN, CD

Mediterranean and DASH
The DASH Diet Mediterranean Solution by Marla Heller, MS, RD
The Mediterranean DASH Diet Cookbook by Abbie Gellman, MS, RD, CDN

For Weight Loss
The 28-Day DASH Diet Weight Loss Program by Andy De Saoris, RD, MPH and Julie Andrews, MS, RDN, CD
The DASH Diet for Weight Loss by Thomas Moore, Megan Murphy, and Mark Jenkins
The DASH Diet Weight Loss Solution by Maria Heller, MS, RD
DASH for Weight Loss by Jennifer Koslo

Hypertension

Hypertension Cookbook for Dummies by Rosanne Rust, MS, RD LDN and Cynthia Kleckner, RDN, LD, FAND

Lower Your Blood Pressure: A 21-Day DASH Diet Meal Plan to Decrease Blood Pressure Naturally by Jennifer Koslo PhD, RDN, CSSD

Dash Diet for Dummies Sarah Samaan, MD, FACC, Rosanne Rust, MS, RDN, LDN and Cynthia Kleckner, RDN, LD, FAND

SUMMARY

DASH has been part of the Dietary Guidelines for Americans for nearly 20 years and embraced by both health professionals and food enthusiasts. It is a research-based effective method for lowering blood pressure as well as reducing risk of all-cause mortality, heart disease, stroke, some types of cancer, type 2 diabetes, cognitive degenerate diseases, gout and kidney disease. The diet achieves its blood pressure lowering effect with moderate sodium limits, and additional benefits may result from further sodium restriction.

The DASH eating style approach is positive and features plenty of fruits, vegetables, and low-fat dairy products. It is rich in minerals and dietary fiber balanced with other food and nutrients that lower blood pressure. It includes fish, poultry, lean meat, legumes, nuts and seeds and deemphasizes sweetened beverages, desserts, and commercial snack foods. Because it is not a restrictive "diet" but rather a lifestyle, individuals may be able to follow the eating plan throughout their life without feeling deprived. DASH provides flexibility and personal choice in daily and weekly food intake.

REFERENCES

2015-2020 Dietary Guidelines | health.gov. (n.d.-a). Retrieved March 15, 2020, from https://health.gov/our-work/food-nutrition/2015-2020-dietary-guidelines/guidelines/

2015-2020 Dietary Guidelines | health.gov. (n.d.-b). Retrieved March 15, 2020, from https://health.gov/our-work/food-nutrition/2015-2020-dietary-guidelines/guidelines/

Appel, L. J., Moore, T. J., Obarzanek, E., Vollmer, W. M., Svetkey, L. P., Sacks, F. M., Bray, G. A., Vogt, T. M., Cutler, J. A., Windhauser, M. M., Lin, P. H., & Karanja, N. (1997). A clinical trial of the effects of dietary patterns on blood pressure. DASH Collaborative Research Group. *The New England Journal of Medicine*, *336*(16), 1117–1124. https://doi.org/10.1056/NEJM199704173361601

Appel, Lawrence J., Champagne, C. M., Harsha, D. W., Cooper, L. S., Obarzanek, E., Elmer, P. J., Stevens, V. J., Vollmer, W. M., Lin, P.-H., Svetkey, L. P., Stedman, S. W., Young, D. R., & Writing Group of the PREMIER Collaborative Research Group. (2003). Effects of comprehensive lifestyle modification on blood pressure control: Main results of the PREMIER clinical trial. *JAMA*, *289*(16), 2083–2093. https://doi.org/10.1001/jama.289.16.2083

Appel Lawrence J., Miller Edgar R., Jee Sun Ha, Stolzenberg-Solomon Rachael, RD null, Lin Pao-Hwa, Erlinger Thomas, Nadeau Marie R., & Selhub Jacob. (2000). Effect of Dietary Patterns on Serum Homocysteine. *Circulation*, *102*(8), 852–857. https://doi.org/10.1161/01.CIR.102.8.852

Appel, Lawrence J., Sacks, F. M., Carey, V. J., Obarzanek, E., Swain, J. F., Miller, E. R., Conlin, P. R., Erlinger, T. P., Rosner, B. A., Laranjo, N. M., Charleston, J., McCarron, P., Bishop, L. M., & OmniHeart Collaborative Research Group. (2005). Effects of protein, monounsaturated fat, and carbohydrate intake on blood pressure and serum lipids: Results of the OmniHeart randomized trial. *JAMA*, *294*(19), 2455–2464. https://doi.org/10.1001/jama.294.19.2455

Arvizu M. (2019). *Adherence to pre-pregnancy DASH dietary pattern and diet recommendations from the American Heart Association and the risk of preeclampsia.* Nutrition 2019.

Asemi, Z., Samimi, M., Tabassi, Z., & Esmaillzadeh, A. (2014). The effect of DASH diet on pregnancy outcomes in gestational diabetes: A randomized controlled clinical trial. *European Journal of Clinical Nutrition*, *68*(4), 490–495. https://doi.org/10.1038/ejcn.2013.296

Chiavaroli, L., Viguiliouk, E., Nishi, S. K., Blanco Mejia, S., Rahelić, D., Kahleová, H., Salas-Salvadó, J., Kendall, C. W., & Sievenpiper, J. L. (2019). DASH Dietary Pattern and Cardiometabolic Outcomes: An Umbrella Review of Systematic

Reviews and Meta-Analyses. *Nutrients*, *11*(2).
https://doi.org/10.3390/nu11020338

Chiu, S., Bergeron, N., Williams, P. T., Bray, G. A., Sutherland, B., & Krauss, R. M. (2016). Comparison of the DASH (Dietary Approaches to Stop Hypertension) diet and a higher-fat DASH diet on blood pressure and lipids and lipoproteins: A randomized controlled trial. *The American Journal of Clinical Nutrition*, *103*(2), 341–347. https://doi.org/10.3945/ajcn.115.123281

Compher C, Elovitz M, Parry S, Chittams J, Griffith C. (2018). *Diet pattern is associated with an increased risk of hypertensive disorders of pregnancy*. *S206*.

Diet-and-the-gut-english-2018.pdf. (n.d.). Retrieved May 25, 2020, from https://www.worldgastroenterology.org/UserFiles/file/guidelines/diet-and-the-gut-english-2018.pdf

Dixit S, DiFiori J. (2020). *Hypertension in Athletes*. https://www.uptodate.com/contents/hypertension-in-athletes

Duarte-Gardea, M. O., Gonzales-Pacheco, D. M., Reader, D. M., Thomas, A. M., Wang, S. R., Gregory, R. P., Piemonte, T. A., Thompson, K. L., & Moloney, L. (2018). Academy of Nutrition and Dietetics Gestational Diabetes Evidence-Based Nutrition Practice Guideline. *Journal of the Academy of Nutrition and Dietetics*, *118*(9), 1719–1742. https://doi.org/10.1016/j.jand.2018.03.014

Elkington, L. J., Gleeson, M., Pyne, D. B., Callister, R., & Wood, L. G. (2015). Inflammation and Immune Function: Can Antioxidants Help the Endurance Athlete? In M. Lamprecht (Ed.), *Antioxidants in Sport Nutrition*. CRC Press/Taylor & Francis. http://www.ncbi.nlm.nih.gov/books/NBK299041/

Epstein, D. E., Sherwood, A., Smith, P. J., Craighead, L., Caccia, C., Lin, P.-H., Babyak, M. A., Johnson, J. J., Hinderliter, A., & Blumenthal, J. A. (2012). Determinants and consequences of adherence to the dietary approaches to stop hypertension diet in African-American and white adults with high blood pressure: Results from the ENCORE trial. *Journal of the Academy of Nutrition and Dietetics*, *112*(11), 1763–1773. https://doi.org/10.1016/j.jand.2012.07.007

Essentials of Nutrition for Chefs. (n.d.). *Culinary Nutrition Publishing*. Retrieved May 25, 2020, from https://culinarynutritionpublishing.com/essentials-nutrition-chefs/

Expert Panel on Integrated Guidelines for Cardiovascular Health and Risk Reduction in Children and Adolescents: Summary Report. (2011). *Pediatrics*, *128*(Suppl 5), S213–S256. https://doi.org/10.1542/peds.2009-2107C

Feng, Q., Fan, S., Wu, Y., Zhou, D., Zhao, R., Liu, M., & Song, Y. (2018). Adherence to the dietary approaches to stop hypertension diet and risk of stroke: A meta-

analysis of prospective studies. *Medicine, 97*(38), e12450.
https://doi.org/10.1097/MD.0000000000012450

Flynn, J. T., Kaelber, D. C., Baker-Smith, C. M., Blowey, D., Carroll, A. E., Daniels, S.
R., de Ferranti, S. D., Dionne, J. M., Falkner, B., Flinn, S. K., Gidding, S. S.,
Goodwin, C., Leu, M. G., Powers, M. E., Rea, C., Samuels, J., Simasek, M.,
Thaker, V. V., Urbina, E. M., & SUBCOMMITTEE ON SCREENING AND
MANAGEMENT OF HIGH BLOOD PRESSURE IN CHILDREN. (2017). Clinical
Practice Guideline for Screening and Management of High Blood Pressure
in Children and Adolescents. *Pediatrics, 140*(3).
https://doi.org/10.1542/peds.2017-1904

Fulay, A. P., Rifas-Shiman, S. L., Oken, E., & Perng, W. (2018). Associations of the
Dietary Approaches To Stop Hypertension (DASH) Diet with Pregnancy
Complications in Project Viva. *European Journal of Clinical Nutrition,
72*(10), 1385–1395. https://doi.org/10.1038/s41430-017-0068-8

Fung, T. T., Hu, F. B., Wu, K., Chiuve, S. E., Fuchs, C. S., & Giovannucci, E. (2010). The
Mediterranean and Dietary Approaches to Stop Hypertension (DASH) diets
and colorectal cancer. *The American Journal of Clinical Nutrition, 92*(6),
1429–1435. https://doi.org/10.3945/ajcn.2010.29242

Gay, H. C., Rao, S. G., Vaccarino, V., & Ali, M. K. (2016). Effects of Different Dietary
Interventions on Blood Pressure: Systematic Review and Meta-Analysis of
Randomized Controlled Trials. *Hypertension (Dallas, Tex.: 1979), 67*(4), 733–
739. https://doi.org/10.1161/HYPERTENSIONAHA.115.06853

Hennessey, L. (2010). *DietaryGuidelines2010.* 112.

Hinderliter, A. L., Babyak, M. A., Sherwood, A., & Blumenthal, J. A. (2011). The DASH
diet and insulin sensitivity. *Current Hypertension Reports, 13*(1), 67–73.
https://doi.org/10.1007/s11906-010-0168-5

Jones-McLean, E., Hu, J., Greene-Finestone, L. S., & de Groh, M. (2015). A DASH
dietary pattern and the risk of colorectal cancer in Canadian adults. *Health
Promotion and Chronic Disease Prevention in Canada : Research, Policy and
Practice, 35*(1), 12–20.

Juraschek, S. P., Gelber, A. C., Choi, H. K., Appel, L. J., & Miller, E. R. (2016). Effects of
the Dietary Approaches To Stop Hypertension (DASH) Diet and Sodium
Intake on Serum Uric Acid. *Arthritis & Rheumatology (Hoboken, N.J.), 68*(12),
3002–3009. https://doi.org/10.1002/art.39813

Karanja, N., Lancaster, K. J., Vollmer, W. M., Lin, P.-H., Most, M. M., Ard, J. D., Swain,
J. F., Sacks, F. M., & Obarzanek, E. (2007). Acceptability of sodium-reduced
research diets, including the Dietary Approaches To Stop Hypertension
diet, among adults with prehypertension and stage 1 hypertension. *Journal
of the American Dietetic Association, 107*(9), 1530–1538.
https://doi.org/10.1016/j.jada.2007.06.013

Larsson, S. C., Wallin, A., & Wolk, A. (2016). Dietary Approaches to Stop Hypertension Diet and Incidence of Stroke: Results From 2 Prospective Cohorts. *Stroke*, *47*(4), 986–990. https://doi.org/10.1161/STROKEAHA.116.012675

Lin, P.-H., Appel, L. J., Funk, K., Craddick, S., Chen, C., Elmer, P., McBurnie, M. A., & Champagne, C. (2007). The PREMIER intervention helps participants follow the Dietary Approaches to Stop Hypertension dietary pattern and the current Dietary Reference Intakes recommendations. *Journal of the American Dietetic Association*, *107*(9), 1541–1551. https://doi.org/10.1016/j.jada.2007.06.019

Lin, P.-H., Ginty, F., Appel, L. J., Aickin, M., Bohannon, A., Garnero, P., Barclay, D., & Svetkey, L. P. (2003). The DASH diet and sodium reduction improve markers of bone turnover and calcium metabolism in adults. *The Journal of Nutrition*, *133*(10), 3130–3136. https://doi.org/10.1093/jn/133.10.3130

Morris, M. C., Tangney, C. C., Wang, Y., Sacks, F. M., Bennett, D. A., & Aggarwal, N. T. (2015). MIND Diet Associated with Reduced Incidence of Alzheimer's Disease. *Alzheimer's & Dementia : The Journal of the Alzheimer's Association*, *11*(9), 1007–1014. https://doi.org/10.1016/j.jalz.2014.11.009

Obarzanek, E., Sacks, F. M., Vollmer, W. M., Bray, G. A., Miller, E. R., Lin, P. H., Karanja, N. M., Most-Windhauser, M. M., Moore, T. J., Swain, J. F., Bales, C. W., Proschan, M. A., & DASH Research Group. (2001). Effects on blood lipids of a blood pressure-lowering diet: The Dietary Approaches to Stop Hypertension (DASH) Trial. *The American Journal of Clinical Nutrition*, *74*(1), 80–89. https://doi.org/10.1093/ajcn/74.1.80

Peairs, A. D., Shah, A. S., Summer, S., Hess, M., & Couch, S. C. (2017). Effects of the dietary approaches to stop hypertension (DASH) diet on glucose variability in youth with Type 1 diabetes. *Diabetes Management (London, England)*, *7*(5), 383–391.

Pingitore, A., Lima, G. P. P., Mastorci, F., Quinones, A., Iervasi, G., & Vassalle, C. (2015). Exercise and oxidative stress: Potential effects of antioxidant dietary strategies in sports. *Nutrition (Burbank, Los Angeles County, Calif.)*, *31*(7–8), 916–922. https://doi.org/10.1016/j.nut.2015.02.005

Rai, S. K., Fung, T. T., Lu, N., Keller, S. F., Curhan, G. C., & Choi, H. K. (2017). The Dietary Approaches to Stop Hypertension (DASH) diet, Western diet, and risk of gout in men: Prospective cohort study. *BMJ (Clinical Research Ed.)*, *357*, j1794. https://doi.org/10.1136/bmj.j1794

Rebholz, C. M., Crews, D. C., Grams, M. E., Steffen, L. M., Levey, A. S., Miller, E. R., Appel, L. J., & Coresh, J. (2016). DASH (Dietary Approaches to Stop Hypertension) Diet and Risk of Subsequent Kidney Disease. *American*

Journal of Kidney Diseases: The Official Journal of the National Kidney Foundation, 68(6), 853–861. https://doi.org/10.1053/j.ajkd.2016.05.019

Sacks, F. M., Obarzanek, E., Windhauser, M. M., Svetkey, L. P., Vollmer, W. M., McCullough, M., Karanja, N., Lin, P. H., Steele, P., & Proschan, M. A. (1995). Rationale and design of the Dietary Approaches to Stop Hypertension trial (DASH). A multicenter controlled-feeding study of dietary patterns to lower blood pressure. *Annals of Epidemiology, 5*(2), 108–118. https://doi.org/10.1016/1047-2797(94)00055-x

Sacks, F. M., Svetkey, L. P., Vollmer, W. M., Appel, L. J., Bray, G. A., Harsha, D., Obarzanek, E., Conlin, P. R., Miller, E. R., Simons-Morton, D. G., Karanja, N., Lin, P. H., & DASH-Sodium Collaborative Research Group. (2001). Effects on blood pressure of reduced dietary sodium and the Dietary Approaches to Stop Hypertension (DASH) diet. DASH-Sodium Collaborative Research Group. *The New England Journal of Medicine, 344*(1), 3–10. https://doi.org/10.1056/NEJM200101043440101

Saneei, P., Salehi-Abargouei, A., Esmaillzadeh, A., & Azadbakht, L. (2014). Influence of Dietary Approaches to Stop Hypertension (DASH) diet on blood pressure: A systematic review and meta-analysis on randomized controlled trials. *Nutrition, Metabolism, and Cardiovascular Diseases: NMCD, 24*(12), 1253–1261. https://doi.org/10.1016/j.numecd.2014.06.008

Schwingshackl, L., Bogensberger, B., & Hoffmann, G. (2018). Diet Quality as Assessed by the Healthy Eating Index, Alternate Healthy Eating Index, Dietary Approaches to Stop Hypertension Score, and Health Outcomes: An Updated Systematic Review and Meta-Analysis of Cohort Studies. *Journal of the Academy of Nutrition and Dietetics, 118*(1), 74-100.e11. https://doi.org/10.1016/j.jand.2017.08.024

Schwingshackl, L., & Hoffmann, G. (2015). Adherence to Mediterranean diet and risk of cancer: An updated systematic review and meta-analysis of observational studies. *Cancer Medicine, 4*(12), 1933–1947. https://doi.org/10.1002/cam4.539

Schwingshackl, L., Missbach, B., König, J., & Hoffmann, G. (2015). Adherence to a Mediterranean diet and risk of diabetes: A systematic review and meta-analysis. *Public Health Nutrition, 18*(7), 1292–1299. https://doi.org/10.1017/S1368980014001542

Shirani, F., Salehi-Abargouei, A., & Azadbakht, L. (2013). Effects of Dietary Approaches to Stop Hypertension (DASH) diet on some risk for developing type 2 diabetes: A systematic review and meta-analysis on controlled clinical trials. *Nutrition (Burbank, Los Angeles County, Calif.), 29*(7–8), 939–947. https://doi.org/10.1016/j.nut.2012.12.021

Siervo, M., Lara, J., Chowdhury, S., Ashor, A., Oggioni, C., & Mathers, J. C. (2015). Effects of the Dietary Approach to Stop Hypertension (DASH) diet on cardiovascular risk factors: A systematic review and meta-analysis. *The British Journal of Nutrition*, *113*(1), 1–15. https://doi.org/10.1017/S0007114514003341

Smith, A. D., Refsum, H., Bottiglieri, T., Fenech, M., Hooshmand, B., McCaddon, A., Miller, J. W., Rosenberg, I. H., & Obeid, R. (2018). Homocysteine and Dementia: An International Consensus Statement. *Journal of Alzheimer's Disease: JAD*, *62*(2), 561–570. https://doi.org/10.3233/JAD-171042

Tangney, C. C., Li, H., Wang, Y., Barnes, L., Schneider, J. A., Bennett, D. A., & Morris, M. C. (2014). Relation of DASH- and Mediterranean-like dietary patterns to cognitive decline in older persons. *Neurology*, *83*(16), 1410–1416. https://doi.org/10.1212/WNL.0000000000000884

Tobias, D. K., Zhang, C., Chavarro, J., Bowers, K., Rich-Edwards, J., Rosner, B., Mozaffarian, D., & Hu, F. B. (2012). Prepregnancy adherence to dietary patterns and lower risk of gestational diabetes mellitus. *The American Journal of Clinical Nutrition*, *96*(2), 289–295. https://doi.org/10.3945/ajcn.111.028266

U.S. Department of Health and Human Services and U.S. Department of Agriculture. (2005). *DGA 2005*. https://health.gov/dietaryguidelines/dga2005/document/html/chapter6.htm

Van Horn, L., Peaceman, A., Kwasny, M., Vincent, E., Fought, A., Josefson, J., Spring, B., Neff, L. M., & Gernhofer, N. (2018). Dietary Approaches to Stop Hypertension Diet and Activity to Limit Gestational Weight: Maternal Offspring Metabolics Family Intervention Trial, a Technology Enhanced Randomized Trial. *American Journal of Preventive Medicine*, *55*(5), 603–614. https://doi.org/10.1016/j.amepre.2018.06.015

Wengreen, H., Munger, R. G., Cutler, A., Quach, A., Bowles, A., Corcoran, C., Tschanz, J. T., Norton, M. C., & Welsh-Bohmer, K. A. (2013). Prospective study of Dietary Approaches to Stop Hypertension- and Mediterranean-style dietary patterns and age-related cognitive change: The Cache County Study on Memory, Health and Aging. *The American Journal of Clinical Nutrition*, *98*(5), 1263–1271. https://doi.org/10.3945/ajcn.112.051276

Whelton, P. K., Carey, R. M., Aronow, W. S., Casey, D. E., Collins, K. J., Himmelfarb, C. D., DePalma, S. M., Gidding, S., Jamerson, K. A., Jones, D. W., MacLaughlin, E. J., Muntner, P., Ovbiagele, B., Smith, S. C., Spencer, C. C., Stafford, R. S., Taler, S. J., Thomas, R. J., Williams, K. A., … Wright, J. T. (2018). 2017 ACC/AHA/AAPA/ABC/ACPM/AGS/APhA/ASH/ASPC/NMA/PCNA Guideline for the Prevention, Detection, Evaluation, and Management of High Blood

Pressure in Adults: A Report of the American College of Cardiology/American Heart Association Task Force on Clinical Practice Guidelines. *Journal of the American College of Cardiology, 71*(19), e127– e248. https://doi.org/10.1016/j.jacc.2017.11.006

THE GLUTEN-FREE DIET

Deborah Kennedy PhD
with Catrina Hidalgo Schick BS
Joy Hutchinson MSc, RD Reviewer

The gluten-free diet became one of the top five food trends in 2014 and continues to be popular to this day. While the diet has been used by many out of medical necessity, two books, *Wheat Belly* by William Davis and *Grain Brain* by David Perlmutter, MD, kick-started the gluten-free diet fad (Pearlman & Casey, 2019). These books spoke negatively about gluten, scaring people into eliminating gluten from their diets. Picked up by influencers and celebrities, the diet is now used by individuals who want to lose weight or just feel healthier, but there hasn't been much data demonstrating that following a gluten-free diet is advantageous for healthy individuals (Gaesser & Angadi, 2012; Lebwohl et al., 2017).

Gluten-containing cereal grains like wheat, barley, and rye, contain fiber, essential vitamins, and minerals along with a balance of protein, carbohydrates, and fats, which makes them a healthful food source. However, for some, these cereals are not healthful. A gluten-free (GF) diet is essential for those who have celiac disease (CD), non-celiac gluten sensitivity (NCGS), gluten ataxia and dermatitis herpetiformis (DH). **A gluten-free diet is not a healthful option for individuals who do not have an allergy or sensitivity as it can potentially lead to various nutritional deficiencies** (Diez-Sampedro et al., 2019; Theethira & Dennis, 2015). This is concerning as the vast majority of individuals following a GF diet in the United States do not have celiac disease (Rubio-Tapia et al., 2012) and about one-third of Americans believe that gluten-free products are healthier than their gluten-containing counterparts and would promote general health (Dunn et al., 2014; Infographics : The Hartman Group, 2015). This chapter will lay out the evidence to describe when a gluten-free diet is appropriate and when it is not.

SECTION 1: WHAT IS GLUTEN?

Gluten is a protein complex found in some grains including wheat, which is the most widely consumed grain in the world, providing 20% of the daily protein for 4.5 billion people (Ludvigsson et al., 2013). Wheat was one of the first cultivated crops 10,000 years ago, and today there are over 25,000 varieties worldwide within five principal classes: spring (hard red spring), winter (hard red and soft red winter), white and durum wheat. Gluten is considered a prolamin protein due to its high proline amino acid content. In addition to wheat, gluten is found in other grains that are dietary staples around the world. These grains are listed in Table 1. For the latest research on wheat, visit the website The Wheat Initiative.

Table 1: Gluten Containing and Gluten-Free Grains

Gluten Containing Grains	Gluten-free Grains
Wheat & wheat derivatives: Durum, Semolina, Spelt, Farro, Atta	Buckwheat
	Millet
Barley	Gluten-free oats
Triticale	Amaranth
Rye	Rice
	Cornmeal, Polenta, Grits
	Quinoa
	Sorghum
	Teff

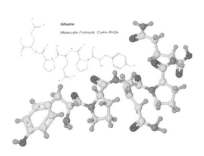

In the United States, approximately one-third of the food found in supermarkets contains gluten (Balakireva & Zamyatnin, 2016). Gluten comes from the Latin word for glue as it is what gives structure and elasticity to baked goods. Gluten is made up of multiple seed storage proteins found in the endosperm of some grains and its purpose is to nourish the grain.

While all gluten proteins act in a different way and cause different damage in individuals with CD, gliadins in wheat are found to be the most harmful while avenins in oats contain a low enough prolamin content to be safe for some patients with CD and those with NCGS (Balakireva & Zamyatnin, 2016). However, individuals with CD must consume gluten-free oats because they are commonly cross-contaminated with other forms of gluten during harvest or processing.

Table 2: Reactivity of Grains Containing Gluten Protein (Prolamin)

Grain	Protein	Reactivity
Wheat	Gliadin, Glutenin	High
Rye	Secalin	High
Barley	Hordein	High
Oat	Avenin	Low

Gluten content in wheat does not seem to have increased over the years, but the amount consumed per person has increased. It is estimated that between 1977 and 2012, gluten consumption per person increased threefold from 0.3 to 0.9 pounds per person per year (Kasarda, 2013). In addition, between 1970 and 2000 consumption of wheat flour increased by 35 pounds per person per year, which accounts for an additional 2.9 pounds of gluten per person per year.

Are oats gluten-free?

Technically, oats are not gluten-free, but many individuals with CD, a wheat allergy, or gluten intolerance can tolerate them without negative health consequences. It is important however to make sure the oats are certified gluten-free as there can often be gluten contamination. Many large brands of commercially rolled oats are often processed in the same facilities that process wheat, barely, and rye. Milling machines are often used for multiple grains, including oats, leading to gluten contamination. Besides the contamination in a factory, there is room for contamination during the cultivation process too. Oats are often grown near other grain fields. This allows for stray gluten grains to enter the oat fields. Due to the high risk of contamination, a GF label is needed, especially if the diet is a medical necessity (Al-Toma et al., 2019).

SECTION 2: TYPES OF GLUTEN SENSITIVITIES AND ALLERGIES

There are three main forms of gluten reactions that cause various bodily reactions, from autoimmune to allergic. These conditions are celiac disease (CD), non-celiac gluten sensitivity (NCGS), and a wheat allergy. Each of these requires a certain level of strictness when following a gluten-free diet.

Celiac disease (CD) is an **autoimmune response** to consuming gluten, as is gluten ataxia (GA) and dermatitis herpetiformis (DH). DH may also occur with CD, causing an itchy blistering rash on the skin. A combination of immunologic (IgA/IgG), genetic, and environmental factors contribute to the development of CD. About 1% of the American population is affected, but many more are assumed to be undiagnosed (Pearlman & Casey, 2019). First-degree relatives of those with CD have a higher liklihood of having CD (Nellikkal et al., 2019). While the cause is still uncertain, CD can develop at any point in life. Two genes, HLA-DQ2 and/or HLA-DQ8, need to be present to develop CD, but alone are not a sufficient trigger, which is evidenced by the fact that 25% to 30% of individuals have the HLA-DQ2 gene but only 1% of the population has CD. When gluten is consumed, an autoimmune reaction causes antibodies to attack the villi and small intestine leading to damage of the villi and subsequent illness. This in turn causes malabsorption of nutrients in the small intestine.

CELIAC DISEASE
DAMAGED SMALL INTESTINE LINING

Diagnosing CD can be a challenge as the list of symptoms is very extensive and just the presence of the genetic markers is not sufficient. In addition, some individuals who have undiagnosed CD may present without any gastrointestinal (GI) issues at all but have persistent **iron deficiency anemia**. Many symptoms, such as abdominal pain and irregular bowel movements, are also symptoms of other conditions like non-celiac gluten sensitivity, irritable bowel disease, and other gastrointestinal conditions. Blood tests to identify the presence of specific antibodies assist in diagnosis. Total tissue transglutaminase (tTG) IgA and deamidated gliadin peptide (DGP) IgG are two blood markers used to detect antibodies. However, an endoscopy with biopsies of the small intestine is needed to confirm CD suspicion.

Wheat allergy is an **allergic reaction** to wheat. Upon consumption, it sets off an IgE-mediated response. No gastrointestinal damage occurs with a wheat allergy. Wheat allergies affect about 0.4% of the American population and can lead to mild symptoms like hives or potentially fatal outcomes like anaphylaxis (Pearlman & Casey, 2019).

For individuals with **non-celiac gluten sensitivity** (**NCGS**), a genetic mutation (HLA-DQ2 or HLA-DQ8) is present in only 50% of cases. Exposure to gluten in NCGS causes similar symptoms to that of CD and include the following (Pinto-Sánchez & Verdú, 2016):

- Abdominal pain
- Eczema or a rash
- Headache and/or foggy mind
- Fatigue
- Diarrhea
- Anemia
- Numbness in legs, arms, or fingers
- Joint pain

NCGS is a condition that does not meet the criteria for CD or wheat allergy. It may be immune mediated, but that is unclear. Individuals with this condition still benefit from removing gluten from their diet. It is estimated that 5% to 6% of the population has NCGS (Sapone et al., 2012). While they may be able to tolerate small amounts of gluten in their diet, most decide to generally avoid it.

There is also a possibility that individuals who believe they have NCGS are actually reacting to fructans, which are fermentable oligo- or polysaccharides that are not well tolerated by some individuals. Oligo- or polysaccharides along with disaccharides, monosaccharides and polyols make up the FODMAP group of carbohydrates. Fructans are often found in foods that also contain gluten, and it just may be that it is the FODMAPs that individuals are reacting to and not the gluten. In fact, in a randomized clinical trial, individuals who self-reported that they had NCGS, actually had more GI distress after eating a bar containing fructans than in one containing gluten (Skodje et al., 2018). More information on the FODMAP diet can be found in the chapter on Gastrointestinal Health.

SECTION 3: POTENTIAL HEALTH BENEFITS OF THE GLUTEN-FREE DIET

There are potential health benefits from following a GF diet for individuals where the diet is medically indicated, which are discussed below. Some symptoms may improve immediately, but for many it may **take months or years to reverse intestinal damage and malabsorption**.

CELIAC DISEASE

For patients with CD, a strict gluten-free diet is essential. Following a gluten-free diet and avoiding cross-contamination will relieve symptoms, heal small intestine damage, and reduce the risk of future damage to the microvilli. Some of the benefits may be due to an improvement in the gut microbiome but data is still limited (Nistal et al., 2012; Tjellström et al., 2013). Consuming gluten after being diagnosed with celiac disease can be detrimental to future health. Untreated celiac disease has been linked to a plethora of health risks including osteoporosis, infertility, nervous system disease, diabetes and intestinal lymphoma (Kooy-Winkelaar YM, Bouwer D, Janssen GMC, Thompson A, Brugman MH, Schmitz F, de Ru AH, Gils, T, Bouma G, van Rood J, van Heelen PA, Mearin ML, Mulder CJ, Koning F, van Bergen J, 2017; Lewis et al., 1996; Shannahan & Leffler, 2017). However, treated CD patients are shown to live normal lives without related additional health concerns.

While the prevalence of CD in the general public is ~1%, the estimated prevalence of CD among those with type 1 diabetes is much higher at ~6%. Patients with both CD and type 1 diabetes may be misdiagnosed as having only one disease. Because of this, after a type 1 diabetes diagnosis, Celiac screening is recommended. And vice versa, after a CD diagnosis screening for type 1 diabetes is warranted (Al-Toma et al., 2019). Both CD and type 1 diabetes are autoimmune related but the reason for the high co-occurrence is still under investigation (Antvorskov et al., 2014; Rewers el al., 2004).

INFLAMMATORY BOWEL DISEASE AND IRRITABLE BOWEL SYNDROME

Inflammatory Bowel Disease (IBD) is used as an all-encompassing term to describe any chronic inflammation along the digestive tract. The two main types of IBD include Crohn's disease and ulcerative colitis. *The Crohn's and Colitis Foundation* states that some IBD patients have found relief from a gluten-free diet, but reduced inflammation has not been confirmed by researchers.

People who suffer from Irritable Bowel Syndrome (IBS) may also benefit from a gluten-free diet, as a significant proportion of these individuals have a sensitivity to gluten (Shahbazkhani et al., 2015). In fact, both CD and IBS present very similarly, making it complicated to diagnose (Elli et al., 2017; Makharia et al., 2015; Niland & Cash, 2018).

It is also difficult to determine that gluten is the sole cause of IBS as it may also be a reaction to FODMAPS (Dieterich & Zopf, 2019; Gibson & Muir, 2013; Junker et al., 2012; McIntosh et al., 2017). This topic is covered more extensively in the chapter on Gastrointestinal Health.

CROHN'S DISEASE

Crohn's disease, similar to CD, deals with intestinal inflammation. Both conditions can cause abdominal pain, irregular bowel movements, and weight loss. In addition, symptoms of Crohn's disease can include rectal bleeding and fever. Crohn's can affect any part of the gastrointestinal tract. Due to the similar symptoms, CD and Crohn's can be difficult to distinguish from each other, which can make testing and diagnosing difficult. Blood tests and endoscopy biopsies are used to determine which disease is present. While the connection between Crohn's and CD is still being investigated, they both share a common genetic risk loci (Festen et al., 2011). In addition, the prevalence of CD is high in patients with Crohn's disease (Tursi et al., 2005). Crohn's disease is covered in more depth in the chapter on Gastrointestinal Health.

AUTOIMMUNE DISEASE

The risk of developing an additional autoimmune disease is increased for CD patients. The *Gluten Intolerance Group* states that the general population has about a 5% to 8% risk of developing an autoimmune disease while the risk with CD increases to around 15% (Lauret & Rodrigo, 2013). The autoimmune diseases that CD patients are more susceptible to include autoimmune thyroiditis, psoriasis, rheumatoid arthritis, Sjögren's syndrome, dermatitis herpetiformis and Addison's disease (Ventura et al., 1999; Viljamaa et al., 2005).

SECTION 4: POTENTIAL RISKS OF FOLLOWING A GLUTEN-FREE DIET

Gluten-free foods tend to have a higher glycemic index and be lower in fiber (Segura & Rosell, 2011), which may contribute to the increased incidence of type 2 diabetes and metabolic syndrome seen in individuals with CD. To limit the spike in blood glucose levels after a meal or snack:

- Choose GF carbohydrate sources rich in fiber like quinoa and sweet potatoes
- Pair GF processed food with a fat or protein to slow the release of simple sugar into the bloodstream

TYPE 2 DIABETES

An observational study conducted by researchers at Harvard that reflected 4.24 million years of follow-up using data from the Nurses' Health Study for women, and the Health Professionals Follow-Up Study for men, found a connecion between the intake of gluten and the risk of developing type 2 diabetes (Zong et al., 2018).

- For men and women, gluten intake was inversely associated with type 2 diabetes risk
- Study participants who ate less gluten also consumed less cereal fiber; intake of cereal fiber is a known protective factor for type 2 diabetes development
- Individuals with the highest 20% of gluten consumption had a 13% lower risk of developing type 2 diabetes

METABOLIC SYNDROME (MetS)

There is more and more evidence indicating that the risk of developing MetS increases on a gluten-free diet due to the increased intake of fats and simple sugars. One year after patients with CD started a gluten-free diet the incidence of MetS increased from 2% to 30% (Tortora et al., 2015). In another study, not only were patients with CD at a higher risk of fatty liver and MetS, but after a year on a GF diet, the incidence of disease increased from 11% to 18% for MetS, and 14% to 30% for fatty liver (Agarwal et al., 2020). MetS and fatty liver among CD patients also increased in a 2019 study after initiation of a GF diet; specifically, an increase in waist circumference, hypertension, high blood sugar, high cholesterol and a BMI>25 was observed (Ciccone et al., 2019).

WEIGHT GAIN

Despite some individuals presenting with symptoms of diarrhea and villous atrophy at diagnosis, there is a range in weight status among patients with CD; some being underweight, the majority being of normal weight, while others are overweight. After 10 years of follow-up, about 80% of those that were compliant on a gluten-free diet gained weight, even in the those that were initially overweight (Dickey & Kearney, 2006).

Weight gain is typical after diagnosis with CD and the switch to a gluten-free diet (Valletta et al., 2010). Individuals may not be eating more necessarily, but as the gut begins to heal, nutrients are better absorbed. In one study, the percentage of children that were overweight at diagnosis (11%) increased to 21% after starting a gluten-free diet (Valletta et al., 2010). Portion sizes and food selection may need to be adjusted to avoid sudden weight gain as many processed GF foods are hypercaloric and low in fiber (Theethira & Dennis, 2015). A visit to a Registered Dietitian may be warranted in order to ensure that the right balance of nutrients is being consumed. A focus on naturally gluten-free foods (vegetables, fruit, non-gluten grains) instead of GF processed food is ideal.

SECTION 5: POTENTIAL MICRONUTRIENT DEFICIENCIES

Nutritional deficiencies in CD are common as the intestinal villi are often shortened or damaged at diagnosis, which leads to nutrient malabsorption in many individuals. The good news is that with a GF diet, the microvilli can return to their original morphology, leading to an improvement in nutrient absorption. With NCGS however the damage to the intestinal wall is not present, therefore technically there should not be nutrient malabsorption. Some studies do suggest that in NCGS, inflammation of the intestinal wall does occur, which can still lead to difficulty absorbing nutrients (Sapone et al., 2011).

Gluten coexists with fiber, vitamins, and minerals in whole grain products. Removing gluten from the diet therefore can lead to unintentional nutrient deficiencies. Monitoring the nutritional status of individuals on a gluten-free diet by a trained Registered Dietitian is crucial to staying healthy. Below in Figure 1 are nutrients individuals following a GF diet are more likely to consume in excess and other nutrients in which individuals are less likely to consume adequate amounts of on a GF diet (Fry et al., 2018; Melini & Melini, 2019; Naik et al., 2018).

Figure 1: Nutrients Consumed in Excess and in Inadequate Amounts When Following a GF Diet

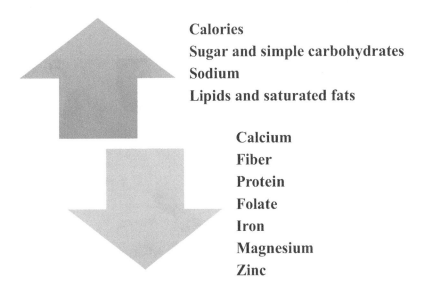

Calories
Sugar and simple carbohydrates
Sodium
Lipids and saturated fats

Calcium
Fiber
Protein
Folate
Iron
Magnesium
Zinc

Table 3: Celiac Disease and Nutrient Deficiencies

Nutrient	Decreased Absorption	Decreased Intake
Iron	X	X
Zinc	X	X
Selenium		X
Calcium	X	X
Potassium		X
Magnesium		X
Folate	X	X
Vitamin B_{12}	X	X
Thiamin		X
Niacin		X
Riboflavin		X
Dietary Fiber		X
Vitamin E		X
Vitamin D	X	X

(Jamieson et al., 2018; Kulai & Rashid, 2014; Miranda et al., 2014; Segura & Rosell, 2011; T. Thompson, 2000;   Thompson: Thiamin, Riboflavin, and Niacin Contents... - Google Scholar, n.d.; Vici et al., 2016.)

At CD diagnosis, the most frequently diagnosed nutrient deficiencies are iron, zinc, calcium, vitamin D, vitamin B_{12} and folic acid (Kreutz et al., 2020). One year after following a GF diet, micronutrient levels may return to normal as the gut heals, but for some, nutrient levels remain low. During long periods of inflammation, the ability to absorb the fat-soluble vitamins — vitamins A, E, and K — is diminished, too (Fasano & Catassi, 2001).

In addition to malabsorption of nutrients causing deficiencies, intake of certain nutrients can be low. Many gluten-free products do not have the same nutrient profile as their gluten containing counterparts. This is partly because gluten-free products like bread and cereal are not enriched and/or fortified as are the gluten containing varieties, and different ratios of micronutrients and macronutrients are used in formulations (Jamieson et al., 2018; Kulai & Rashid, 2014; Segura & Rosell, 2011). In general, **gluten-free foods are lower in the following nutrients**:

- Fiber
- Protein
- B Vitamins — Folate, thiamin, riboflavin, vitamin B_{12} and niacin
- Minerals — Selenium, magnesium, iron, zinc and potassium
- Vitamins D and E

B VITAMINS

In the United States, breads are fortified with certain vitamins and minerals. But only 5% of GF breads contain four fortified nutrients — calcium, iron, niacin and thiamin — and only 28% of GF breads are fortified with calcium and iron.

A study from a Swedish university that took place over 10 years assessed patients' vitamin nutritional status (Hallert et al., 2002). The monitored vitamins were vitamin B_6 and vitamin B_{12} along with related plasma vitamin levels and total plasma homocysteine levels, a metabolic marker of folate deficiency. There were higher total plasma homocysteine levels in study patients compared to the general public, which suggests poor vitamin status. Folate levels were low in 36% of patients and 5'-phosphate, an active form of vitamin B_6, was found to be low in 20% of patients. In addition, the daily consumption of folate and vitamin B_{12} was found to be significantly lower in the patients tested than in the controls. Several reviews summarized the findings on vitamin levels in patients with CD, with one finding that 30% had deficient vitamin B_{12} levels (Caruso et al., 2013; Rondanelli et al., 2019).

IRON AND CALCIUM

> **Iron + vitamin C = increases absorption of iron**

Anemia has been found in approximately 46% of CD patients, most likely because of inadequate iron stores. The reason for this is that the main site of iron absorption is in the duodenum, which is damaged by the body's reaction to gluten in patients with CD. The good news is that iron absorption can be improved with the implementation of a GF diet, but it takes six to 12 months of consuming a GF diet to reverse the damage to the intestinal villi (Annibale et al., 2001). If the intestinal villi are not damaged as is postulated in a wheat allergy or NCGS, the reason for a low iron status would most likely be from inadequate intake.

> **Calcium + vitamin D = increases absorption of calcium**

Calcium deficiencies and metabolic bone diseases can appear in CD patients. About 75% of untreated adults suffer from low bone mineral density. Young patients can experience growth problems while older patients can experience bone fracturing. Similar to iron absorption, calcium and vitamin D are both absorbed in the duodenum.

FATS

Lipid-rich ingredients are a common addition to gluten-free products. The total and saturated fat content found in GF breads, pastas, and bakery products is found to be higher than the gluten-containing equivalents (Di Nardo et al., 2019). Below is an example of the comparison of gluten-free breads and gluten-containing breads. For both types of bread, total fat and sodium percentage is higher in the gluten-free version. The GF hamburger buns also contain lower calcium and iron while the GF bread contains lower iron.

Figure 2: Nutrient Comparison of Gluten-Free versus Gluten Containing Rolls and Bread

GF Classic Hamburger Buns	Classic Hamburger Buns	GF White Bread	White Bread

GF Classic Hamburger Buns

200 CALORIES · 0g SAT FAT · 360mg SODIUM · 5g SUGARS

Nutrition Facts
Serving Size 1.0 bun
Servings Per Container 4

Amount Per Serving
Calories 200
Calories from Fat 50

	% Daily Value*
Total Fat 5g	8%
Saturated Fat 0g	0%
Trans Fat 0g	
Cholesterol 0mg	0%
Sodium 360mg	15%
Total Carbohydrate 36g	11%
Dietary Fiber 4g	16%
Sugars 5g	
Protein 4g	

Vitamin A 0%   Vitamin C 0%
Calcium 2%   Iron 4%

*Percent Daily Values are based on a 2,000 calorie diet.

Classic Hamburger Buns

140 CALORIES · 0.5g SAT FAT · 210mg SODIUM · 4g SUGARS

Nutrition Facts
Serving Size 1.8 oz
Servings Per Container 8

Amount Per Serving
Calories 140
Calories from Fat

	% Daily Value*
Total Fat 2g	3%
Saturated Fat 0.5g	3%
Trans Fat 0g	
Polyunsaturated Fat 1g	
Monounsaturated Fat 0g	
Cholesterol 0mg	0%
Sodium 210mg	9%
Potassium 40mg	0%
Total Carbohydrate 26g	9%
Dietary Fiber 1g	4%
Sugars 4g	
Protein 6g	

Calcium 6%   Iron 6%

*Percent Daily Values are based on a 2,000 calorie diet.

GF White Bread

140 CALORIES · 0g SAT FAT · 270mg SODIUM · 3g SUGARS

Nutrition Facts
Serving Size 2.0 slices
Servings Per Container 7

Amount Per Serving
Calories 140
Calories from Fat 35

	% Daily Value*
Total Fat 4g	6%
Saturated Fat 0g	0%
Trans Fat 0g	
Cholesterol 0mg	0%
Sodium 270mg	11%
Total Carbohydrate 23g	8%
Dietary Fiber 1g	2%
Sugars 3g	
Protein 3g	

Vitamin A 0%   Vitamin C 0%
Calcium 2%   Iron 0%

*Percent Daily Values are based on a 2,000 calorie diet.

White Bread

130 CALORIES · 0g SAT FAT · 230mg SODIUM · 2g SUGARS

Nutrition Facts
Serving Size 2.0 slices
Servings Per Container 9

Amount Per Serving
Calories 130
Calories from Fat

	% Daily Value*
Total Fat 1.5g	2%
Saturated Fat 0g	0%
Trans Fat 0g	
Cholesterol 0mg	0%
Sodium 230mg	10%
Potassium 40mg	0%
Total Carbohydrate 24g	9%
Dietary Fiber 0g	0%
Sugars 2g	
Protein 4g	

Calcium 2%   Iron 6%

*Percent Daily Values are based on a 2,000 calorie diet.

FIBER

Fiber content in gluten-free flours is often very low, and the reason is that during the production process, the highest concentration of fiber found in the outer layer of the grain is removed (Lamacchia et al., 2014). Because of this, fiber is usually added to GF foods in the form of β-glucan, inulin, oligofructose, linseed mucilage, apple pomace, carob fiber, bamboo fiber, polydextrose and resistant starch (El Khoury et al., 2018).

SECTION 6: CULINARY COMPETENCIES FOR FOLLOWING A GLUTEN-FREE DIET

In addition to following the culinary competencies for Fruit, Vegetables, Grains, Dairy, Fats & Oils, Protein and Sodium, individuals who wish to follow a GF diet will do well if they can:

1. Describe the GF diet, including foods to avoid and foods to focus on
2. List the types of reactions to wheat and/or gluten that necessitate following a GF diet
3. List the benefits and risks of following a GF diet
4. List the benefits and risks of not following a GF diet when medically indicated

5. Choose nutrient of concern when following a GF diet and food sources of those nutrients
6. Model consumption of a GF diet
7. Buy certified GF products
8. Bake and cook with GF alternatives
9. Serve a combination of macronutrients to reduce post-prandial spikes in blood sugar levels
10. Include good sources of fiber at meals and snacks
11. Design a weekly menu that aligns with the GF diet
12. Create a safe space in the kitchen for storing and preparing GF food in order to prevent cross contamination
13. Refer to a registered dietitian or clinician when medically appropriate

SECTION 7: AT THE STORE

The production of gluten-free foods in the last 10 to 20 years has advanced to such a degree that finding gluten-free options is relatively easy in most larger towns and cities. One can find pasta, cookies, bread, cake and muffins as well as many other products that are produced without gluten. While the availability of GF foods has increased dramatically, shopping for GF foods can still be difficult as gluten is hidden in many products.

WHAT TO LOOK FOR ON THE LABEL

The labeling of gluten-free foods provides comfort to many who need to avoid cross-contamination. However, the array of labels and certifications can lead to some confusion. Some foods do not need a label due to their naturally gluten-free nature. For example, an apple would not need a gluten-free label as no type of fresh, raw apple would ever contain gluten. In 2004, the Center for Food Safety and

Applied Nutrition (CFSAN), a branch of the Food and Drug Administration (FDA), passed the 2004 <u>Food Allergen Labeling and Consumer Protection Act (FALCPA)</u>. This required nutrition labels to display "contains" for any of the eight main allergens, including wheat. While this was a huge step in ensuring food safety, more labeling and transparency was needed for gluten-free food as gluten is found in other grains besides wheat.

Different dietary restrictions may require different necessities. For example, a food suitable for a gluten intolerant person may not be sufficient for those who have CD. The FDA has established a rule for using the term "gluten-free," "no gluten," "free of gluten" or "without gluten." If a food is labeled with these words it must be one of the following: contains no gluten-containing grain ingredients, contains no ingredient derived from gluten-containing grain without removing the gluten, or the presence of any gluten must be under 20 parts per million (ppm).

Even though these guidelines are in place, there is no requirement for testing food for gluten. In a systematic review of 23 studies, **13% of industrial food products were contaminated** and **42% of non-industrial food products were contaminated** (Falcomer et al., 2020). The uncertainty of testing and labeling has pushed third-party organizations to establish more strict guidelines and testing for specific labels. The advocacy website, *Beyond Celiac* endorsed the <u>Gluten-Free Certification Program</u> (GFCP), which tests products and allows the claim **gluten-free** if the product contains 20 ppm or less of gluten. *The National Sanitation Foundation* (NSF) certifies products that contain 15 ppm or less. *The Gluten Intolerance Group's* Gluten-Free Certification Organization (GFCO) requires the product to contain 10 ppm or less. *The National Celiac Association* (NCA) has gone a step farther and requires tested foods to contain less than 5 ppm of gluten, if any. Certification organizations provide customers with more confidence in their food. Below are two tables showing the certifications in addition to FDA standards.

Table 4: Gluten-Free Symbols on Packages

Certification	Label	Allowed ppm
Beyond Celiac Gluten-Free Certification Program (GFCP)		20 ppm or less

National Sanitation Foundation (NSF)		15 ppm or less
Gluten Intolerance Group's Gluten-Free Certification Organization (GFCO)		10 ppm or less
National Celiac Association (NCA)		5 ppm or less

Table 5: Definition of Gluten-Free Levels Around the World

Country	Level of gluten in parts per million (ppm)
USA	< 20 ppm
Australia & New Zealand	< 5 ppm
European Union & United Kingdom	< 20 ppm
Canada	< 20 ppm

Reference: https://glutenfreepassport.com/pages/understand-global-gluten-free-amp-food-allergy-product-labeling

GLUTEN-FREE FOOD ACCESS

Not everyone has good access to GF products. Individuals living in rural areas may have a harder time finding processed GF items due to more limited selection in grocery stores. The price of GF products is also often a concern.

- Gluten-free products are 200% to 500% more expensive than their gluten containing counterparts, making them less available to those on a limited budget (Lambert & Ficken, 2016; Lee et al., 2007; Singh & Whelan, 2011)
- Up to 85% of individuals with CD have a hard time identifying GF ingredients and products (Halmos et al., 2018; Zarkadas et al., 2006)

A great resource for staying up to date on contamination of gluten in GF products is the Gluten Free Watchdog run by registered dietitian Tricia Thompson, MS RD (Note: there is a cost for this service).

HIDDEN SOURCES OF GLUTEN

There are several common places where gluten can hide, which can lead to a negative reaction after consumption. Naturally gluten-free grains can be contaminated during the cultivation or production process. A 2010 study examined 22 different types of grains, seeds, and flours that should have been naturally gluten-free, e.g. millet. Upon testing, 32% of the packages contained gluten levels over the safe level of 20 ppm. None of the packages were required to mark an allergy advisory statement, leading to contamination and misguidance. Out of the tested foods, the lowest contained 8.5 ppm and the highest contained 2,925 ppm (Thompson et al., 2010).

In addition, some gluten containing ingredients are not that obvious. Derivatives of barley and rye can be hidden in a long list of ingredients. Malt and malt derivatives are common ingredients made from barley. An example of a product with hidden gluten is shown below:

Ingredients
Rice, Sugar, Contains 2% Or Less Of Salt, Malt Flavor.

Look for gluten-containing grains on the food label along with **flavorings** and **hydrolyzed vegetable protein**. Great resources for hidden sources of gluten can be found **here** and **here**. Below are foods that commonly contain gluten:

- Soy sauce
- Processed meats and meat alternatives — breadcrumbs are often used as fillers and binders
- Soups — wheat flour is often used as a thickener
- Restaurant eggs — pancake batter can be used as a thickener. Order fried, boiled, or poached eggs instead
- Salad dressing

- Beer

Other products: anything that goes near the mouth and contains gluten is not safe for individuals with CD. These include topical products like:
- Lipstick or Chapstick
- Toothpaste and mouthwash
- Medications

Cross-contact: It's important that any kitchen tools that are used to prepare gluten-containing foods are not also used to prepare gluten-free foods due to the risk of cross-contamination. This includes the:
- Toaster
- Colander
- Cutting board
- Wooden utensils (spoons, rolling pin, cutting board)
- Dish rags and sponges (these need to be swapped after cleaning the counter and washing dishes)
- Grill
- Any surface that had gluten
- Foods fried in oil also used for breaded foods
- Condiments — can be contaminated with utensils that were used on bread then double-dipped
- Bulk bins at grocery stores

Overall, it is important to check into **everything** that is consumed or touches consumed food. It may be tedious but it will help to avoid any illness related to cross-contamination.

Checklist for Food Service to Prevent Cross Contamination with Gluten.

FOODS TO FOCUS ON

Preparing a daily GF diet requires knowledge of which nutrients are low or absent in a GF diet and in GF alternatives. For an individual on a GF diet, it is important to make sure that they are consuming enough of the nutrients listed in Table 6.

Table 6: Nutrients of Concern When Following a Gluten-Free Diet

Nutrient	Food Sources*
Iron	Oysters, white beans (cooked), lentils (cooked), spinach (boiled), tofu, kidney beans (cooked), sardines, chickpeas (cooked), tomatoes (stewed), beef, potatoes (baked) and cashews (roasted)
Zinc	Oysters, beef, crab, lobster, pork chop, baked beans, chicken, pumpkin seeds, yogurt, cashews (dry roasted), chickpeas (cooked), Swiss cheese and oatmeal (cooked)
Selenium	Brazil nuts, tuna, halibut, sardines, ham, shrimp, beef, turkey, chicken, cottage cheese, rice (parboiled), eggs (hard boiled), lentils (boiled), baked beans, milk and yogurt
Calcium	Yogurt, milk, and cheeses like cheddar, mozzarella, and cottage cheese; orange juice (fortified with calcium), tofu (only if made with calcium sulfate), salmon, dairy, dairy alternatives like soy and almond milk (only if fortified) and kale
Magnesium	Spinach, dark chocolate, and nuts like almonds, cashews, and peanuts; legumes like black, soy, and kidney beans; rice, potato, soymilk and yogurt
Folate	Spinach (boiled and raw), black eyed peas (boiled), rice (parboiled), asparagus (boiled), Brussels sprouts (boiled), lettuce, avocado, broccoli (cooked), mustard greens (boiled), green peas (boiled), kidney beans and enriched GF pasta
Vitamin B_6	Chickpeas, tuna, salmon, chicken, potatoes (boiled), turkey, banana, beef, cottage cheese and winter squash (baked)
Vitamin B_{12}	Clams, trout, salmon, tuna, Nutritional yeast, beef, haddock, milk, yogurt, Swiss cheese, egg (hard boiled), ham and chicken
Thiamin	Enriched rice (parboiled), enriched egg noodles, pork chop, trout, black beans (boiled), mussels, tuna and acorn squash (baked)
Vitamin C	Red and green pepper, oranges, grapefruit, kiwifruit, broccoli (cooked and raw), Brussels sprouts (cooked), strawberries, tomato (raw), cantaloupe, cabbage

	(cooked), cauliflower, tomato juice, potato (baked) and spinach (cooked)
Dietary Fiber **	Whole GF grains like quinoa, amaranth, millet, buckwheat, oats and sorghum, legumes, pears, prunes, dried figs, berries, oranges, avocado, deep green leafy vegetables, seeds, almonds, pinon nuts and pistachios
Vitamin D	Cod liver oil, trout, salmon, white mushrooms (exposed to UV light), milk (fortified), soy, oat or almond milk (fortified)

*Information from ODS Fact Sheets for Professionals. All foods listed are gluten-free and provide 10% or more DV for the specific nutrient. All food listed is raw or frozen unless otherwise stated.

** (The Top Fiber-Rich Foods List, 2008.)

GLUTEN-FREE WHOLE-GRAINS

Besides the standard GF options – corn, rice and oats (for some) – below are some great tasting GF whole grains. Experiment with different varieties and use them as substitutes in recipes that call for gluten-containing grains, like wheat, barley, rye, triticale, and oats (for some).

Figure 3: The Flavor of Gluten-Free Whole Grain Alternatives

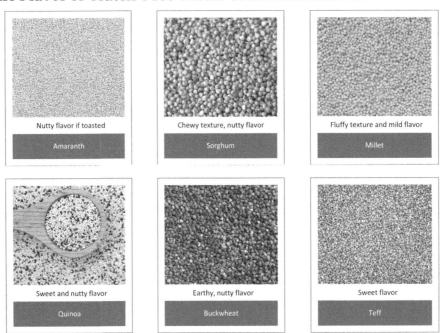

Nutty flavor if toasted	Chewy texture, nutty flavor	Fluffy texture and mild flavor
Amaranth	Sorghum	Millet
Sweet and nutty flavor	Earthy, nutty flavor	Sweet flavor
Quinoa	Buckwheat	Teff

- Dry cooking grains in a pan (toasting) before adding liquid can bring out a nutty taste

- Sorghum is a great substitute for couscous
- Always rinse quinoa to remove a bitter tasting coating
- The toasted/roasted version of buckwheat is called kasha

SECTION 8: IN THE KITCHEN

Gluten provides the structure and elasticity in baked goods, but this structure and elasticity must come from elsewhere when making GF products. Use the following guidance when baking or cooking with non-wheat flour-based recipes.

Building structure when baking:
- Add eggs as they add structure
- Different combinations of GF flours work best for different baking projects — do some researching before you bake
- Use xanthan gum as a binder to give texture
- Mix the batter for a longer period of time to build structure, which is the opposite of what one would do when mixing a batter with a gluten-containing flour
- Let the batter rest for 30 minutes before baking, a tip from America's Test Kitchen
- Cook for the required length of time using a timer. Using traditional methods like a clean toothpick or a firmness to the touch do not work well for telling if GF baked products are ready to be taken out of the oven. The firmness occurs when the baked product cools and the starches finish setting up.

STEPS TO MAKING A GLUTEN-FREE DOUGH THAT WORKS

Step 1: Choose one or a combination of gluten-free flours: oats, rice, buckwheat, maize (corn), quinoa, sorghum, teff, chickpea, pea, carob germ, carob, chia, marama bean and soy flour. There are lots to choose from and an infinite variety of

combinations. Khoury et al has a <u>great review</u> of the properties of various flours when making bread.

Step 2: Add fiber to add the following properties: water-binding, viscosity-increasing, and gel-forming capacities. Options include chia or flax seeds, rice or corn bran. Added fiber found in processed food include: β-glucan, inulin, oligofructose, linseed mucilage, apple pomace, carob fiber, bamboo fiber, polydextrose and resistant starch.

Step 3: Choose a hydrocolloid to increase viscosity and therefore the ability to form a structure that traps gas. The most popular are xanthan gum, guar gum, and hydroxypropyl methyl cellulose (HPMC) but others that have been used include pectin, locust bean gum, agarose, tragacanth gum, cress seed gum and carboxymethyl cellulose.

<u>King Arthur Flour Gluten-free Baking</u> has more information on GF baking.

Gums

Both guar and xanthan gum are a thickening agent, an emulsifier and a stabilizer that are used frequently in GF cooking and baking. Guar gum is best used in cold dishes unless the dish contains acid (lemon or lime juice and/or vinegars). Xanthan gum is best for cooked dishes and it is what helps build structure in bread-like products. The following are the amounts of xanthan gum to be used in GF recipes suggested by <u>Bobs Red Mills</u>:

Table 7: Amount of Xanthan Gum Used in Recipes

Baked Item	Teaspoon per cup of GF flour
Cookies	¼ tsp
Cakes and pancakes	½ tsp
Muffins and quick bread	¾ tsp
Bread	1 to 1 ½ tsp
Pizza dough	2 tsp

For cold items like salad dressing, a fruit sauce or compote use:
- Salad dressing (8 oz): ½ teaspoon xanthan gum or guar gum
- Fruit compote or sauces (8 oz): start with ½ teaspoon xanthan gum or guar gum. The thickening agent has an added benefit in that the recipe can be made with less sugar as the gums provide the thickening.

GLUTEN-FREE BREADCRUMBS

It is super easy to make homemade breadcrumbs. Most GF premade bread has two ends that are small and are usually tossed out. Instead of throwing them away, leave the ends out on a cookie sheet where they will dry out. When the pile gets large and the ends are dried, grind them in a food processor and add salt and pepper and dried spices, herbs, or aromatics like ground turmeric and garlic powder, for example. Do not add any wet ingredients as it will cause spoiling. The options are endless. Make an Italian breadcrumb with dried garlic and oregano and maybe a little rosemary. Make a curried inspired mix with curry powder, turmeric, and black pepper.

Making Breaded Meat Cutlets

Option 1: Dip pounded chicken in egg wash and then roll in a plate with crushed toasted pecans or almonds. Bake on a cookie sheet with canola oil. (Note: This wouldn't hold up to deep frying).

Option 2: Follow the traditional method except replace with GF flour and GF breadcrumbs. Begin by rolling chicken in GF flour, followed by a dip in egg wash and finally a roll in GF breadcrumbs.

Option 3: When in a rush, just roll pounded chicken cutlets in breadcrumbs.

For all options cook on baking sheet that has a thin layer of oil at 375°F/190°C until done (depends on the thickness of the cutlet). Cook until an internal temperature of 165°F/74°C is reached.

GLUTEN-FREE GRANOLA

Depending on a person's reaction to GF oats, a traditional granola can be made with GF rolled oats, nuts, seeds and dried fruit. If oats are to be avoided, a granola can be made with no grains or quinoa flakes with the nuts, seeds, and dried fruit.

SAUCES WITHOUT GLUTEN

To thicken sauces, follow the advice below:
- In soups and stews use shaved cooked potato or cooked rice to thicken the sauce
- Mixing 1 tablespoon of water with 1 teaspoon of either cassava or corn flour and adding that to soups and stews will thicken the base
- For a white sauce, use pureed cooked cauliflower, cashews, or white beans as the thickener
- Use a GF flour without gums (guar or xanthan gum) in the same amount when a recipe calls for using all-purpose wheat flour – for example, sweet rice flour, bean flour, or other GF alternatives work well
- Make sure not to overheat the mixture as it will break down and separate

BUILD A NUTRIENT PACKED SMOOTHIE

The following smoothie provides many of the nutrients that are low or missing in a gluten-free diet. Make this **Chocolate Pear Smoothie** or make your own from any of the GF foods listed below.

- 1/3 cup cashews or 2 tbsp nut butter
- 2 large kale leaves or 1 cup baby kale
- 1 cup milk fortified with calcium and vitamin D
- 2 tsp unsweetened dark chocolate
- 1 pear, chopped
- 1 tbsp ground flax seeds
- ½ tsp nutritional yeast
- Handful of ice
- 1 mint leaf (optional)

Mix all in a blender and enjoy!

Components to Build a GF Friendly Smoothie

1 cup liquid	1 cup fresh fruit	1 cup vegetables
Low fat milk	Raspberries	Kale
Almond or soy milk (fortified with calcium and vitamin D)	Blackberries	Collard or mustard greens
	Pears	Broccoli
	Apples	Spinach
	Oranges	
Protein	**Fiber**	**Additions**
Tofu or legumes	GF Flax seeds	Nutritional yeast
GF nut butter	GF Chia seeds	Sunflower seeds
GF almonds	Avocado	Unsweetened cocoa
GF cashews		Hemp hearts
Yogurt unsweetened		

SECTION 9: AT THE TABLE

A healthful diet is one that is full of a variety of fruits, vegetables, whole grains, low-fat dairy and protein sources. Just because someone is on a gluten-free diet though doesn't necessarily mean that they are opting for fruits and vegetables over processed gluten-free products. In fact, many are consuming processed GF products because they think that they are healthful just because they don't contain gluten.

The healthfulness or unhealthfulness of a product doesn't have anything to do with the presence or absence of gluten. In fact, replacing gluten with gluten-free alternatives can actually lead to weight gain due to the increase in sugar, fat, and calories used to mimic the texture of gluten in processed foods. Plus, prepared gluten-free foods tend to be less filling because they are usually lower in fiber.

Being GF doesn't mean that one has a license to eat whatever they want as long as it is GF. Within most types of diets there are both healthful, nutrient-dense options, and energy dense, not very healthful options. The goal is to consume the healthful options most of the time and consume the less nutrient dense options occasionally. In figure 4 are examples of gluten-free meals and a snack that are higher in nutrient density and a snack and meals that are lower in nutrient density.

Figure 4: Two Days of Gluten-Free Meals and a Snack

VERSUS

It is obvious from the pictures above that a GF diet can look just as processed as a standard American diet. Here is a Sample meal plan for gluten-free living.

SECTION 10: EATING OUT

HOW TO ORDER AT A RESTAURANT

Eating out can on a gluten-free diet can be an intimidating adventure. The fear of contamination and judgment can get in the way of having a relaxing meal. Here are some ways of cutting back on the stress:

1. **Call the restaurant before going to learn about how the kitchen handles gluten-free requests and avoids contamination.** First, it is helpful to ask if the restaurant has GF options. This is a great starting point as the answer will show their attitude towards gluten-free. If they do have GF options, the next step would be asking about kitchen safety procedures. Questions about if they keep a separate preparation area and keep GF ingredients away from gluten containing foods will help with feeling more comfortable and confident in the restaurant's ability to serve GF food. If they have many options or are open to making accommodations, the staff is most likely well-versed. If the response is negative or comes across as unsure, the staff most likely has not been properly trained. While the response over the phone is not always a definite answer, it can help when deciding to dine at the restaurant or not.

2. **Inquire as to the gluten-free training of the servers at a restaurant**. This can be done beforehand on the phone or while at the restaurant. If the server does not seem well versed, ask to speak to the manager. The manager *should*

know the proper answers and will be able to direct the kitchen staff to make safe accommodations.

3. The internet is a great and easy way of figuring out how the restaurant handles a gluten-free request. **Simply searching for the menu** will show if the foods appears to be GF. Some menus will have a symbol next to the food item depicting if it has gluten or if it is GF. These restaurants will most likely be aware of the needs of a GF patron and can make accommodations if needed. Gluten-free finder apps are also a new and innovative way of finding safe establishments. This allows for past patrons to vote and comment on their care. Reading reviews will provide honest opinions and experiences.

4. Ask specific questions while at the restaurant. When you go to the restaurant and have selected your meal, ask questions to determine that your meal will be safe. For example, if you order a steak with steamed vegetables and French fries you could ask: Is the steak grilled on a separate, clean surface? Are clean utensils used for the vegetables? Have the fries been cooked in a deep fryer which is only used for GF foods?

For more guidelines and tips, visit the follow sites:
https://celiac.org/gluten-free-living/dining-and-social-eating/
https://www.beyondceliac.org/gluten-free-diet/dining-tips/
https://www.gastrocenter.org/our-centers/celiac-center-at-gcc/tips-dining-celiac-disease/

GLUTEN-FREE PREFERENCE OR REQUEST?

Restaurants will sometimes ask if the gluten-free request is a preference or medically necessary. The answer will tell them what precautions need to be taken in the kitchen. If the staff does not ask, it is always a good idea to tell them. Saying GF food is medically necessary should tell them cross-contamination is not safe. It is always best to reiterate that point and explain specific needs. For example, ensure the GF pasta is not boiled in the same water as gluten containing pasta. Saying "preference" will mean cross-contamination does not matter. For example, fries fried in the same oil as wheat-based breaded chicken is dangerous for someone with CD or a wheat allergy but might be fine for someone with a GF preference.

SECTION 11: RESOURCES

https://www.findmeglutenfree.com/
https://gf-finder.com/
https://www.yelp.com/nearme/gluten-free-restaurants
https://www.allergyeats.com/

Apps:
The Gluten-free Scanner
Dedicated Gluten-free

SECTION 12: TIPS FOR FOLLOWING A GLUTEN-FREE DIET

As can be seen through pictures in a previous section, *At the Table*, a GF diet can be a healthful diet if individuals who need to be on a GF diet select fruits, vegetables, whole GF grains, healthful fats and low-fat protein sources as their main staples. If one chooses instead to switch GF products for gluten containing products and follow a typical Standard American Diet (SAD) with a high consumption of processed foods and the salt, sugar, and solid fat that accompanies it, that will not lead down a path towards health. In fact, it will increase an individual's risk of excessive weight gain and developing chronic diseases like heart disease, diabetes, and cancer.

Swap gluten containing grains for **whole grains that do not contain gluten** — millet, quinoa, sorghum, buckwheat, amaranth — instead of switching to GF processed products like GF breads, pasta, cookies and crackers.

When deciding what to eat, the Celiac Disease Foundation has the following suggestions:

- **Rotate whole grains**: avoid rotating rice, corn, and potato every day. Add certified GF grains like buckwheat, quinoa, and amaranth.
- **Institute "Meatless Mondays" or "Fatty Fish Fridays":** don't miss plant-based proteins (beans, legumes) for omega-3 and omega-6 fatty acids. They are low in saturated fat and have no cholesterol. Studies show two servings of fatty fish per week deliver fatty acids needed to calm inflammation.
- **Eat at least one leafy green per day and the darker the better!** A serving of kale, chard, spinach or mustard greens will supply significant amounts of vitamins A, C, K and folate — all can be used to combat oxidative stress.

Lightly cook the greens with a fat source (olive oil) or serve in a salad or smoothie.

- **Vary cooking oils and salad dressings:** flaxseed, hemp, pumpkin seed, and walnut oils are great for salads, but too delicate for heat. Olive, grapeseed, and sesame oils are good for sautéing. Coconut, avocado, safflower, canola oils are stable for frying and baking. Varying oils will give a good balance of monounsaturated, polyunsaturated, and saturated fats in the right proportions.

SUMMARY

Many Americans believe that gluten-free products are more healthful and that they promote general health. This is concerning as a gluten-free diet can be an unbalanced diet and therefore should not be undertaken unless there is a medical reason to do so. A GF diet is necessary for individuals with celiac disease, a wheat allergy, and non-celiac gluten sensitivity, and it may also be beneficial for those with irritable bowel syndrome or an autoimmune disease. Working with a Registered Dietitian is often advised as a GF diet is a very complex lifestyle change and it should not be adopted lightly. While the diet can be helpful, even essential, there are many factors to consider like the micronutrient deficiencies that can occur when following a GF diet.

REFERENCES

Agarwal, A., Singh, A., Mehtab, W., Gupta, V., Chauhan, A., Rajput, M. S., Singh, N., Ahuja, V., & Makharia, G. K. (2020). Patients with celiac disease are at high risk of developing metabolic syndrome and fatty liver. *Intestinal Research*. https://doi.org/10.5217/ir.2019.00136

Al-Toma, A., Volta, U., Auricchio, R., Castillejo, G., Sanders, D. S., Cellier, C., Mulder, C. J., & Lundin, K. E. A. (2019). European Society for the Study of Coeliac Disease (ESsCD) guideline for coeliac disease and other gluten-related disorders. *United European Gastroenterology Journal*, *7*(5), 583–613. https://doi.org/10.1177/2050640619844125

Annibale, B., Severi, C., Chistolini, A., Antonelli, G., Lahner, E., Marcheggiano, A., Iannoni, C., Monarca, B., & Delle Fave, G. (2001). Efficacy of gluten-free diet alone on recovery from iron deficiency anemia in adult celiac patients. *The American Journal of Gastroenterology*, *96*(1), 132–137. https://doi.org/10.1111/j.1572-0241.2001.03463.x

Antvorskov, J. C., Josefsen, K., Engkilde, K., Funda, D. P., & Buschard, K. (2014). Dietary gluten and the development of type 1 diabetes. *Diabetologia*, *57*(9), 1770–1780. https://doi.org/10.1007/s00125-014-3265-1

Balakireva, A. V., & Zamyatnin, A. A. (2016). Properties of Gluten Intolerance: Gluten Structure, Evolution, Pathogenicity and Detoxification Capabilities. *Nutrients*, *8*(10). https://doi.org/10.3390/nu8100644

Caruso, R., Pallone, F., Stasi, E., Romeo, S., & Monteleone, G. (2013). Appropriate nutrient supplementation in celiac disease. *Annals of Medicine*, *45*(8), 522–531. https://doi.org/10.3109/07853890.2013.849383

Ciccone, A., Gabrieli, D., Cardinale, R., Di Ruscio, M., Vernia, F., Stefanelli, G., Necozione, S., Melideo, D., Viscido, A., Frieri, G., & Latella, G. (2019). Metabolic Alterations in Celiac Disease Occurring after Following a Gluten-Free Diet. *Digestion*, *100*(4), 262–268. https://doi.org/10.1159/000495749

Di Nardo, G., Villa, M. P., Conti, L., Ranucci, G., Pacchiarotti, C., Principessa, L., Raucci, U., & Parisi, P. (2019). Nutritional Deficiencies in Children with Celiac Disease Resulting from a Gluten-Free Diet: A Systematic Review. *Nutrients*, *11*(7). https://doi.org/10.3390/nu11071588

Dickey, W., & Kearney, N. (2006). Overweight in celiac disease: Prevalence, clinical characteristics, and effect of a gluten-free diet. *The American Journal of Gastroenterology*, *101*(10), 2356–2359. https://doi.org/10.1111/j.1572-0241.2006.00750.x

Dieterich, W., & Zopf, Y. (2019). Gluten and FODMAPS-Sense of a Restriction/When Is Restriction Necessary? *Nutrients*, *11*(8). https://doi.org/10.3390/nu11081957

Diez-Sampedro, A., Olenick, M., Maltseva, T., & Flowers, M. (2019). A Gluten-Free Diet, Not an Appropriate Choice without a Medical Diagnosis. *Journal of Nutrition and Metabolism, 2019.* https://doi.org/10.1155/2019/2438934

Dunn, C., House, L., & Shelnutt, K. P. (2014). Consumer Perceptions of Gluten-Free Products and the Healthfulness of Gluten-Free Diets. *Journal of Nutrition Education and Behavior, 46*(4), S184–S185. https://doi.org/10.1016/j.jneb.2014.04.280

El Khoury, D., Balfour-Ducharme, S., & Joye, I. J. (2018). A Review on the Gluten-Free Diet: Technological and Nutritional Challenges. *Nutrients, 10*(10). https://doi.org/10.3390/nu10101410

Elli, L., Villalta, D., Roncoroni, L., Barisani, D., Ferrero, S., Pellegrini, N., Bardella, M. T., Valiante, F., Tomba, C., Carroccio, A., Bellini, M., Soncini, M., Cannizzaro, R., & Leandro, G. (2017). Nomenclature and diagnosis of gluten-related disorders: A position statement by the Italian Association of Hospital Gastroenterologists and Endoscopists (AIGO). *Digestive and Liver Disease: Official Journal of the Italian Society of Gastroenterology and the Italian Association for the Study of the Liver, 49*(2), 138–146. https://doi.org/10.1016/j.dld.2016.10.016

Falcomer, A. L., Santos Araújo, L., Farage, P., Santos Monteiro, J., Yoshio Nakano, E., & Puppin Zandonadi, R. (2020). Gluten contamination in food services and industry: A systematic review. *Critical Reviews in Food Science and Nutrition, 60*(3), 479–493. https://doi.org/10.1080/10408398.2018.1541864

Fasano, A., & Catassi, C. (2001). Current approaches to diagnosis and treatment of celiac disease: An evolving spectrum. *Gastroenterology, 120*(3), 636–651. https://doi.org/10.1053/gast.2001.22123

Festen, E. A. M., Goyette, P., Green, T., Boucher, G., Beauchamp, C., Trynka, G., Dubois, P. C., Lagacé, C., Stokkers, P. C. F., Hommes, D. W., Barisani, D., Palmieri, O., Annese, V., Heel, D. A. van, Weersma, R. K., Daly, M. J., Wijmenga, C., & Rioux, J. D. (2011). A Meta-Analysis of Genome-Wide Association Scans Identifies IL18RAP, PTPN2, TAGAP, and PUS10 As Shared Risk Loci for Crohn's Disease and Celiac Disease. *PLOS Genetics, 7*(1), e1001283. https://doi.org/10.1371/journal.pgen.1001283

Fry, L., Madden, A. M., & Fallaize, R. (2018). An investigation into the nutritional composition and cost of gluten-free versus regular food products in the UK. *Journal of Human Nutrition and Dietetics: The Official Journal of the British Dietetic Association, 31*(1), 108–120. https://doi.org/10.1111/jhn.12502

Gaesser, G. A., & Angadi, S. S. (2012). Gluten-free diet: Imprudent dietary advice for the general population? *Journal of the Academy of Nutrition and Dietetics, 112*(9), 1330–1333. https://doi.org/10.1016/j.jand.2012.06.009

Gibson, P. R., & Muir, J. G. (2013). Not all effects of a gluten-free diet are due to removal of gluten. *Gastroenterology*, *145*(3), 693. https://doi.org/10.1053/j.gastro.2013.06.056

Hallert, C., Grant, C., Grehn, S., Grännö, C., Hultén, S., Midhagen, G., Ström, M., Svensson, H., & Valdimarsson, T. (2002). Evidence of poor vitamin status in coeliac patients on a gluten-free diet for 10 years. *Alimentary Pharmacology & Therapeutics*, *16*(7), 1333–1339. https://doi.org/10.1046/j.1365-2036.2002.01283.x

Halmos, E. P., Deng, M., Knowles, S. R., Sainsbury, K., Mullan, B., & Tye-Din, J. A. (2018). Food knowledge and psychological state predict adherence to a gluten-free diet in a survey of 5310 Australians and New Zealanders with coeliac disease. *Alimentary Pharmacology & Therapeutics*, *48*(1), 78–86. https://doi.org/10.1111/apt.14791

Infographics: The Hartman Group. (n.d.). Retrieved May 5, 2020, from https://www.hartman-group.com/infographics/1852467713/gluten-free-trend

Jamieson, J. A., Weir, M., & Gougeon, L. (2018). Canadian packaged gluten-free foods are less nutritious than their regular gluten-containing counterparts. *PeerJ*, *6*, e5875. https://doi.org/10.7717/peerj.5875

Junker, Y., Zeissig, S., Kim, S.-J., Barisani, D., Wieser, H., Leffler, D. A., Zevallos, V., Libermann, T. A., Dillon, S., Freitag, T. L., Kelly, C. P., & Schuppan, D. (2012). Wheat amylase trypsin inhibitors drive intestinal inflammation via activation of toll-like receptor 4. *The Journal of Experimental Medicine*, *209*(13), 2395–2408. https://doi.org/10.1084/jem.20102660

Kasarda, D. D. (2013). Can an Increase in Celiac Disease Be Attributed to an Increase in the Gluten Content of Wheat as a Consequence of Wheat Breeding? *Journal of Agricultural and Food Chemistry*, *61*(6), 1155–1159. https://doi.org/10.1021/jf305122s

Kooy-Winkelaar YM, Bouwer D, Janssen GMC, Thompson A, Brugman MH, Schmitz F, de Ru AH, Gils, T, Bouma G, van Rood J, van Heelen PA, Mearin ML, Mulder CJ, Koning F, van Bergen J. (2017). CD4 T-cell cytokines synergize to induce proliferation of malignant and nonmalignant innate intraepithelial lymphocytes. *PNAS*, 1–10.

Kreutz, J. M., Adriaanse, M. P. M., van der Ploeg, E. M. C., & Vreugdenhil, A. C. E. (2020). Narrative Review: Nutrient Deficiencies in Adults and Children with Treated and Untreated Celiac Disease. *Nutrients*, *12*(2), 500. https://doi.org/10.3390/nu12020500

Kulai, T., & Rashid, M. (2014). Assessment of Nutritional Adequacy of Packaged Gluten-free Food Products. *Canadian Journal of Dietetic Practice and Research: A Publication of Dietitians of Canada = Revue Canadienne De La*

Pratique Et De La Recherche En Dietetique: Une Publication Des Dietetistes Du Canada, *75*(4), 186–190. https://doi.org/10.3148/cjdpr-2014-022

Lamacchia, C., Camarca, A., Picascia, S., Di Luccia, A., & Gianfrani, C. (2014). Cereal-Based Gluten-Free Food: How to Reconcile Nutritional and Technological Properties of Wheat Proteins with Safety for Celiac Disease Patients. *Nutrients*, *6*(2), 575–590. https://doi.org/10.3390/nu6020575

Lambert, K., & Ficken, C. (2016). Cost and affordability of a nutritionally balanced gluten-free diet: Is following a gluten-free diet affordable? *Nutrition & Dietetics*, *73*(1), 36–42. https://doi.org/10.1111/1747-0080.12171

Lauret, E., & Rodrigo, L. (2013). *Celiac Disease and Autoimmune-Associated Conditions* [Review Article]. BioMed Research International; Hindawi. https://doi.org/10.1155/2013/127589

Lebwohl, B., Cao, Y., Zong, G., Hu, F. B., Green, P. H. R., Neugut, A. I., Rimm, E. B., Sampson, L., Dougherty, L. W., Giovannucci, E., Willett, W. C., Sun, Q., & Chan, A. T. (2017). Long term gluten consumption in adults without celiac disease and risk of coronary heart disease: Prospective cohort study. *The BMJ*, *357*. https://doi.org/10.1136/bmj.j1892

Lee, A. R., Ng, D. L., Zivin, J., & Green, P. H. R. (2007). Economic burden of a gluten-free diet. *Journal of Human Nutrition and Dietetics: The Official Journal of the British Dietetic Association*, *20*(5), 423–430. https://doi.org/10.1111/j.1365-277X.2007.00763.x

Lewis, H. M., Renaula, T. L., Garioch, J. J., Leonard, J. N., Fry, J. S., Collin, P., Evans, D., & Fry, L. (1996). Protective effect of gluten-free diet against development of lymphoma in dermatitis herpetiformis. *The British Journal of Dermatology*, *135*(3), 363–367.

Ludvigsson, J. F., Leffler, D. A., Bai, J. C., Biagi, F., Fasano, A., Green, P. H. R., Hadjivassiliou, M., Kaukinen, K., Kelly, C. P., Leonard, J. N., Lundin, K. E. A., Murray, J. A., Sanders, D. S., Walker, M. M., Zingone, F., & Ciacci, C. (2013). The Oslo definitions for coeliac disease and related terms. *Gut*, *62*(1), 43–52. https://doi.org/10.1136/gutjnl-2011-301346

Makharia, A., Catassi, C., & Makharia, G. K. (2015). The Overlap between Irritable Bowel Syndrome and Non-Celiac Gluten Sensitivity: A Clinical Dilemma. *Nutrients*, *7*(12), 10417–10426. https://doi.org/10.3390/nu7125541

McIntosh, K., Reed, D. E., Schneider, T., Dang, F., Keshteli, A. H., De Palma, G., Madsen, K., Bercik, P., & Vanner, S. (2017). FODMAPs alter symptoms and the metabolome of patients with IBS: A randomised controlled trial. *Gut*, *66*(7), 1241–1251. https://doi.org/10.1136/gutjnl-2015-311339

Melini, V., & Melini, F. (2019). Gluten-Free Diet: Gaps and Needs for a Healthier Diet. *Nutrients*, *11*(1). https://doi.org/10.3390/nu11010170

Miranda, J., Lasa, A., Bustamante, M. A., Churruca, I., & Simon, E. (2014). Nutritional differences between a gluten-free diet and a diet containing equivalent products with gluten. *Plant Foods for Human Nutrition (Dordrecht, Netherlands)*, *69*(2), 182–187. https://doi.org/10.1007/s11130-014-0410-4

Naik, R. D., Seidner, D. L., & Adams, D. W. (2018). Nutritional Consideration in Celiac Disease and Nonceliac Gluten Sensitivity. *Gastroenterology Clinics of North America*, *47*(1), 139–154. https://doi.org/10.1016/j.gtc.2017.09.006

Nellikkal, S. S., Hafed, Y., Larson, J. J., Murray, J. A., & Absah, I. (2019). High Prevalence of Celiac Disease Among Screened First-Degree Relatives. *Mayo Clinic Proceedings*, *94*(9), 1807–1813. https://doi.org/10.1016/j.mayocp.2019.03.027

Niland, B., & Cash, B. D. (2018). Health Benefits and Adverse Effects of a Gluten-Free Diet in Non–Celiac Disease Patients. *Gastroenterology & Hepatology*, *14*(2), 82–91.

Nistal, E., Caminero, A., Herrán, A. R., Arias, L., Vivas, S., de Morales, J. M. R., Calleja, S., de Miera, L. E. S., Arroyo, P., & Casqueiro, J. (2012). Differences of small intestinal bacteria populations in adults and children with/without celiac disease: Effect of age, gluten diet, and disease. *Inflammatory Bowel Diseases*, *18*(4), 649–656. https://doi.org/10.1002/ibd.21830

Pearlman, M., & Casey, L. (2019). Who Should Be Gluten-Free? A Review for the General Practitioner. *The Medical Clinics of North America*, *103*(1), 89–99. https://doi.org/10.1016/j.mcna.2018.08.011

Pinto-Sánchez, M. I., & Verdú, E. F. (2016). Non-coeliac gluten sensitivity: Are we closer to separating the wheat from the chaff? *Gut*, *65*(12), 1921–1922. https://doi.org/10.1136/gutjnl-2016-312471

Rewers, M., Liu, E., Simmons, J., Redondo, M. J., & Hoffenberg, E. J. (2004). Celiac disease associated with type 1 diabetes mellitus. *Endocrinology and Metabolism Clinics of North America*, *33*(1), 197–214, xi. https://doi.org/10.1016/j.ecl.2003.12.007

Rondanelli, M., Faliva, M. A., Gasparri, C., Peroni, G., Naso, M., Picciotto, G., Riva, A., Nichetti, M., Infantino, V., Alalwan, T. A., & Perna, S. (2019). Micronutrients Dietary Supplementation Advices for Celiac Patients on Long-Term Gluten-Free Diet with Good Compliance: A Review. *Medicina (Kaunas, Lithuania)*, *55*(7). https://doi.org/10.3390/medicina55070337

Rubio-Tapia, A., Ludvigsson, J. F., Brantner, T. L., Murray, J. A., & Everhart, J. E. (2012). The prevalence of celiac disease in the United States. *The American Journal of Gastroenterology*, *107*(10), 1538–1544; quiz 1537, 1545. https://doi.org/10.1038/ajg.2012.219

Sapone, A., Bai, J. C., Ciacci, C., Dolinsek, J., Green, P. H., Hadjivassiliou, M., Kaukinen, K., Rostami, K., Sanders, D. S., Schumann, M., Ullrich, R., Villalta,

D., Volta, U., Catassi, C., & Fasano, A. (2012). Spectrum of gluten-related disorders: Consensus on new nomenclature and classification. *BMC Medicine*, *10*, 13. https://doi.org/10.1186/1741-7015-10-13

Sapone, A., Lammers, K. M., Casolaro, V., Cammarota, M., Giuliano, M. T., De Rosa, M., Stefanile, R., Mazzarella, G., Tolone, C., Russo, M. I., Esposito, P., Ferraraccio, F., Cartenì, M., Riegler, G., de Magistris, L., & Fasano, A. (2011). Divergence of gut permeability and mucosal immune gene expression in two gluten-associated conditions: Celiac disease and gluten sensitivity. *BMC Medicine*, *9*, 23. https://doi.org/10.1186/1741-7015-9-23

Segura, M. E. M., & Rosell, C. M. (2011). Chemical composition and starch digestibility of different gluten-free breads. *Plant Foods for Human Nutrition (Dordrecht, Netherlands)*, *66*(3), 224–230. https://doi.org/10.1007/s11130-011-0244-2

Shahbazkhani, B., Sadeghi, A., Malekzadeh, R., Khatavi, F., Etemadi, M., Kalantri, E., Rostami-Nejad, M., & Rostami, K. (2015). Non-Celiac Gluten Sensitivity Has Narrowed the Spectrum of Irritable Bowel Syndrome: A Double-Blind Randomized Placebo-Controlled Trial. *Nutrients*, *7*(6), 4542–4554. https://doi.org/10.3390/nu7064542

Shannahan, S., & Leffler, D. A. (2017). Diagnosis and Updates in Celiac Disease. *Gastrointestinal Endoscopy Clinics of North America*, *27*(1), 79–92. https://doi.org/10.1016/j.giec.2016.08.011

Singh, J., & Whelan, K. (2011). Limited availability and higher cost of gluten-free foods. *Journal of Human Nutrition and Dietetics: The Official Journal of the British Dietetic Association*, *24*(5), 479–486. https://doi.org/10.1111/j.1365-277X.2011.01160.x

Skodje, G. I., Sarna, V. K., Minelle, I. H., Rolfsen, K. L., Muir, J. G., Gibson, P. R., Veierød, M. B., Henriksen, C., & Lundin, K. E. A. (2018). Fructan, Rather Than Gluten, Induces Symptoms in Patients With Self-Reported Non-Celiac Gluten Sensitivity. *Gastroenterology*, *154*(3), 529-539.e2. https://doi.org/10.1053/j.gastro.2017.10.040

The Top Fiber-Rich Foods List. (n.d.). Retrieved June 3, 2020, from https://www.todaysdietitian.com/newarchives/063008p28.shtml

Theethira, T. G., & Dennis, M. (2015). Celiac disease and the gluten-free diet: Consequences and recommendations for improvement. *Digestive Diseases (Basel, Switzerland)*, *33*(2), 175–182. https://doi.org/10.1159/000369504

Thompson et al. (1999). *Thompson: Thiamin, riboflavin, and niacin contents... - Google Scholar*. https://scholar.google.com/scholar_lookup?hl=en&volume=99&publication _year=1999&pages=858-

862&journal=J+Am+Diet+Assoc.&author=Thompson+T.&title=Thiamin%2C+
riboflavin%2C+and+niacin+contents+of+the+gluten-free

Thompson, T. (2000). Folate, iron, and dietary fiber contents of the gluten-free diet. *Journal of the American Dietetic Association, 100*(11), 1389–1396. https://doi.org/10.1016/S0002-8223(00)00386-2

Thompson, T., Lee, A. R., & Grace, T. (2010). Gluten contamination of grains, seeds, and flours in the United States: A pilot study. *Journal of the American Dietetic Association, 110*(6), 937–940. https://doi.org/10.1016/j.jada.2010.03.014

Tjellström, B., Högberg, L., Stenhammar, L., Fälth-Magnusson, K., Magnusson, K.-E., Norin, E., Sundqvist, T., & Midtvedt, T. (2013). Faecal short-chain fatty acid pattern in childhood coeliac disease is normalised after more than one year's gluten-free diet. *Microbial Ecology in Health and Disease, 24.* https://doi.org/10.3402/mehd.v24i0.20905

Tortora, R., Capone, P., De Stefano, G., Imperatore, N., Gerbino, N., Donetto, S., Monaco, V., Caporaso, N., & Rispo, A. (2015). Metabolic syndrome in patients with coeliac disease on a gluten-free diet. *Alimentary Pharmacology & Therapeutics, 41*(4), 352–359. https://doi.org/10.1111/apt.13062

Tursi, A., Giorgetti, G. M., Brandimarte, G., & Elisei, W. (2005). High prevalence of celiac disease among patients affected by Crohn's disease. *Inflammatory Bowel Diseases, 11*(7), 662–666. https://doi.org/10.1097/01.mib.0000164195.75207.1e

Valletta, E., Fornaro, M., Cipolli, M., Conte, S., Bissolo, F., & Danchielli, C. (2010). Celiac disease and obesity: Need for nutritional follow-up after diagnosis. *European Journal of Clinical Nutrition, 64*(11), 1371–1372. https://doi.org/10.1038/ejcn.2010.161

Ventura, A., Magazzù, G., & Greco, L. (1999). Duration of exposure to gluten and risk for autoimmune disorders in patients with celiac disease. SIGEP Study Group for Autoimmune Disorders in Celiac Disease. *Gastroenterology, 117*(2), 297–303. https://doi.org/10.1053/gast.1999.0029900297

Vici, G., Belli, L., Biondi, M., & Polzonetti, V. (2016). Gluten free diet and nutrient deficiencies: A review. *Clinical Nutrition (Edinburgh, Scotland), 35*(6), 1236–1241. https://doi.org/10.1016/j.clnu.2016.05.002

Viljamaa, M., Kaukinen, K., Huhtala, H., Kyrönpalo, S., Rasmussen, M., & Collin, P. (2005). Coeliac disease, autoimmune diseases and gluten exposure. *Scandinavian Journal of Gastroenterology, 40*(4), 437–443. https://doi.org/10.1080/00365520510012181

Zarkadas, M., Cranney, A., Case, S., Molloy, M., Switzer, C., Graham, I. D., Butzner, J. D., Rashid, M., Warren, R. E., & Burrows, V. (2006). The impact of a gluten-free diet on adults with coeliac disease: Results of a national survey. *Journal of*

Human Nutrition and Dietetics: The Official Journal of the British Dietetic Association, 19(1), 41–49. https://doi.org/10.1111/j.1365-277X.2006.00659.x

Zong, G., Lebwohl, B., Hu, F. B., Sampson, L., Dougherty, L. W., Willett, W. C., Chan, A. T., & Sun, Q. (2018). Gluten intake and risk of type 2 diabetes in three large prospective cohort studies of US men and women. *Diabetologia, 61*(10), 2164–2173. https://doi.org/10.1007/s00125-018-4697-9

KETOGENIC METABOLIC THERAPY

Denise Potter RDN, CSP, CDCES,
Lisa Vanatta MS, RDN, CSP,
and Jasna Robinson Wright MSc, RD, CDE, CIEC

Modern researchers first utilized ketogenic metabolic therapy (KMT) in 1921 for epilepsy. Dr. Hugh W. Conklin and Dr. H. Rawle Geyelin studied the beneficial effects of fasting on children with epilepsy and discovered fasting improved seizures in patients with epilepsy. Dr. Geyelin reported long-term seizure freedom in 18% of fasted children and improvements in many others (Geyelin, 1921). While fasting proved helpful for epilepsy, it was unsustainable. However, as these reports emerged, the success of fasting generated more research, including that of Dr. Russell Wilder at the Mayo Clinic who postulated an alternative plan to mimic the effects of fasting. He suggested, "to provoke ketogenesis by feeding diets which are rich in fats and low in carbohydrates" (Wilder, 1921). Subsequently, Dr. M.G. Peterman, also from the Mayo Clinic, picked up the proverbial "ball" and developed the "Classic Ketogenic Diet", a 4:1 ratio of fat to protein plus carbohydrate, which is still in use today as one version of KMT.

Physicians commonly utilized KMT as a treatment for epilepsy in the 1920s, 1930s, and 1940s, but KMT waned in popularity after the development of medications such as Dilantin® in 1937. As new anti-epileptic medications became available, physicians more commonly used these new medications rather than KMT, and over the next several decades KMT faded from view (Wheless, 2008).

In 1993, Jim Abrahams, a very determined parent of a child with medication-resistant epilepsy, sought out ketogenic therapy across the country and found that it was being offered at The Johns Hopkins Hospital (Baltimore, MD). Jim, and his wife Nancy, took their son Charlie to Johns Hopkins in spite of resistance from their medical team. Charlie was experiencing anywhere from dozens to up to 100 seizures per day. After a few days of ketogenic therapy, his seizures stopped.

The impressive and immediate resolution of Charlie's seizures led the Abrahams down a road that changed the world in relation to the ketogenic diet as a medical treatment for epilepsy and more recently as a potential treatment in several other conditions. They founded The Charlie Foundation and have worked tirelessly for more than 25 years to promote education and training for both families and health care professionals. Hundreds of ketogenic diet centers exist today, largely because of their ongoing efforts.

SECTION 1: KETOGENIC METABOLIC THERAPY

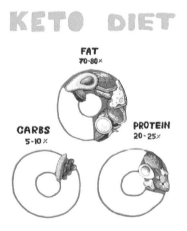

KMTs are high-fat, moderate-protein, low-carbohydrate metabolic therapies. Carbohydrates are typically the body's first choice for fuel and energy, but in the absence of significant carbohydrates, the body utilizes fat for energy, which induces a state of "ketosis" in the body. The resultant by-products of fat metabolism are ketone bodies or "ketones." Ketones can be measured in the blood, breath, and urine.

> Nutritional ketosis is achieved when blood ketone levels > 0.5 mmol/L

KMT mimics a state of fasting in the body and is referred to as nutritional ketosis. Without food for 24 to 48 hours, the body will naturally go into a state of ketosis. Once in ketosis, internal stores of fat are used as the primary source of energy instead of carbohydrates. To induce more rapid ketosis, one can fast for 48 hours before initiating KMT. However, this may cause a condition commonly referred to as "Keto Flu," and should only be done under the guidance of a health care professional.

How does KMT therapy work to reduce seizures?

The goal of KMT is to induce nutritional ketosis. When the body is not in ketosis, it uses glucose as its primary source of fuel. Glucose is a form of sugar that comes from carbohydrates in the diet. Once consumed, the body breaks carbohydrates down into glucose, and with the release of the hormone insulin, the body then uses glucose for fuel. However, when carbohydrates are restricted in the diet, the body turns to fat as a fuel source instead. Fat is broken down into ketone bodies instead of glucose, and ketone bodies do not require the release of insulin. Some proteins can be broken down into glucose as well, which is why protein needs to also be partially restricted in KMT. Research shows that for those with epilepsy, a high level of ketone bodies in the blood is associated with good seizure control. In the brain, ketone bodies inhibit the activity of a class of proteins called vesicular glutamate transporters, or VGLUT. The job of VGLUT is to transport glutamate, an excitatory neurotransmitter, from inside cells where it is made to the outside. If VGLUT cannot function because of a high level of ketone bodies, there is a decreased level of glutamate released, likely leading to decreased seizure activity.

Source: Rho & Kim, 2008

The following describes foods permitted and disallowed for KMT.

PROTEIN

Allowable sources include all animal meat including poultry, eggs, beef, pork, as well as seafood and fish. Protein foods that also contain carbohydrates such as processed meats should be limited.

Vegetarian protein options include hemp hearts, nuts and seeds, meat substitutes with nominal carbohydrates (such as soy or pea protein-based meat substitutes), unsweetened soy milk and brewer's yeast.

DAIRY/DAIRY ALTERNATIVES

Allowable sources include cheese, vegan cheese, unsweetened almond milk, heavy whipping cream, canned coconut cream, butter, ghee and almond, coconut and macadamia nut milks. Unsweetened yogurt may be included in small quantities. Avoid cow's milk (any fat content) and other milk alternatives such as soy milk, half and half, sweetened yogurt and ice cream.

VEGETABLES

Allowable sources include most non-starchy vegetables such as broccoli, cauliflower, green beans, artichokes, tomatoes, onions and leafy greens. Other vegetables can be within the established daily limit for carbohydrates. Avoid potatoes, sweet potatoes, corn and peas.

FRUIT

Allowable sources include strawberries, raspberries, and blackberries in small quantities. Other fruit can be consumed occasionally within the established daily limit for carbohydrates. Avoid fruit juice and dried fruit.

GRAINS

Grains are not permitted. Fiber is provided by the high fiber vegetables and occasional fruit that is allowed on the KMT.

FATS AND OILS

Allowable sources include butter, mayonnaise, and all oils including olive, macadamia, avocado, MCT and coconut oils. Polyunsaturated fats like corn, safflower, and sunflower oil should be limited as they are high in omega-6 fatty acids that can lead to increased inflammation if consumed in excess. Hydrogenated fats such as margarine or shortening (or foods fried in these) are to be avoided.

SWEETS AND SWEETENERS

Keto-friendly desserts with high-fat content and either no or limited artificial sweeteners are allowed. Limit or eliminate erythritol, monk fruit, stevia and sucralose. Artificial sweeteners including aspartame and saccharine should also be avoided. Avoid sugar in all its forms such as honey, maple syrup, and agave syrup (unless a dietitian has demonstrated how to include a tiny amount on rare occasions).

BEVERAGES

Allowable beverages include water, coffee, and tea but limit beverages sweetened with erythritol, monk fruit, stevia and sucralose. Avoid sugar-sweetened drinks such as regular soft drinks, sports drinks, fruit juice as well as drinks containing aspartame and saccharine.

OTHER

Avoid balsamic vinegar, vinegar glazes, and seasoning mixes. Apple cider vinegar, red wine vinegar, and white vinegar are very low in carbohydrates and fine to utilize.

How does KMT differ from the Paleo Diet?

By design, KMTs induce a state of ketosis, largely by limiting carbohydrates, but also by limiting protein to only that which is necessary for growth and tissue maintenance. The types of carbohydrates in KMT are limited mostly to low carbohydrate vegetables and occasional fruits. The limitations on dairy and grains are solely based on carbohydrate content. Due to the limited carbohydrate and protein, and to provide fuel for ketogenesis, a large proportion of fat is recommended.

The Paleo Diet, on the other hand, is based on what is presumed to have been eaten by early humans and limits foods to those which can be "hunted and gathered." Therefore, this diet does not allow dairy or grains and also excludes legumes and processed foods (https://www.healthline.com/nutrition/paleo-diet-meal-plan-and-menu). Protein and carbohydrates are not intentionally limited in a Paleo Diet. Carbohydrates and protein eaten in the wrong proportions and without liberal fat will inhibit ketosis. The Paleo Diet is not designed to promote ketogenesis.

SECTION 2: CLINICAL MONITORING

KMT is often used as "medical nutrition therapy" and should be treated as such. All ketogenic therapies restrict carbohydrates which in turn limits essential nutrients. Over time, if not well-monitored and supplemented, KMT may cause nutritional deficiencies or unwanted side effects. In order to safely follow a therapeutic ketogenic diet, utilize a Registered Dietitian Nutritionist (RDN) (or Registered Dietitian (RD) if you are outside of the U.S.) with training in this area, as well as a physician well-versed on KMT.

The following is an overview of the clinical course of KMT implementation:
1. Assessment: The physician and RDN/RD assess the patient to assure he/she/they is a good candidate for KMT. The person should be evaluated for one of the numerous conditions that KMT has been shown to benefit.
2. Prior to treatment, the health care providers will conduct a full nutritional assessment as well as a review of pre-ketogenic labs to assure there are no contraindications to initiating ketogenic therapy. Recommended pre-ketogenic labs include a complete blood count, complete metabolic panel, fasting lipid profile, 25-OH vitamin D level and total and free carnitine levels. For children, a zinc and selenium level, as well as serum amino acids, are often also assessed. Contraindications for the diet include:
   - Fat metabolism defects
   - Carnitine deficiency disorders
   - Inability to maintain adequate nutrition and/or hydration
   - A surgical option is available to treat seizures
   - Caregiver noncompliance to the restrictions of ketogenic therapy
3. Once the patient is deemed eligible to initiate KMT, the RDN and physician determine the right type of **ketogenic therapy**. The RDN/RD takes into account the age of the patient, and any current diet modifications (e.g., on a

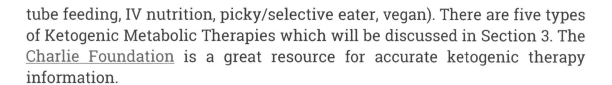

tube feeding, IV nutrition, picky/selective eater, vegan). There are five types of Ketogenic Metabolic Therapies which will be discussed in Section 3. The Charlie Foundation is a great resource for accurate ketogenic therapy information.

Topics the clinician specializing in KMT will educate patients on include:
- Diet selection — recommendations for KMT and why it is recommended
- Diet implementation — preparation and initiation
- Nutrient tracking — guidance on apps to track carbohydrate intake
- Meal planning — provision of sample meals and resources
- Ketone testing — method (blood, urine, or breath) and frequency
- Nutrient balance — provision of Daily Recommended Intakes (DRI) for all nutrients
- Supplementation — nutrient deficiencies and common supplements
- Fluid intake — adequacy and effects
- Side effects — causes and prevention
- Sick-day management — guidance and management
- Laboratory studies — importance and evaluation
- Medication — indications and effects

How long can an individual stay on KMT?

The answer to this is unknown. Metabolically, the human body was created to function properly by metabolizing carbohydrates, proteins, and fats. To date, there is no research to validate a lifelong state of ketosis. There are many anecdotal reports of people following their own version of the ketogenic diet for decades, however, scientific evidence in this area is lacking.

In epilepsy, KMT is frequently used for a minimum of two years with rare adverse effects, and often patients with gastrostomy tubes continue the diet for many years due to improved seizure control and ease of administration.

SECTION 3: TYPES OF KETOGENIC METABOLIC THERAPY

KMT is defined by a ratio of macronutrients, specifically the ratio of grams of fat to grams of protein plus (net) carbohydrate. At the high end of the spectrum is the classic KD at a 4:1 ratio — four times as much fat as protein plus carbohydrates. Below are the five types of ketogenic metabolic therapies with their respective ratios. The therapies work best when they are tailored to the individual, which is one reason why having a professional who specializes in ketogenic therapy is essential.

- **Classic Ketogenic Diet (KD):** Individualized and structured diet where food is weighed on a gram scale to a 3:1 or 4:1 ratio.
- **Modified Ketogenic Diet (MKD):** Individualized and structured diet where food is weighed on a gram scale or measured with household measures, to a 1:1 to 2:1 ratio.
- **Modified Atkins Diet (MAD):** Tracks carbohydrates only; fat is encouraged.
- **Medium Chain Triglyceride (MCT) Oil Die**t: 50% of kcals from MCT Oil, and 21% from long chain triglycerides (LCT). MCT oil produces ketones more readily than LCT.
- **Low Glycemic Index Treatment (LGIT):** Complex, low glycemic index carbohydrates; 40 gm to 60 gm of total carbohydrate/day. It is not intended to promote ketosis.

Table 1: Levels Of Macronutrients (Percentage of Calories) In Various Types Of Ketogenic Therapies

The Diet	Fat	Protein	Carbs	Ratio
Classic KD	87% to 90%	7% to 10%	3%	4:1, 3:1
MKD	70% to 82%	12% to 15%	6% to 15%	2:1, 1:1
MAD	65%	29% to 32%	3 to 6%	~1:1
MCT Oil Diet	71%	19%	10%	~1::1
LGIT	60%	28%	12%	n/a

Source: *The Charlie Foundation*

Because the diet of children under the age of five years is largely controlled by an adult, more restrictive diets can be used — the classic KD or MCT oil diet. The same applies to anyone fed by an enteral feeding tube as enteral formula can be easily manipulated. For those who find it hard to follow the restrictive diets, such as older children and adults, a less restrictive diet like the MAD or LGIT may be more sustainable and lead to better compliance. A practitioner may also combine or switch back and forth among the various KMTs.

Table 2: A Comparison Of The Ketogenic Diets

Questions	Classic and Modified KDs	MCT Oil Diet	Low Glycemic Index Treatment	Modified Atkins
Is medical supervision required	Yes	Yes	Yes	Yes
Is diet high in fat?	Yes	Yes	Yes	Yes
Is diet low in carbohydrate?	Yes	Yes	Yes	Yes
What is the ratio of fat to carbohydrate & protein?	4:1, 3:1, 2:1, 1:1	Approximately 1:1	Approximately 1:1	Approximately 2:1
How much carbohydrate is allowed on a 1000 calorie diet?	8gm carb on a 4:1 16gm carb on a 3:1 30gm carb on a 2:1 40-60gm carb on a 1:1	40-50gm	40-60gm	10-15g children and adolescents or 20 gm adults
How are foods measured?	Weighed	Weighed or measured	Measured or estimated	Estimated
Are meal plans used?	Yes	Yes	Yes	Optional
Where is the diet started?	Hospital or home under supervision	Hospital or home under supervision	Home	Home
Are calories controlled?	Yes	Yes	Yes	When needed
Are vitamin and mineral supplements required?	Yes	Yes	Yes	Yes
Are liquids (fluids) restricted?	No	No	No	No
Is a pre-diet laboratory evaluation required?	Yes	Yes	Yes	Yes
Can there be side-effects?	Yes	Yes	Yes	Yes
What is the overall difference in design of these diets?	This is an individualized and structured diet that provides specific meal plans. Foods are weighed and meals should be consumed in their entirety for best results. The ratio of this diet can be adjusted to effect better seizure-control and also liberalized for better tolerance. This diet is also considered a low glycemic therapy and results in steady glucose levels.	An individualized and structured diet containing Medium Chain Triglycerides (MCT) which are highly ketogenic. This allows more carbohydrate and protein than the Classic KD. A 2008 study showed that both diets are equal in eliminating seizures. A source of essential fatty acids must be included with this diet.	This is individualized but less structured diet than the KD. It uses exchange lists for planning meal and emphasizes complex carbohydrates. The balance of low glycemic carbohydrates in combination with fat result in steady glucose levels. It is not intended to promote ketosis.	This diet focuses on limiting the amount of carbohydrate while encouraging fat. Carbohydrate may be consumed at any time during the day as long as it is within limits and should be consumed with fat. Suggested meal plans are used as a guide. Protein is not limited but too much is discouraged.

Copyright permission provided by author Beth Zupec-Kania 1/2020

SECTION 4: THE SCIENCE ON KETOGENIC METABOLIC THERAPIES

STRONG EVIDENCE

Children with Epilepsy
Epilepsy affects about 7.6 of every 1,000 people in the world (Fiest et al., 2017). A Cochrane review from 2018 found 30% of children do not achieve seizure freedom with pharmacotherapy. KMT has been well-established through clinical studies as a legitimate treatment for medically refractory epilepsy (Kossoff et al., 2018). Of children treated with KMT, 50% to 70% achieved a reduction in seizure frequency, with some achieving seizure freedom (Kossoff et al., 2018, Consensus Recommendations, Martin-McGill et al., 2018). Thousands of children have reduced and or eliminated seizures by diligently following this treatment. Long-term adherence, though challenging due to limited food choices and adverse effects, can be managed successfully with appropriate medical supervision. In fact, many adverse effects are fully avoided or mitigated when therapy is initiated by a well-trained Registered Dietitian Nutritionist. Modified versions of the ketogenic therapies allow for more carbohydrate intake and more dietary flexibility, while still being effective in seizure reduction (D'Andrea et al., 2019).

WEAK EVIDENCE

The use of KMT for numerous other medical conditions shows promising preclinical evidence to support its use. Human studies are underway but it will take many years to fully determine the benefit of this therapy in all of the studied conditions. Below is a discussion of several areas where research is showing KMT as a potential treatment.

Psychiatric Disorders
Psychiatric conditions, such as depression, bipolar disorder, and schizophrenia, are neurometabolic diseases that share several common mechanisms. They all involve decreased glucose metabolism, neurotransmitter imbalances, oxidative stress and inflammation. KMT has the potential to influence these pathways (Norwitz et al., 2020; Brietzke et al., 2018; Campbell & Campbell, 2019; Phelps et al., 2013). A review by Kovács et al. (2019) suggests that supplement-induced ketosis causes changes in metabolism such as mitochondrial function and inflammatory processes that can benefit psychiatric diseases. To date, there have been few studies other than case studies. A systematic review by Bostock et al. (2017) found 15 studies on psychiatric disorders and ketogenic therapy, including nine animal models, four case studies, and two open-label studies.

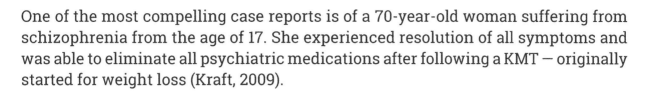

One of the most compelling case reports is of a 70-year-old woman suffering from schizophrenia from the age of 17. She experienced resolution of all symptoms and was able to eliminate all psychiatric medications after following a KMT — originally started for weight loss (Kraft, 2009).

Another case report shows two women with type II bipolar disorder treated with KMT experiencing mood stabilization that exceeded any prior results with medication. They experienced no adverse effects and followed KMT for two and three years respectively.

This author (Denise Potter) has worked with patients with depression, bipolar disorder, and schizophrenia and has noted results from KMT that also far exceed that of prior medications. She notes several patients that have had life-changing benefits from KMT and hopes to one day publish her experiences.

Overall, there have been mixed results to date and most studies involving the ketogenic diet and psychiatric conditions are animal models which may or may not be generalizable to humans. Studies in human populations are needed to better understand the relationship and effects of a ketogenic diet in psychiatric conditions.

Heart Disease

KMT has been viewed with concern when discussing heart disease as it is known to cause a substantial rise in low-density lipoprotein (LDL) cholesterol, largely due to the high saturated and total fat intake central to the diet (O'Neill and Raggi, 2020). In studies using very low carbohydrate diets, increases in LDL cholesterol were 18 mg/dL in one study (Westman, 2002) and >10% increase in over 30% of participants (Yancy, 2004) in a six-month time span, despite losing weight while following the diet. Other studies have found similar results (Stern, 2004; Hallberg et al., 2018; Athinarayanan et al., 2019).

In contrast, a landmark study examining data from 18 countries over a seven-year time span showed that total fat and type of fat were not significantly associated with cardiovascular disease risk, heart attacks, or heart disease mortality and instead high carbohydrate intake was associated with a higher risk of total mortality (Dehghan et al., 2017). On the other hand, very low carbohydrate diets, such as the ketogenic diet, tend to be low in carbohydrate-containing foods that have been shown to be protective in epidemiologic studies such as legumes, fruits, and whole grains.

Cardioprotective nutrients such as fiber, folate, magnesium, potassium, calcium and phytonutrients are also often low in the ketogenic diet (Liu, 2013; Slavin and Lloyd, 2012; Patterson et al., 2020; Freedman et al., 2001). Because some nutrients may be lacking on a strict KMT, this therapy should be guided by a Registered Dietitian. If there are concerns about the LDL rise that may occur during KMT, a more complete profile should be obtained to determine the "type" of LDL particles. LDL particle size must be further analyzed to determine if there is cause for concern. As with any therapy or medication, a risk/benefit analysis should be done and consistent laboratory monitoring completed.

Weight Loss

Perhaps the most widely advertised claim of KMT is weight loss. Many people no longer have a healthful relationship with food while simultaneously idealizing thinness, and people are constantly looking for an easy fix. "Keto" has become the latest craze. But is it a legitimate claim?

A number of studies have found that following a ketogenic-type diet does elicit substantial short-term weight loss (Mohoko et al., 2019; Castellana et al., 2020; Dashti et al., 2004; Westman et al., 2008; Foster et al., 2003; Dashti et al., 2006). A study by Mohorko et al. (2019) found that a 12-week keto diet resulted in an 18 kg weight loss for men and 11 kg weight loss for women on average. Two recent systematic reviews and meta-analyses by Castellana et al. (2020) and Chawla et al. (2020) found a weight loss of 10 kg to 15 kg using low calorie/low carbohydrate diets for an average of six to 12 months. Most of the studies included in these reviews met the criteria for a ketogenic diet. However, it's important to note that **many individuals who try ketogenic diets on a whim do not meet the macronutrient criteria outlined for true KMT.**

Appetite suppression may be one possible mechanism for the initial weight loss seen on ketogenic diets (Westman et al., 2007). The high fat intake contributes to satiety, as does the production of ketones. Low-calorie diets and high-carbohydrate/low-fat diets have also been found to suppress appetite (Gibson et al., 2015; Hall et al., 2021; Academy of Nutrition and Dietetics Evidence Analysis Library, 2021). In randomized controlled trials, low-carbohydrate diets seem similarly effective at inducing short-term weight loss as other food restriction methods such as calorie-restriction and low-fat vegetarian diets (Academy of Nutrition and Dietetics Evidence Analysis Library, 2021; Gardner et al., 2007; Dansinger et al., 2005). A meta-analysis comparing low-carbohydrate diets to moderate fat diets (fat <30% Kcal) found more weight loss at one year among the low-carb diets but no difference by two years (Bueno et al., 2013). Meng et al. (2017) found similar results in their meta-analysis.

Furthermore, research suggests that the ketogenic diet, like any restrictive diet, can elicit weight loss in the short term, however, when food is restricted in any form of diet, there is a series of biological control mechanisms that adjust appetite and metabolic processes to help the body defend against famine and ultimately lead to regaining of the lost weight — known as set point theory or set-range theory/dual intervention point model (Harris, 1990; Keesey et al., 1997; Ghanemi et al., 2018). Dieters often experience overeating/binge eating of the previously taboo food (carbohydrates in the case of the ketogenic diet), further propelling their weight back to pre-diet size (or higher). The choice to try a ketogenic diet with a patient/client wanting to control their body size should include a discussion around possible disordered eating behaviors and how to manage these if they arise as well as a discussion of possible adverse effects of the diet, as described later in this chapter. When undertaking a ketogenic diet for weight loss, it is important to guide people into the understanding that this involves a sustainable lifestyle change. If they plan to follow this for only a few months and then revert to their previous diet, the weight will most likely be regained (as it would no matter which "diet" they followed for a short time). A long-term ketogenic therapy/lifestyle for weight loss will likely involve a higher carbohydrate content than one undertaken for other medical conditions.

Athletic Performance

Some groups of athletes have turned to a ketogenic diet/lifestyle in attempts to enhance their athletic performance. Volek reports no differences in glycogen concentrations, utilization, and post-exercise synthesis between keto-adapted athletes and "high-carb" athletes' endurance, while also noting a two-fold increase in fat utilization for the keto-adapted athletes. (Volek et al., 2016). A review by Bailey et al. (2020) found seven studies that included VO_2 max as well as secondary performance outcomes — time to exhaustion, race time, rating of perceived exertion, and peak power. The studies included in the review showed mixed results in terms of athletic performance using a ketogenic diet. More randomized controlled trials are needed to fully assess the benefits and risks of ketosis on athletes.

Diabetes

Type 1 Diabetes

Following a ketogenic diet can improve blood glucose management in children with type 1 diabetes, however, they are not often used in this age group due to the high risk of malnutrition, poor linear growth, low bone density, hyperlipidemia, amenorrhea, poor sleep and hypoglycemia (McClean et al., 2019; Kanikarla-Marie & Jain, 2016). Since KMT has been utilized successfully for 100 years in treating pediatric epilepsy, further research into this population is warranted. This has led to the formation of an interdisciplinary committee to create a protocol for medical providers to safely implement KMTs for children with type 1 diabetes. (Rydin et al., 2021).

Type 2 Diabetes

For people with type 2 diabetes, the use of KMT has been shown to provide numerous benefits. Several studies have reported improvements in appetite regulation, improved blood glucose management, lower hemoglobin A1c and improved insulin sensitivity independent of weight loss (Westman et al., 2008; Yancy et al., 2005; Dashti et al., 2007; Hussain et al., 2012; Goday et al., 2016; Colica et al., 2017; Saslow et al., 2017; McKenzie et al., 2017; Murphy et al., 2019; Brouns et al., 2018).

A two-year study by Athinarayanan et al. (2019) found that there was a 54% reversal rate for type 2 diabetes diagnosis and an 18% remission rate for patients following KMT compared to no remission or reversal in the usual care arm of the study. This is groundbreaking news as for many years people with type 2 diabetes have been told that there was no chance of cure or remission. This research shows that patients adhering to a low carbohydrate diet for six months may experience remission of diabetes without adverse consequences. (Goldenberg et al., 2021). Other research has shown that people following KMT may be able to reduce or even eliminate the use of anti-hyperglycemic medications (Yancy et al., 2005; Hussain et al., 2012; McKenzie et al., 2017).

It is unknown whether the beneficial effects of following KMT persist over time due to the progressive nature of diabetes and difficulty with ongoing adherence to the diet. Some may also experience regain of lost weight even when remaining on the diet due to a slowed metabolism from the weight loss process and changes to appetite (for more information on this see the Weight Loss subsection above). There have not been significant adverse effects in the short term of following a ketogenic diet for people with type 2 diabetes, but further studies are needed to investigate any longer-term adverse effects.

Cancer

The Warburg effect is the predominant use of glucose anaerobically by cancer cells, and it is a potential metabolic pathway that may be targeted during cancer treatment. Otto Warburg first discussed this in the early 20th century and in recent years Dr. Thomas Seyfried and others have taken up his mantel to learn if KMT is in fact effective, and if so, how to use this alongside conventional and/or nonconventional treatments and exactly how should this therapy be implemented. Changing the diet to change fuel oxidation is a potential strategy that requires further investigation in cancer treatment. Given its low carbohydrate content, KMT could theoretically be used as a therapy to starve cancer cells, as cancer cells use glucose at a higher rate than noncancerous cells. Furthermore, ketone bodies produced on KMT are available for energy production in normal cells but not in cancerous cells which theoretically have downregulated oxidative phosphorylation (Vergati et al., 2017; Huebner et al., 2014; Liberti and Locasale, 2016; Kalamian, 2017).

Few studies have tested the Warburg theory to evaluate the effect in cancer management in practice. A review by Oliveira et al. (2018) found that the use of KMT in cancer shows promising but inconsistent results to date. There have been few studies with inconsistent designs which limits the ability to draw good-quality conclusions. Further studies are needed in the area of oncology and the potential therapeutic use of the ketogenic diet.

A review of available literature on glioblastoma multiforme (GBM) revealed only case series evidence, which did show KMT to be safe in this population (Martin-McGill, et al., 2018). Many cases noted overall or progression-free survival, but the effectiveness of KMT could not be established. Enough evidence was presented to encourage research to continue, and even Dr. Seyfried suggested that the medical community consider adding KMT to the Standard of Care for GBM. KMT continues to be utilized and studied as a cancer treatment.

A 2020 systematic review looked at 13 studies of KMT used as a complementary therapy in various types of cancer. The studies included in the review were small and found that there were few adverse events and no major adverse events among the patients following KMT. Beneficial effects of KMT were seen in four of the 13 studies. The findings were inconsistent in terms of slowing the progression of cancer and improving survival (Klement et al., 2020). Research to date is promising, and numerous patients with cancer are utilizing KMTs to supplement their treatments of this multifactorial disease. There is a continuous need for more well-designed studies to further evaluate the use of KMT in cancer treatment.

POTENTIAL AREAS FOR FUTURE RESEARCH

Anorexia Nervosa

There is a sparsity of available literature to fully evaluate KMT as a treatment for anorexia nervosa. However, scattered anecdotal reports have been circulated and some researchers feel this area is worth investigating. For example, there is a case report noting full remission of chronic anorexia nervosa with a ketogenic diet and ketamine, and the same researchers have additional studies in process (Scolnick, et al., 2020).

Multiple Sclerosis

KMT is currently being researched as a potential treatment for Multiple Sclerosis (MS), an autoimmune condition. The trial underway by Bahr et al. (2020) aims to randomize people with MS to 18 months of either ketogenic diet (20 g to 40 g of carbohydrate per day), a seven-day fast every six months and 14-hour intermittent fast, and a fat-modified standard diet. This trial is proposed since rodent studies have suggested that ketones could be an alternative and more efficient fuel source for the brain. The mouse studies found that ketogenic and fasting diets improved disease progression, disability, cognition and inflammatory markers likely through regeneration of demyelinated axons (Storoni and Plant, 2015; Kim et al., 2012; Choi et al., 2016; Piccio et al., 2008; Kafami et al., 2010; Razaghi et al., 2016). More clinical trials are needed to evaluate the potential for use of a low-carbohydrate/high-fat diet in MS.

Alzheimer's Disease

In patients with Alzheimer's disease (AD), the brain has difficulty using glucose effectively, and so the use of ketones to fuel the brain has been proposed as a possible method to improve symptoms of AD (Broom et al., 2019). A review of small clinical trials found that supplementing medium-chain triglycerides to increase blood ketone concentration improves cognitive functioning in some people with AD, but not in those with APOE+4 variation (Wlodarek, 2019). Most studies to date have been shorter-term (one to three months). Another recent review of short-term trials looking at older adults following KMT and/or using ketone supplements found somewhat mixed results, with some trials showing significant improvements in cognitive functioning while others showing no difference between intervention and control groups (Lilamand et al., 2020).

While a ketogenic diet shows potential in the management of AD, further studies are needed to more specifically look at the relationship between following different types of ketogenic diets and the risk of developing AD. Overall, it appears that a high-fat/low-carb and especially a high animal food diet may increase the risk of developing AD, but the use of ketones to fuel neurons in people with established AD can help improve symptoms, at least in the short-term (Grant, 2016).

Perinatal Period — Preconception and Pregnancy
Almost half of the pregnancies in the United States are unplanned (Ahrens et al., 2018). Therefore, messaging around healthful and balanced eating patterns targeted toward women in their child-bearing years is of particular importance. Furthermore, this is an age and gender group which is also the focus of many harmful body-dissatisfaction and dieting messages, leading many young women to restrict their eating in the search for the thin ideal. Preconception weight loss has been suggested as a possible way to increase fertility among higher-weight women and as a way to reduce the risk of complications during pregnancy and delivery. Many women turn to popular diets — including a ketogenic diet — to lose weight quickly in the hopes of conceiving.

Few studies have examined the effects of the ketogenic diet in preconception and pregnancy. Among the studies done to date, it appears that a low-carbohydrate intake in the peri-conception period is associated with an increased risk of birth defects and gestational diabetes. The National Birth Defects Prevention Study found that women who reported consuming low-carb diets in the one year prior to conception (fifth percentile of carbohydrate intake or 95 g of carb or less per day) were slightly more likely to have an infant with a neural tube defect (Desrosiers et al., 2018). In this study, folate supplement use among those following a low-carbohydrate diet did not decrease the risk of birth defects. A study by Shaw and Yang (2019) also suggests that mechanisms other than simply lower intake of folate-fortified grain foods may be responsible for the higher rates of neural tube defects in the offspring of women recently following low-carbohydrate diets.

A prospective cohort study by Bao et al. (2014) found that women following a low carbohydrate diet in the peri-conception period had a 27% increased risk of developing gestational diabetes when corrections were made for body mass index (BMI) and other risk factors. Among the women, those with the highest intake of animal products had the highest risk for gestational diabetes (36% higher risk), while those following a plant-based low-carbohydrate diet were not associated with an increased risk of gestational diabetes. An alternative diet option for women trying to conceive may be to follow a more balanced Low Glycemic Index diet (promotes replacing refined carbohydrates with higher fiber and lower glycemic load whole foods), which has been shown to improve maternal and fetal outcomes (Mahajan et al., 2019).

Women who are pregnant or desire to become pregnant should consider all factors when considering KMT. In women with epilepsy, the risk of a well-managed KMT should be weighed against the teratogenic effects of anti-epileptic medications and the life-threatening impact of potential seizures, and this treatment should certainly be discussed with their health care providers.

SECTION 5: RISKS OF FOLLOWING KETOGENIC METABOLIC THERAPY

NUTRITIONAL DEFICIENCIES

Due to the limited intake of foods containing carbohydrates (fruits, vegetables, enriched grains, and dairy), all KMTs are deficient in vitamins and minerals (Kossoff et al., 2018). In an analysis of 24 micronutrients in a classic nutritionally dense KMT, 19 of the nutrients analyzed were below the Dietary Reference Intakes (DRI), and 11 of those were provided at < 50% of the DRI (Zupec-Kania, 2007). This analysis emphasizes that all KMT requires supplementation with appropriate low carbohydrate complete vitamins and minerals. Some specific nutrients of concern include:

Carnitine
Carnitine is required for the metabolism of fat, and an increase in fat intake (particularly long-chain fats) results in a theoretical need for increased carnitine. In the presence of high fat intake, carnitine may become depleted (Berry-Kravis et al., 2001).

Selenium
There have been case reports of low selenium, leading to cardiomyopathy (Bergqvist et al., 2003, Bank et al., 2008, Sirikonda et al., 2012). Patients beginning KMT should have selenium levels measured at baseline and every three months for the first year.

Calcium and Sodium Bicarbonate
Additional nutrients may be needed to manage the side effects of the diet. Acidosis, as a result of excess ketone production, may require bicarbonate replacement to maintain acid-base balance in the blood. Additionally, acidosis causes calcium to be leached out of the bones increasing the risk of developing kidney stones (McNally et al., 2009).

Other common vitamin and mineral deficiencies seen with KMT are summarized in Table 3.

Table 3: Common Vitamin And Mineral Deficiencies On KMTs

Nutrient	Deficiency Symptoms
B vitamins	Fatigue, poor cognition, edema of feet/legs, cramps, chronic abdominal pain
Vitamin D	Lethargy, impaired resistance to infections, muscle/bone pain, mood issues
Calcium and phosphorus	Bone fractures
Potassium	Weakness, anorexia, nausea, heart arrhythmias
Iron	Fatigue, anemia
Selenium	Muscle pain, cardiomyopathy
Magnesium	Nausea, weakness, cognitive impairments, arrhythmias, constipation, muscle cramps
Zinc	Poor growth, diarrhea, hair loss, rash, anorexia, poor sleep

Sources: Bergqvist et al., 2007; Bergqvist et al., 2008

SUPPLEMENTATION

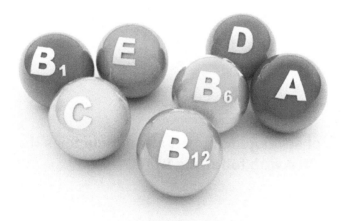

Due to the risk of many nutrient deficiencies, vitamin and mineral supplementation is recommended for all individuals receiving KMT: (Kossoff et al., 2018; Roehl and Sewak, 2017). All supplementation should be discussed with a health care provider well versed in KMT prior to initiating the diet.

1. Universal recommendations:
    a. Complete multivitamin with minerals (including trace minerals, especially selenium)
    b. Calcium — meeting daily Recommended Dietary Allowances (RDA)

c. Vitamin D — meeting daily RDA
2. Optional recommendations:
    a. Oral Citrates — may start prophylactically to decrease the risk for renal stones
    b. Potassium — excreted with ketones in urine; may need to replace if low
    c. Phosphorus — can act as a buffer to prevent acidosis
    d. Carnitine — low levels may decrease fat metabolism with decreased ketone production
    e. Salt — excreted with ketones in urine; may need to replace if low
    f. Selenium — found to be low in several case reports; supplement if necessary

OTHER RISKS AND COMPLICATIONS

In addition to the risk of developing nutritional deficiencies the information below lists other **risks associated with following KMT**:

Constipation

Clinical definition: Irregular frequency (> three days without stooling), difficult to pass stool, and/or abdominal distension. Constipation in KMT is often the result of high fat and low fiber intake. Constipation may cause a lower seizure threshold, causing an increase in seizures, even if well-controlled with KMT.

Common or rare: Most common

Treatable/avoidable: Yes

Treatment: Soluble and insoluble fiber, probiotics, MCT oil, avocado, flax, hemp or chia seeds, fluids, reduce or eliminate constipating medications

References: (Sampaio et al., 2017; El-Rashidy et al., 2013; Dressler et al., 2020)

Acidosis

Clinical definition: Increased acid load due to conversion of fat to ketone bodies. The body tries to maintain a balance between acids and bases in the blood within a very narrow range for optimal physiological function. An increase in ketones in the blood causes metabolic acidosis, which can lead to lethargy, sleepiness, nausea, vomiting and eventually deep pause-less breathing known as "Kussmaul respirations." If left untreated, chronic metabolic acidosis can lead to kidney stone formation and bone demineralization.

Common or rare: Common, especially during initiation

Treatable/avoidable: Yes

Treatment: Slow diet initiation, sodium bicarbonate supplementation, adequate hydration

References: (Bjurulf et al., 2020; Zupec-Kania et al., 2006)

Renal Stones

Clinical definition: Hard deposits made of minerals and salts that form inside the kidneys. Other names for kidney stones are renal calculi, nephrolithiasis, or urolithiasis. Chronic metabolic acidosis, increased ketones or acids, and increased calcium along with low levels of citrates in the urine from KMT predisposes patients to the development of kidney stones.

Common or rare: Common; 1.4% to 8.7% reported in children on KMT

Treatable/avoidable: Yes

Treatment: Medical attention, adequate fluids, treat acidosis with citrates

References: (McNally et al., 2009; Paul et al., 2010; Furth et al., 2000)

Hyperlipidemia

Clinical definition: Abnormally high levels of fats (lipids) in the blood. The two primary forms of fat in the blood are triglycerides and cholesterol. Triglycerides are formed when the body has extra calories it doesn't need for energy. It is the major form of fat stored in the body. Some foods, including red meat and whole-fat dairy products, also contain triglycerides.

Cholesterol, on the other hand, is produced naturally in the liver and is found in the blood and all cells of the body. There are two main types of cholesterol, low-density lipoprotein (LDL) and high-density lipoprotein (HDL). HDL is typically considered "good" cholesterol since it moves fat away from the arteries and back to the liver to be excreted. LDL is considered the "bad" cholesterol. However, not all LDL cholesterol is "bad." LDL can occur as small dense particles or large buoyant particles. The small and dense LDL is the "bad" cholesterol that builds up in the artery walls, resulting in hardening and narrowing the vessels, increasing the risk for cardiovascular disease. Foods containing cholesterol include eggs, meat, shellfish and dairy foods such as cheese, but these foods do not necessarily need to be avoided.

Common or rare: Common

Treatable/avoidable: Yes

Treatment: Assess necessity of treatment, utilize a balance of monounsaturated and saturated fats, monitor over time, utilize a lower ratio of the diet, carnitine supplementation, fish oil supplementation, and adding soluble fiber (flax, chia, hemp seeds)

References: (Sharman et al., 2002; Diamond et al., 2020)

Hypoglycemia

Clinical definition: Condition in which blood sugar (glucose) level is lower than normal. Glucose is the body's main source of energy as it is primarily derived from carbohydrates. As carbohydrate intake is decreased and fat intake is increased, blood sugar levels can drop below normal range. This usually happens during initiation of KMT before the body has adapted to using ketones for fuel. Once keto-adapted, a normal blood sugar range is 50 to 80 mg/dL.

Common or rare: usually only during initiation or with fasting

Treatable/avoidable: Yes

Treatment: 2 grams of simple carbohydrate = 15 mL fruit juice for blood sugar < 40 mg/dL. Prevent with slow diet initiation

References: (Lin et al., 2017; Kang et al., 2004)

Dehydration

Clinical definition: The loss of too much water and other fluids the body needs to work normally. When the body uses fat for energy, the liver produces ketones, resulting in increased loss of body fluids through frequent and increased urination. Loss of water and electrolytes may lead to dehydration. Additionally, decreased circulating insulin from restricted carbohydrate intake results in reduced sodium reabsorption in the kidneys.

Common or rare: Common during initiation, fasting, or with illness (diarrhea, vomiting)

Treatable/avoidable: Yes

Treatment: Drink adequate fluids. Additional sources of electrolytes (such as sodium and potassium) may also be needed. Urine should be pale yellow.

References: (Kang et al., 2004; Tiwari et al., 2007)

Bone Loss

Clinical definition: Occurs when the body loses too much bone mass, makes too little bone, or both. If severe or prolonged, bone loss can progress to **osteoporosis**. It often develops without any symptoms or pain, and frequently is not discovered until there is bone pain or a fracture due to weakened bones. Patients with epilepsy are at increased risk from both inadequate intake as well as seizure treatment (anti-seizure medications) that may negatively impact nutrient metabolism and bone health.

Common or rare: Common on long-term ketogenic therapy

Treatable/avoidable: Yes

Treatment: Treat with adequate calcium, phosphorus, and vitamin D_3. Prevent with adequate supplementation at the start of the diet. Prevent and treat acidosis.

References: (Kossoff et al., 2018; Berggvist et al., 2008)

Growth Deceleration

Clinical definition: Slowed weight and/or height gain resulting from caloric restriction or excessive energy expenditure. There is mixed data on the effect of KMT on growth, particularly in children. Classic KMT appears to have negative effects with weight loss during the first few months of initiating diet and over time may cause height deceleration as well. The MCT oil diet did not result in better growth patterns, even with higher protein content.

Common or rare: Uncommon (unless initiating diet for weight loss)

Treatable/avoidable: Yes

Treatment: Adequate caloric intake

References: (Neal et al., 2008; Kossoff et al., 2018; Vestergaard, 2015)

Irregular Menses

Clinical definition: When the length of the menstrual cycle is > 35 days or if the duration varies from normal. Change in menstrual cycles is more likely related to weight loss associated with the diet, although some reports note the irregularities may not be attributed to weight loss alone. Estrogen levels significantly decrease with weight loss resulting in irregular menstrual cycles.

Common or rare: Unknown

Treatable/avoidable: Unknown

Treatment: Consider increased carbohydrate intake or small weight gain

References: (Kossoff, et al., 2016; pg 129; no published recommendations — only anecdotal)

> **Can KMT be implemented with only healthful sources of fat?**
> **Yes** — the ketogenic diet encourages healthful fats in appropriate combinations to meet essential fatty acid needs. In patients where there is concern for elevated lipids, the types of fats can be switched to predominately unsaturated fats to decrease the risk of further elevation of LDL cholesterol. However, in most cases saturated fat does not need to be completely avoided, and it is not considered a bad fat for KMT depending on the source. In fact, foods that contain saturated fat such as red meat, butter, and cream are often a standard part of KMT and help contribute variety to a diet. If someone prefers not to eat red meat, it can be replaced with other sources of fat. Ultimately, when KMT is indicated, there is a higher risk to a patient's health to continue eating a high-carbohydrate diet than to avoid eating a diet high in saturated fat.

SECTION 6: CULINARY COMPETENCIES

In addition to following the culinary competencies for Fruit, Vegetables, Dairy, Fats and Oils, Protein and Sodium (with the caveat that additional ingredients in these chapters may not be permitted while following KMT), individuals who wish to follow a KMT diet will do well if they can:

1. Describe ketogenic metabolic therapies, including specific amounts of macronutrients recommended for the different therapies
2. Model consumption of the KMT
3. List possible side effects of KMT
4. List nutrient deficiencies most common with KMT
5. Buy healthful no- and low-carbohydrate products
6. Calculate net carbs
7. Plan and eat a meal with limited carbohydrates
8. Plan and eat a snack with limited carbohydrates
9. Weigh and measure ingredients
10. Prepare recipes with permitted amounts of vegetables and fruit
11. Design a weekly menu that aligns with KMT
12. Work under the guidance of a registered dietitian or a clinician who specializes in KMT

SECTION 7: AT THE STORE

IN THE PANTRY

It is important to stock the pantry with foods that are allowed on the KMT before starting the diet as it requires foods that may not already be in the household.

Nuts and seeds: Almonds, macadamia, pecans, brazil, cashews, filberts, pistachios, walnuts, pumpkin seeds, sesame seeds, sunflower seeds, chia seeds and flax seeds (small amounts)

Fats: Oils (olive, coconut, walnut, grape seed, flaxseed, avocado), avocados, olives, mayonnaise, coconut milk and full-fat salad dressing (with no added sugar)

Proteins: Eggs, chicken, turkey, pork, lamb, beef (all cuts), game meats and seafood (salmon, tuna, halibut, etc.)

Dairy: Heavy cream, butter, full-fat sour cream, full-fat cream cheese, full-fat plain yogurt, full-fat cottage cheese, ricotta cheese, buttermilk and cheeses

Vegetables: Broccoli, cabbage, carrots, cauliflower, green beans, tomatoes, onions, spinach, cucumber, Brussel sprouts, asparagus and leafy greens

Fruits: Raspberries, blackberries and strawberries (limited amount)

KETO FLOUR

Wheat flour

✓ Peanut flour

✓ Almond flour

✓ Coconut flour

✓ Flaxseed meal

✓ Sunflower seed flour

99

Baking ingredients: coconut flour, shredded coconut (unsweetened), almond flour, psyllium husks, baking powder, baking soda, Bickford flavorings

Sweeteners: erythritol and monk fruit

Miscellaneous: Miracle and shirataki noodles, Walden Farm's products, low-carb baking mixes, low-carb bread and tortillas

For keto-friendly milk, look for brands with 1 gram or less of net carbohydrate per eight ounces (240 ml).

Table 4: Keto-Friendly Milks

Milks*
Almond milk
Coconut milk in cartons not canned**
Cashew milk
Hemp milk
Flax milk
Soy milk
Heavy cream

*Select only the unsweetened varieties
** Canned coconut milk has more net carbs than coconut milk found in cartons. It is best to always check the label.

BUDGETING TIPS

- **Buy in bulk.** Nuts and seeds can be found in bulk containers at most stores. Oils can be purchased online much cheaper in large quantities than in the store.
- **Look for sales and stock up.** Most perishables can be put in the freezer, including meats, vegetables, berries and even avocados.
- **Buy vegetables in season.** Out-of-season vegetables tend to be more expensive. Choose vegetables that grow above the ground to avoid those that are high in starch.
- **Buy frozen over fresh.** Frozen produce, such as berries, cauliflower, and broccoli, are often more affordable than fresh varieties.
- **Make a meal plan and prep routine** to prevent making unnecessary purchases. Planning ahead may also increase diet compliance.
- **Choose cheaper protein sources.** Eggs are an affordable keto-friendly food you can use in a variety of ways. Also, save money buying whole cooked chickens, or getting cheaper cuts of meat (ground beef, chicken thighs, etc.).

- **Skip packaged foods labeled as "keto" friendly**. It is much cheaper to buy the ingredients to make an even fancier treat at home than to pay the high price of the convenience item.

SELECTING LOW-CARBOHYDRATE FOODS

On the Nutrition Facts Panel, the total carbs (carbohydrate) listed is a combination of starches, sugars, sugar alcohol and fiber. Net carbs are those carbohydrates that the body is able to fully digest into glucose. While many labels show the 'Net Carbs', there is no FDA definition for this. The manufacturers use numerous and different methods to count 'Net Carbs', many of which are incorrect and will confound your KMT by raising your blood glucose levels. Although many labels will subtract the sugar alcohols out of the total carbohydrate, it is not an accurate representation. Use the calculation below for best results:

Figure 1: A Nutrition Facts Panel

Net carbs (g) = total carbohydrate (g) – fiber (g)

Figure 1 depicts a Nutrition Facts Label. Using this as an example, the calculation for determining net carbs in this product is:

Net Carbs = 15 g – 5 g = 10 grams

SECTION 8: IN THE KITCHEN

- **Keep meals simple.** When starting a KMT, start slowly, gradually decreasing carbohydrates in current meals while increasing fat intake.
- **Purchase and use the right equipment.** Some staple tools include a skillet, good quality knife, food processor or blender, parchment paper, food containers and a **food scale**.
- **Weigh and measure appropriate portions for KMT.** Some KMTs requires patients to weigh and measure all food on a scale. Other KMTs use household

measurements and exchanges, while others simply require tracking total carbohydrate intake while allowing unlimited fat and protein.

- **Batch cook** and portion out meals for a few days ahead of time.
- **Double the recipe** for a meal and save the extra in a container for another meal.

BUILD A KMT SNACK

Figure 2: Keto Friendly Ingredients for Snacking

Protein	Fat	Other
• Fatty meat • Fish • Bacon • Hard boiled eggs, or deviled eggs • Full-fat Greek yogurt • Nuts, nut butter or seeds • Cheese	• Heavy (whipping) cream • Mayonnaise • Butter • Olive oil • Cream cheese • Sour cream • MCT oil	• Olives • Celery • Peppers • Avacado • Berries (small portion) • Salsa

Select an item from each of the columns in Figure 2. Examples of snacks:
- Deviled eggs made with mayonnaise and celery or pepper slices
- Piece of fish or chicken with mayonnaise and salsa
- Cheese slices and peppers with a sour cream dip

Recipes from www.Ruled.me can give you some more great ideas for snacks and meals.

BUILD A CHIA PUDDING

Add 2 tablespoons of chia seeds to 1 cup canned coconut milk. Stir and let rest for 2 hours (you can always add more seeds a teaspoon at a time until the desired thickness is achieved). The pudding tastes great either warm or cold and the following can also be added to the mix: berries, nut butter, matcha, unsweetened cocoa, cinnamon or vanilla extract (that has no added sweeteners). Top with nuts and seeds.

RECIPES
Recipes from the Charlie Foundation

SECTION 9: AT THE TABLE

For classic and modified ketogenic therapy, the RDN/RD provides meals with exact gram weights of each food to provide a specific macronutrient ratio (4:1, 3:1, 2:1, 1:1 etc.). Usually about one month after initiating KMT, the RDN/RD trains the patient or family how to use the Keto Diet Calculator (KDC) program to calculate their meals moving forward. See the example below of a meal calculated using the KDC.

For all other KMTs, a sample meal plan may be provided by the RDN/RD, but it is up to the patient to track carbohydrate intake using a web-based app or using exchanges and household measurements to manage their macronutrient intake. Specific meals typically are not provided for these KMTs.

MEAL PLANNING

Example Meals:

Figures three and four depict two meals with their nutrition and serving information displayed using two separate online calculators.

Figure 3: Classic/Modified Ketogenic Diet — Using a Gram Scale

#73 Chicken Breast & Broccoli

☑ Verified by Nutritionist & ready for print or email

(unchecking will remove from meal planner)

| Add New Foods | | Save Changes | | Meal List | | Reset |

Blue font = your administrator

Del	Food Item	Grams	Fat	Pro	Net Carb	Fiber *=NA	Calories	Pro+Carb	Ratio
☐	Cream, 36%	30	▲▼ 10.8	0.6	0.9	0	103		
☐	Broccoli, raw then steamed	140	▲▼ 0.57	3.33	5.43	4.62	40		
☐	Chicken, breast, no skin - cooked	55	▲▼ 1.96	17.06	0	0	86		
☐	Butter	23	▲▼ 18.66	0.2	0.01	0	169		
☐	Oil, Olive	23	▲▼ 23	0	0	0	207		
	Actual		54.99	21.19	6.34	4.62	605	27.53	2:1
	GOAL		54.55	20.00	7.27		600	27.27	2:1

Suggested accuracy: achieve within 4 calories of GOAL calories AND on or slightly above the ratio.

www.ketodietcalculator.org

Figure 4: Modified Keto or Modified Atkins Diet Meal — Using a Cronometer App

Description	Amount	Unit	Calories
Chicken Breast, Skin Removed Before Cooking	3	oz	147.13
Broccoli, Cooked From Fresh	1	cup, chopped	54.6
Cream, Fluid, Heavy Whipping	2	tbsp	102
Butter, Salted	1.5	tbsp	152.59
Olive Oil	1.5	tbsp	179.01

Calories Summary			Macronutrient Targets	
635 kcal CONSUMED	1992 kcal BURNED	857 Calories Remaining BUDGET	Energy	635.3 kcal / 1493 kcal (42%)
			Protein	31.0 g / 55.0 g (56%)
			Net Carbs	6.9 g / 30.0 g (22%)
			Fat	52.8 g / 128.1 g (41%)

www.cronometer.com

Simplified Ketogenic Meals:

Keep it simple: **Protein + Vegetables + Fats**
- Begin with 2 to 4 ounces of protein (fish, chicken, beef, pork)
- Add low carb vegetables (1 to 2 cups or more if leafy greens included)
- Incorporate 2 to 3 tablespoons of high-quality olive oil, butter, mayonnaise, MCT oil* or heavy whipping cream**

*MCT Oil should be added to one's diet gradually — talk with your dietitian for guidance
**heavy whipping cream has less fat than oil and should be increased proportionately

Meal example:
- 4 ounces chicken thigh
- 1 to 2 cups steamed broccoli topped with 1 tablespoon butter
- 2 cups fresh organic spinach topped with 1 to 2 tablespoons olive oil

- 2 to 3 tablespoons heavy whipping cream stirred into 1 cup unsweetened almond milk

SECTION 10: RESOURCES

- Atkins for Seizures: https://atkinsforseizures.com/ - provides information, recipes, articles and resources on MAD
- Dietary Therapies, LLC: https://www.dietarytherapies.com/ - provides information and resources for cancer and ketogenic therapy
- Dom D'Agostino PhD Website: https://www.ketonutrition.org/- provides accurate information to the public on nutrition and metabolic therapies through their blog, resources, and podcasts
- Epilepsy Foundation: https://www.epilepsy.com/ - provides community services, public education, federal and local advocacy, seizure first aid training and research funding into new treatments and therapies for epilepsy
- Matthew's Friends: https://www.matthewsfriends.org/ — provides community support with ketogenic resources, including professional tutorial films, a cooking channel and keto events, based in the U.K.
- The Charlie Foundation: https://charliefoundation.org/ — provides community support with ketogenic resources, including recipes, resources, and KDC, based in the U.S.
- Virta Health: https://www.virtahealth.com/ — provides support for patients with type 2 diabetes who want to follow carbohydrate-restricted diet
- KetoCook: http://ketocook.com/ — Provides recipes and lifestyle tips for children following a ketogenic diet

SUMMARY

What has long been considered an alternative therapy for treating seizures and is respected as a "nonpharmacologic" treatment for epilepsy, has now become a trendy, popular diet for weight loss. Where there used to be just one ketogenic therapy, there are now multiple ways ketogenic metabolic therapies are implemented. With the advent of many "keto" friendly products on the market, the diet is very palatable with many food options available in nearly every grocery store.

Though ketogenic metabolic therapies are highly popular today, it remains vitally important that all KMTs must be done under the supervision of a trained neurologist and dietitian who are familiar with the risks and benefits of these therapies. The KMT is not without its risks — constipation, stress on the liver and kidney, nutrient deficiencies, and high intake of saturated fat that is linked to heart disease. Following a ketogenic-type diet short-term to lose weight may be beneficial as long as there are no underlying medical issues. However, the risk of nutrient deficiencies and the risk of consuming an abundance of fat (especially if the fat source is not a plant-based oil) is substantial and may make KMT an unsustainable weight loss diet.

REFERENCES

Academy of Nutrition and Dietetics Evidence Analysis Library. (2006). In Adults, How Effective, in Terms of Weight Loss and Maintenance, are Low Carbohydrate Diets (Defined as <35% kcals From Carbohydrate)? Available online at: https://www.andeal.org/topic.cfm?cat=2891&evidence_ (accessed January 29, 2021).

Ahrens, K. A., Thoma, M. E., Copen, C. E., Frederiksen, B. N., Decker, E. J., & Moskosky, S. (2018). Unintended pregnancy and interpregnancy interval by maternal age, National Survey of Family Growth. *Contraception, 98*(1), 52–55. https://doi-org./10.1016/j.contraception.2018.02.013

Athinarayanan, S. J., Adams, R. N., Hallberg, S. J., McKenzie, A. L., Bhanpuri, N. H., Campbell, W. W., Volek, J. S., Phinney, S. D., & McCarter, J. P. (2019). Long-Term Effects of a Novel Continuous Remote Care Intervention Including Nutritional Ketosis for the Management of Type 2 Diabetes: A 2-Year Non-randomized Clinical Trial. *Frontiers in endocrinology, 10*, 348. https://doi.org/10.3389/fendo.2019.00348

Bahr, L. S., Bock, M., Liebscher, D., Bellmann-Strobl, J., Franz, L., Prüß, A., Schumann, D., Piper, S. K., Kessler, C. S., Steckhan, N., Michalsen, A., Paul, F., & Mähler, A. (2020). Ketogenic diet and fasting diet as Nutritional Approaches in Multiple Sclerosis (NAMS): protocol of a randomized controlled study. *Trials, 21*(1), 3. https://doi.org/10.1186/s13063-019-3928-9

Bailey, C. P., & Hennessy, E. (2020). A review of the ketogenic diet for endurance athletes: performance enhancer or placebo effect?. *Journal of the International Society of Sports Nutrition, 17*(1), 33. https://doi.org/10.1186/s12970-020-00362-9

Bank, I. M., Shemie, S. D., Rosenblatt, B., Bernard, C., & Mackie, A. S. (2008). Sudden cardiac death in association with the ketogenic diet. *Pediatric neurology, 39*(6), 429–431. https://doi.org/10.1016/j.pediatrneurol.2008.08.013

Bao, W., Bowers, K., Tobias, D. K., Olsen, S. F., Chavarro, J., Vaag, A., Kiely, M., & Zhang, C. (2014). Prepregnancy low-carbohydrate dietary pattern and risk of gestational diabetes mellitus: a prospective cohort study. *The American journal of clinical nutrition, 99*(6), 1378–1384. https://doi.org/10.3945/ajcn.113.082966

Bergqvist, A. G., Schall, J. I., & Stallings, V. A. (2007). Vitamin D status in children with intractable epilepsy, and impact of the ketogenic diet. *Epilepsia, 48*(1), 66–71. https://doi.org/10.1111/j.1528-1167.2006.00803.x

Bergqvist, A. G., Schall, J. I., Stallings, V. A., & Zemel, B. S. (2008). Progressive bone mineral content loss in children with intractable epilepsy treated with the ketogenic diet. *The American journal of clinical nutrition*, *88*(6), 1678–1684. https://doi.org/10.3945/ajcn.2008.26099

Bergqvist, A. G., Chee, C. M., Lutchka, L., Rychik, J., & Stallings, V. A. (2003). Selenium deficiency associated with cardiomyopathy: a complication of the ketogenic diet. *Epilepsia*, *44*(4), 618–620. https://doi.org/10.1046/j.1528-1157.2003.26102.x

Berry-Kravis, E., Booth, G., Sanchez, A. C., & Woodbury-Kolb, J. (2001). Carnitine levels and the ketogenic diet. *Epilepsia*, *42*(11), 1445–1451. https://doi.org/10.1046/j.1528-1157.2001.18001.x

Bjurulf, B., Magnus, P., Hallböök, T., & Strømme, P. (2020). Potassium citrate and metabolic acidosis in children with epilepsy on the ketogenic diet: a prospective controlled study. *Developmental medicine and child neurology*, *62*(1), 57–61. https://doi.org/10.1111/dmcn.14393

Bostock, E. C., Kirkby, K. C., & Taylor, B. V. (2017). The Current Status of the Ketogenic Diet in Psychiatry. *Frontiers in psychiatry*, *8*, 43. https://doi.org/10.3389/fpsyt.2017.00043

Brietzke, E., Mansur, R. B., Subramaniapillai, M., Balanzá-Martínez, V., Vinberg, M., González-Pinto, A., Rosenblat, J. D., Ho, R., & McIntyre, R. S. (2018). Ketogenic diet as a metabolic therapy for mood disorders: Evidence and developments. *Neuroscience and biobehavioral reviews*, *94*, 11–16. https://doi.org/10.1016/j.neubiorev.2018.07.020

Broom, G. M., Shaw, I. C., & Rucklidge, J. J. (2019). The ketogenic diet as a potential treatment and prevention strategy for Alzheimer's disease. *Nutrition (Burbank, Los Angeles County, Calif.)*, *60*, 118–121. https://doi.org/10.1016/j.nut.2018.10.003

Brouns F. (2018). Overweight and diabetes prevention: is a low-carbohydrate-high-fat diet recommendable?. *European journal of nutrition*, *57*(4), 1301–1312. https://doi.org/10.1007/s00394-018-1636-y

Bueno, N. B., de Melo, I. S., de Oliveira, S. L., & da Rocha Ataide, T. (2013). Very-low-carbohydrate ketogenic diet v. low-fat diet for long-term weight loss: a meta-analysis of randomised controlled trials. *The British journal of nutrition*, *110*(7), 1178–1187. https://doi.org/10.1017/S0007114513000548

Campbell, I. H., & Campbell, H. (2019). Ketosis and bipolar disorder: controlled analytic study of online reports. *BJPsych open*, *5*(4), e58. https://doi.org/10.1192/bjo.2019.49

Castellana, M., Conte, E., Cignarelli, A., Perrini, S., Giustina, A., Giovanella, L., Giorgino, F., & Trimboli, P. (2020). Efficacy and safety of very low calorie ketogenic diet (VLCKD) in patients with overweight and obesity: A systematic review and meta-analysis. *Reviews in endocrine & metabolic disorders*, *21*(1), 5–16. https://doi.org/10.1007/s11154-019-09514-y

Charlie Foundation for Ketogenic Therapies. (2021). Retrieved December 4, 2021, from https://charliefoundation.org/.

Chawla, S., Tessarolo Silva, F., Amaral Medeiros, S., Mekary, R. A., & Radenkovic, D. (2020). The Effect of Low-Fat and Low-Carbohydrate Diets on Weight Loss and Lipid Levels: A Systematic Review and Meta-Analysis. *Nutrients, 12*(12), 3774. https://doi.org/10.3390/nu12123774

Choi, I. Y., Piccio, L., Childress, P., Bollman, B., Ghosh, A., Brandhorst, S., Suarez, J., Michalsen, A., Cross, A. H., Morgan, T. E., Wei, M., Paul, F., Bock, M., & Longo, V. D. (2016). A Diet Mimicking Fasting Promotes Regeneration and Reduces Autoimmunity and Multiple Sclerosis Symptoms. *Cell reports, 15*(10), 2136–2146. https://doi.org/10.1016/j.celrep.2016.05.009

Colica, C., Merra, G., Gasbarrini, A., De Lorenzo, A., Cioccoloni, G., Gualtieri, P., Perrone, M. A., Bernardini, S., Bernardo, V., Di Renzo, L., & Marchetti, M. (2017). Efficacy and safety of very-low-calorie ketogenic diet: a double blind randomized crossover study. *European review for medical and pharmacological sciences, 21*(9), 2274–2289.

D'Andrea Meira, I., Romão, T. T., Pires do Prado, H. J., Krüger, L. T., Pires, M., & da Conceição, P. O. (2019). Ketogenic Diet and Epilepsy: What We Know So Far. *Frontiers in neuroscience, 13*, 5. https://doi.org/10.3389/fnins.2019.00005

Dansinger, M. L., Gleason, J. A., Griffith, J. L., Selker, H. P., & Schaefer, E. J. (2005). Comparison of the Atkins, Ornish, Weight Watchers, and Zone diets for weight loss and heart disease risk reduction: a randomized trial. *JAMA, 293*(1), 43–53. https://doi.org/10.1001/jama.293.1.43

Dashti, H. M., Mathew, T. C., Hussein, T., Asfar, S. K., Behbahani, A., Khoursheed, M. A., Al-Sayer, H. M., Bo-Abbas, Y. Y., & Al-Zaid, N. S. (2004). Long-term effects of a ketogenic diet in obese patients. *Experimental and clinical cardiology, 9*(3), 200–205.

Dashti, H. M., Mathew, T. C., Khadada, M., Al-Mousawi, M., Talib, H., Asfar, S. K., Behbahani, A. I., & Al-Zaid, N. S. (2007). Beneficial effects of ketogenic diet in obese diabetic subjects. *Molecular and cellular biochemistry, 302*(1-2), 249–256. https://doi.org/10.1007/s11010-007-9448-z

Dashti, H. M., Al-Zaid, N. S., Mathew, T. C., Al-Mousawi, M., Talib, H., Asfar, S. K., & Behbahani, A. I. (2006). Long term effects of ketogenic diet in obese subjects with high cholesterol level. *Molecular and cellular biochemistry, 286*(1-2), 1–9. https://doi.org/10.1007/s11010-005-9001-x

Dehghan, M., Mente, A., Zhang, X., Swaminathan, S., Li, W., Mohan, V., Iqbal, R., Kumar, R., Wentzel-Viljoen, E., Rosengren, A., Amma, L. I., Avezum, A., Chifamba, J., Diaz, R., Khatib, R., Lear, S., Lopez-Jaramillo, P., Liu, X., Gupta, R., Mohammadifard, N., … Prospective Urban Rural Epidemiology (PURE) study investigators (2017). Associations of fats and carbohydrate intake with cardiovascular disease and mortality in 18 countries from five continents (PURE): a prospective cohort study. *Lancet (London, England)*, *390*(10107), 2050–2062. https://doi.org/10.1016/S0140-6736(17)32252-3

Desrosiers, T. A., Siega-Riz, A. M., Mosley, B. S., Meyer, R. E., & National Birth Defects Prevention Study (2018). Low carbohydrate diets may increase risk of neural tube defects. *Birth defects research*, *110*(11), 901–909. https://doi.org/10.1002/bdr2.1198

Diamond, D. M., O'Neill, B. J., & Volek, J. S. (2020). Low carbohydrate diet: are concerns with saturated fat, lipids, and cardiovascular disease risk justified?. *Current opinion in endocrinology, diabetes, and obesity*, *27*(5), 291–300. https://doi.org/10.1097/MED.0000000000000568

Dressler, A., Häfele, C., Giordano, V., Benninger, F., Trimmel-Schwahofer, P., Gröppel, G., Samueli, S., Feucht, M., Male, C., & Repa, A. (2020). The Ketogenic Diet Including Breast Milk for Treatment of Infants with Severe Childhood Epilepsy: Feasibility, Safety, and Effectiveness. *Breastfeeding medicine : the official journal of the Academy of Breastfeeding Medicine*, *15*(2), 72–78. https://doi.org/10.1089/bfm.2019.0190

El-Rashidy, O. F., Nassar, M. F., Abdel-Hamid, I. A., Shatla, R. H., Abdel-Hamid, M. H., Gabr, S. S., Mohamed, S. G., El-Sayed, W. S., & Shaaban, S. Y. (2013). Modified Atkins diet vs classic ketogenic formula in intractable epilepsy. *Acta neurologica Scandinavica*, *128*(6), 402–408. https://doi.org/10.1111/ane.12137

Fiest, K. M., Sauro, K. M., Wiebe, S., Patten, S. B., Kwon, C. S., Dykeman, J., Pringsheim, T., Lorenzetti, D. L., & Jetté, N. (2017). Prevalence and incidence of epilepsy: A systematic review and meta-analysis of international studies. *Neurology*, *88*(3), 296–303. https://doi.org/10.1212/WNL.0000000000003509

Freedman, M. R., King, J., & Kennedy, E. (2001). Popular diets: a scientific review. *Obesity research*, *9 Suppl 1*, 1S–40S. https://doi.org/10.1038/oby.2001.113

Furth, S. L., Casey, J. C., Pyzik, P. L., Neu, A. M., Docimo, S. G., Vining, E. P., Freeman, J. M., & Fivush, B. A. (2000). Risk factors for urolithiasis in children on the ketogenic diet. *Pediatric nephrology (Berlin, Germany)*, *15*(1-2), 125–128. https://doi.org/10.1007/s004670000443

Gardner, C. D., Kiazand, A., Alhassan, S., Kim, S., Stafford, R. S., Balise, R. R., Kraemer, H. C., & King, A. C. (2007). Comparison of the Atkins, Zone, Ornish, and LEARN diets for change in weight and related risk factors among overweight premenopausal women: the A TO Z Weight Loss Study: a

randomized trial. *JAMA*, *297*(9), 969–977.
https://doi.org/10.1001/jama.297.9.969

Geyelin, H. R. (1921). Fasting as a method for treating epilepsy. *Med Rec,* 99:1037-1039.

Ghanemi, A., Yoshioka, M., & St-Amand, J. (2018). Broken Energy Homeostasis and Obesity Pathogenesis: The Surrounding Concepts. *Journal of clinical medicine*, *7*(11), 453. https://doi.org/10.3390/jcm7110453

Gibson, A. A., Seimon, R. V., Lee, C. M., Ayre, J., Franklin, J., Markovic, T. P., Caterson, I. D., & Sainsbury, A. (2015). Do ketogenic diets really suppress appetite? A systematic review and meta-analysis. *Obesity reviews : an official journal of the International Association for the Study of Obesity*, *16*(1), 64–76. https://doi.org/10.1111/obr.12230

Goday, A., Bellido, D., Sajoux, I., Crujeiras, A. B., Burguera, B., García-Luna, P. P., Oleaga, A., Moreno, B., & Casanueva, F. F. (2016). Short-term safety, tolerability and efficacy of a very low-calorie-ketogenic diet interventional weight loss program versus hypocaloric diet in patients with type 2 diabetes mellitus. *Nutrition & diabetes*, *6*(9), e230. https://doi.org/10.1038/nutd.2016.36

Goldenberg, J. Z., Day, A., Brinkworth, G. D., Sato, J., Yamada, S., Jönsson, T., Beardsley, J., Johnson, J. A., Thabane, L., & Johnston, B. C. (2021). Efficacy and safety of low and very low carbohydrate diets for type 2 diabetes remission: systematic review and meta-analysis of published and unpublished randomized trial data. *BMJ (Clinical research ed.)*, *372*, m4743. https://doi.org/10.1136/bmj.m4743

Grant W. B. (2016). Using Multicountry Ecological and Observational Studies to Determine Dietary Risk Factors for Alzheimer's Disease. *Journal of the American College of Nutrition*, *35*(5), 476–489. https://doi.org/10.1080/07315724.2016.1161566

Hall, K. D., Guo, J., Courville, A. B., Boring, J., Brychta, R., Chen, K. Y., Darcey, V., Forde, C. G., Gharib, A. M., Gallagher, I., Howard, R., Joseph, P. V., Milley, L., Ouwerkerk, R., Raisinger, K., Rozga, I., Schick, A., Stagliano, M., Torres, S., Walter, M., ... Chung, S. T. (2021). Effect of a plant-based, low-fat diet versus an animal-based, ketogenic diet on ad libitum energy intake. *Nature medicine*, *27*(2), 344–353. https://doi.org/10.1038/s41591-020-01209-1

Hallberg, S. J., McKenzie, A. L., Williams, P. T., Bhanpuri, N. H., Peters, A. L., Campbell, W. W., Hazbun, T. L., Volk, B. M., McCarter, J. P., Phinney, S. D., & Volek, J. S. (2018). Effectiveness and Safety of a Novel Care Model for the Management of Type 2 Diabetes at 1 Year: An Open-Label, Non-Randomized, Controlled Study. *Diabetes therapy : research, treatment and education of diabetes and related disorders*, *9*(2), 583–612. https://doi.org/10.1007/s13300-018-0373-9

Harris R. B. (1990). Role of set-point theory in regulation of body weight. *FASEB journal : official publication of the Federation of American Societies for Experimental Biology*, *4*(15), 3310–3318. https://doi.org/10.1096/fasebj.4.15.2253845

Huebner, J., Marienfeld, S., Abbenhardt, C., Ulrich, C., Muenstedt, K., Micke, O., Muecke, R., & Loeser, C. (2014). Counseling patients on cancer diets: a review of the literature and recommendations for clinical practice. *Anticancer research*, *34*(1), 39–48.

Hussain, T. A., Mathew, T. C., Dashti, A. A., Asfar, S., Al-Zaid, N., & Dashti, H. M. (2012). Effect of low-calorie versus low-carbohydrate ketogenic diet in type 2 diabetes. *Nutrition (Burbank, Los Angeles County, Calif.)*, *28*(10), 1016–1021. https://doi.org/10.1016/j.nut.2012.01.016

Kraft, B. D., & Westman, E. C. (2009). Schizophrenia, gluten, and low-carbohydrate, ketogenic diets: a case report and review of the literature. *Nutrition & metabolism*, *6*, 10. https://doi.org/10.1186/1743-7075-6-10

Kafami, L., Raza, M., Razavi, A., Mirshafiey, A., Movahedian, M., & Khorramizadeh, M. R. (2010). Intermittent feeding attenuates clinical course of experimental autoimmune encephalomyelitis in C57BL/6 mice. *Avicenna journal of medical biotechnology*, *2*(1), 47–52.

Keesey, R. E., & Hirvonen, M. D. (1997). Body weight set-points: determination and adjustment. *The Journal of nutrition*, *127*(9), 1875S–1883S. https://doi.org/10.1093/jn/127.9.1875S

Kalamian, M. (2017). *Keto For Cancer: Ketogenic Metabolic Therapy as a Targeted Nutritional Strategy*. Chelsea Green Publishing.

Kang, H. C., Chung, D. E., Kim, D. W., & Kim, H. D. (2004). Early- and late-onset complications of the ketogenic diet for intractable epilepsy. *Epilepsia*, *45*(9), 1116–1123. https://doi.org/10.1111/j.0013-9580.2004.10004.x

Kanikarla-Marie, P., & Jain, S. K. (2016). Hyperketonemia and ketosis increase the risk of complications in type 1 diabetes. *Free radical biology & medicine*, *95*, 268–277. https://doi.org/10.1016/j.freeradbiomed.2016.03.020

Kim, D. Y., Hao, J., Liu, R., Turner, G., Shi, F. D., & Rho, J. M. (2012). Inflammation-mediated memory dysfunction and effects of a ketogenic diet in a murine model of multiple sclerosis. *PloS one*, *7*(5), e35476. https://doi.org/10.1371/journal.pone.0035476

Kim, D. Y., & Rho, J. M. (2008). The ketogenic diet and epilepsy. *Current opinion in clinical nutrition and metabolic care*, *11*(2), 113–120. https://doi.org/10.1097/MCO.0b013e3282f44c06

Klement, R. J., Brehm, N., & Sweeney, R. A. (2020). Ketogenic diets in medical oncology: a systematic review with focus on clinical outcomes. *Medical oncology (Northwood, London, England)*, *37*(2), 14. https://doi.org/10.1007/s12032-020-1337-2

Kossoff, E. H., Turner, Z., Doerrer, S., Cervenka, M. C., & Henry, B. J. (2016). *The Ketogenic and Modified Atkins Diets: Treatments for Epilepsy and Other Disorders* (6th ed.). Demos Health.

Kossoff, E. H., Zupec-Kania, B. A., Auvin, S., Ballaban-Gil, K. R., Christina Bergqvist, A. G., Blackford, R., Buchhalter, J. R., Caraballo, R. H., Cross, J. H., Dahlin, M. G., Donner, E. J., Guzel, O., Jehle, R. S., Klepper, J., Kang, H. C., Lambrechts, D. A., Liu, Y., Nathan, J. K., Nordli, D. R., Jr, Pfeifer, H. H., … Practice Committee of the Child Neurology Society (2018). Optimal clinical management of children receiving dietary therapies for epilepsy: Updated recommendations of the International Ketogenic Diet Study Group. *Epilepsia open*, *3*(2), 175–192. https://doi.org/10.1002/epi4.12225

Kovács, Z., D'Agostino, D. P., Diamond, D., Kindy, M. S., Rogers, C., & Ari, C. (2019). Therapeutic Potential of Exogenous Ketone Supplement Induced Ketosis in the Treatment of Psychiatric Disorders: Review of Current Literature. *Frontiers in psychiatry*, *10*, 363. https://doi.org/10.3389/fpsyt.2019.00363

Liberti, M. V., & Locasale, J. W. (2016). The Warburg Effect: How Does it Benefit Cancer Cells?. *Trends in biochemical sciences*, *41*(3), 211–218. https://doi.org/10.1016/j.tibs.2015.12.001

Lilamand, M., Porte, B., Cognat, E., Hugon, J., Mouton-Liger, F., & Paquet, C. (2020). Are ketogenic diets promising for Alzheimer's disease? A translational review. *Alzheimer's research & therapy*, *12*(1), 42. https://doi.org/10.1186/s13195-020-00615-4

Lin, A., Turner, Z., Doerrer, S. C., Stanfield, A., & Kossoff, E. H. (2017). Complications During Ketogenic Diet Initiation: Prevalence, Treatment, and Influence on Seizure Outcomes. *Pediatric neurology*, *68*, 35–39. https://doi.org/10.1016/j.pediatrneurol.2017.01.007

Mahajan, A., Donovan, L. E., Vallee, R., & Yamamoto, J. M. (2019). Evidenced-Based Nutrition for Gestational Diabetes Mellitus. *Current diabetes reports*, *19*(10), 94. https://doi.org/10.1007/s11892-019-1208-4

Liu R. H. (2013). Health-promoting components of fruits and vegetables in the diet. *Advances in nutrition (Bethesda, Md.)*, *4*(3), 384S–92S. https://doi.org/10.3945/an.112.003517

Martin-McGill, K. J., Jackson, C. F., Bresnahan, R., Levy, R. G., & Cooper, P. N. (2018). Ketogenic diets for drug-resistant epilepsy. *The Cochrane database of*

systematic reviews, *11*(11), CD001903.
https://doi.org/10.1002/14651858.CD001903.pub4

Martin-McGill, K. J., Srikandarajah, N., Marson, A. G., Tudur Smith, C., & Jenkinson, M. D. (2018). The role of ketogenic diets in the therapeutic management of adult and paediatric gliomas: a systematic review. *CNS oncology*, *7*(2), CNS17. https://doi.org/10.2217/cns-2017-0030

McClean, A. M., Montorio, L., McLaughlin, D., McGovern, S., & Flanagan, N. (2019). Can a ketogenic diet be safely used to improve glycaemic control in a child with type 1 diabetes?. *Archives of disease in childhood*, *104*(5), 501–504. https://doi.org/10.1136/archdischild-2018-314973

McNally, M. A., Pyzik, P. L., Rubenstein, J. E., Hamdy, R. F., & Kossoff, E. H. (2009). Empiric use of potassium citrate reduces kidney-stone incidence with the ketogenic diet. *Pediatrics*, *124*(2), e300–e304. https://doi.org/10.1542/peds.2009-0217

Meng, Y., Bai, H., Wang, S., Li, Z., Wang, Q., & Chen, L. (2017). Efficacy of low carbohydrate diet for type 2 diabetes mellitus management: A systematic review and meta-analysis of randomized controlled trials. *Diabetes research and clinical practice*, *131*, 124–131. https://doi.org/10.1016/j.diabres.2017.07.006

Mohorko, N., Černelič-Bizjak, M., Poklar-Vatovec, T., Grom, G., Kenig, S., Petelin, A., & Jenko-Pražnikar, Z. (2019). Weight loss, improved physical performance, cognitive function, eating behavior, and metabolic profile in a 12-week ketogenic diet in obese adults. *Nutrition research (New York, N.Y.)*, *62*, 64–77. https://doi.org/10.1016/j.nutres.2018.11.007

McKenzie, A. L., Hallberg, S. J., Creighton, B. C., Volk, B. M., Link, T. M., Abner, M. K., Glon, R. M., McCarter, J. P., Volek, J. S., & Phinney, S. D. (2017). A Novel Intervention Including Individualized Nutritional Recommendations Reduces Hemoglobin A1c Level, Medication Use, and Weight in Type 2 Diabetes. *JMIR diabetes*, *2*(1), e5. https://doi.org/10.2196/diabetes.6981

Murphy, E. A., & Jenkins, T. J. (2019). A ketogenic diet for reducing obesity and maintaining capacity for physical activity: hype or hope?. *Current opinion in clinical nutrition and metabolic care*, *22*(4), 314–319. https://doi.org/10.1097/MCO.0000000000000572

Neal, E. G., Chaffe, H. M., Edwards, N., Lawson, M. S., Schwartz, R. H., & Cross, J. H. (2008). Growth of children on classical and medium-chain triglyceride ketogenic diets. *Pediatrics*, *122*(2), e334–e340. https://doi.org/10.1542/peds.2007-2410

Norwitz, N. G., Dalai, S. S., & Palmer, C. M. (2020). Ketogenic diet as a metabolic treatment for mental illness. *Current opinion in endocrinology, diabetes, and obesity*, *27*(5), 269–274. https://doi.org/10.1097/MED.0000000000000564

Oliveira, C., Mattingly, S., Schirrmacher, R., Sawyer, M. B., Fine, E. J., & Prado, C. M. (2018). A Nutritional Perspective of Ketogenic Diet in Cancer: A Narrative Review. *Journal of the Academy of Nutrition and Dietetics*, *118*(4), 668–688. https://doi.org/10.1016/j.jand.2017.02.003

O'Neill, B., & Raggi, P. (2020). The ketogenic diet: Pros and cons. *Atherosclerosis*, *292*, 119–126. https://doi.org/10.1016/j.atherosclerosis.2019.11.021

Patterson, M. A., Maiya, M., & Stewart, M. L. (2020). Resistant Starch Content in Foods Commonly Consumed in the United States: A Narrative Review. *Journal of the Academy of Nutrition and Dietetics*, *120*(2), 230–244. https://doi.org/10.1016/j.jand.2019.10.019

Paul, E., Conant, K. D., Dunne, I. E., Pfeifer, H. H., Lyczkowski, D. A., Linshaw, M. A., & Thiele, E. A. (2010). Urolithiasis on the ketogenic diet with concurrent topiramate or zonisamide therapy. *Epilepsy research*, *90*(1-2), 151–156. https://doi.org/10.1016/j.eplepsyres.2010.04.005

Phelps, J. R., Siemers, S. V., & El-Mallakh, R. S. (2013). The ketogenic diet for type II bipolar disorder. *Neurocase*, *19*(5), 423–426. https://doi.org/10.1080/13554794.2012.690421

Piccio, L., Stark, J. L., & Cross, A. H. (2008). Chronic calorie restriction attenuates experimental autoimmune encephalomyelitis. *Journal of leukocyte biology*, *84*(4), 940–948. https://doi.org/10.1189/jlb.0208133

Roehl, K., & Sewak, S. L. (2017). Practice Paper of the Academy of Nutrition and Dietetics: Classic and Modified Ketogenic Diets for Treatment of Epilepsy. *Journal of the Academy of Nutrition and Dietetics*, *117*(8), 1279–1292. https://doi.org/10.1016/j.jand.2017.06.006

Rydin, A. A., Spiegel, G., Frohnert, B. I., Kaess, A., Oswald, L., Owen, D., & Simmons, K. M. (2021). Medical management of children with type 1 diabetes on low-carbohydrate or ketogenic diets. *Pediatric diabetes*, *22*(3), 448–454. https://doi.org/10.1111/pedi.13179

Sampaio, L., Takakura, C., & Manreza, M. (2017). The use of a formula-based ketogenic diet in children with refractory epilepsy. *Arquivos de neuro-psiquiatria*, *75*(4), 234–237. https://doi.org/10.1590/0004-282X20170028

Saslow, L. R., Mason, A. E., Kim, S., Goldman, V., Ploutz-Snyder, R., Bayandorian, H., Daubenmier, J., Hecht, F. M., & Moskowitz, J. T. (2017). An Online Intervention Comparing a Very Low-Carbohydrate Ketogenic Diet and Lifestyle Recommendations Versus a Plate Method Diet in Overweight Individuals With Type 2 Diabetes: A Randomized Controlled Trial. *Journal of medical Internet research*, *19*(2), e36. https://doi.org/10.2196/jmir.5806

Scolnick, B., Zupec-Kania, B., Calabrese, L., Aoki, C., & Hildebrandt, T. (2020). Remission from Chronic Anorexia Nervosa With Ketogenic Diet and

Ketamine: Case Report. *Frontiers in psychiatry*, *11*, 763.
https://doi.org/10.3389/fpsyt.2020.00763

Sharman, M. J., Kraemer, W. J., Love, D. M., Avery, N. G., Gómez, A. L., Scheett, T. P., & Volek, J. S. (2002). A ketogenic diet favorably affects serum biomarkers for cardiovascular disease in normal-weight men. *The Journal of nutrition*, *132*(7), 1879–1885. https://doi.org/10.1093/jn/132.7.1879

Shaw, G. M., & Yang, W. (2019). Women's periconceptional lowered carbohydrate intake and NTD-affected pregnancy risk in the era of prefortification with folic acid. *Birth defects research*, *111*(5), 248–253. https://doi.org/10.1002/bdr2.1466

Sirikonda, N. S., Patten, W. D., Phillips, J. R., & Mullett, C. J. (2012). Ketogenic diet: rapid onset of selenium deficiency-induced cardiac decompensation. *Pediatric cardiology*, *33*(5), 834–838. https://doi.org/10.1007/s00246-012-0219-6

Slavin, J. L., & Lloyd, B. (2012). Health benefits of fruits and vegetables. *Advances in nutrition (Bethesda, Md.)*, *3*(4), 506–516. https://doi.org/10.3945/an.112.002154

Stern, L., Iqbal, N., Seshadri, P., Chicano, K. L., Daily, D. A., McGrory, J., Williams, M., Gracely, E. J., & Samaha, F. F. (2004). The effects of low-carbohydrate versus conventional weight loss diets in severely obese adults: one-year follow-up of a randomized trial. *Annals of internal medicine*, *140*(10), 778–785. https://doi.org/10.7326/0003-4819-140-10-200405180-00007

Storoni, M., & Plant, G. T. (2015). The Therapeutic Potential of the Ketogenic Diet in Treating Progressive Multiple Sclerosis. *Multiple sclerosis international*, *2015*, 681289. https://doi.org/10.1155/2015/681289

Tiwari, S., Riazi, S., & Ecelbarger, C. A. (2007). Insulin's impact on renal sodium transport and blood pressure in health, obesity, and diabetes. *American journal of physiology. Renal physiology*, *293*(4), F974–F984. https://doi.org/10.1152/ajprenal.00149.2007

Vergati, M., Krasniqi, E., Monte, G. D., Riondino, S., Vallone, D., Guadagni, F., Ferroni, P., & Roselli, M. (2017). Ketogenic Diet and Other Dietary Intervention Strategies in the Treatment of Cancer. *Current medicinal chemistry*, *24*(12), 1170–1185. https://doi.org/10.2174/0929867324666170116122915

Vestergaard P. (2015). Effects of antiepileptic drugs on bone health and growth potential in children with epilepsy. *Paediatric drugs*, *17*(2), 141–150. https://doi.org/10.1007/s40272-014-0115-z

Volek, J. S., Freidenreich, D. J., Saenz, C., Kunces, L. J., Creighton, B. C., Bartley, J. M., Davitt, P. M., Munoz, C. X., Anderson, J. M., Maresh, C. M., Lee, E. C., Schuenke, M. D., Aerni, G., Kraemer, W. J., & Phinney, S. D. (2016). Metabolic characteristics of keto-adapted ultra-endurance runners. *Metabolism:*

clinical and experimental, *65*(3), 100–110.
https://doi.org/10.1016/j.metabol.2015.10.028

Westman, E. C., Yancy, W. S., Edman, J. S., Tomlin, K. F., & Perkins, C. E. (2002). Effect of 6-month adherence to a very low carbohydrate diet program. *The American journal of medicine*, *113*(1), 30–36. https://doi.org/10.1016/s0002-9343(02)01129-4

Westman, E. C., Feinman, R. D., Mavropoulos, J. C., Vernon, M. C., Volek, J. S., Wortman, J. A., Yancy, W. S., & Phinney, S. D. (2007). Low-carbohydrate nutrition and metabolism. *The American journal of clinical nutrition*, *86*(2), 276–284. https://doi.org/10.1093/ajcn/86.2.276

Westman, E. C., Yancy, W. S., Jr, Mavropoulos, J. C., Marquart, M., & McDuffie, J. R. (2008). The effect of a low-carbohydrate, ketogenic diet versus a low-glycemic index diet on glycemic control in type 2 diabetes mellitus. *Nutrition & metabolism*, *5*, 36. https://doi.org/10.1186/1743-7075-5-36

Wheless J. W. (2008). History of the ketogenic diet. *Epilepsia*, *49 Suppl 8*, 3–5. https://doi.org/10.1111/j.1528-1167.2008.01821.x

Wilder, R. M. (1921). High fat diets in epilepsy. *Mayo Clin Bull*, *2*, 308.

Włodarek D. (2019). Role of Ketogenic Diets in Neurodegenerative Diseases (Alzheimer's Disease and Parkinson's Disease). *Nutrients*, *11*(1), 169. https://doi.org/10.3390/nu11010169

Yancy, W. S., Jr, Olsen, M. K., Guyton, J. R., Bakst, R. P., & Westman, E. C. (2004). A low-carbohydrate, ketogenic diet versus a low-fat diet to treat obesity and hyperlipidemia: a randomized, controlled trial. *Annals of internal medicine*, *140*(10), 769–777. https://doi.org/10.7326/0003-4819-140-10-200405180-00006

Yancy, W. S., Jr, Foy, M., Chalecki, A. M., Vernon, M. C., & Westman, E. C. (2005). A low-carbohydrate, ketogenic diet to treat type 2 diabetes. *Nutrition & metabolism*, *2*, 34. https://doi.org/10.1186/1743-7075-2-34

Zupec-Kania, B. A. (2007). *Micronutrient composition of the classic ketogenic diet.* KetoPag Conference, London, England.

Zupec-Kania, B. A. (2006). *Keto news for health care professionals*, Volume 1, Issue 3.

THE MEDITERRANEAN DIET

Julia Hilbrands MS, MPH, RD
Kelly Toups MLA, RD, LDN Reviewer

"I think the Mediterranean diet is one of the healthiest … lots of nuts, vegetables, fruits, fresh fish, lean meats, and yogurt."
Quote by Cat Cora

While the Mediterranean diet has been the subject of many headlines in the past few decades, it is far from a new diet. In fact, if the word "diet" brings to mind descriptions such as "restrictive," "limiting," or "rigid," the Mediterranean diet is hardly a diet at all. Rather, it is habitual eating pattern developed over thousands of years by rural communities with limited resources scattered throughout the Mediterranean basin. It is a mostly a plant-based eating pattern but it does also include some animal products, primarily in the form of fish and seafood as well as fermented dairy products. The primary source of fat in the Mediterranean diet is olive oil, and a moderate amount of alcohol is included as well, mainly in the form of red wine.

The Mediterranean diet began receiving attention when researchers were noticing that the people of this region have historically experienced low rates of chronic disease, including heart disease, some cancers, and diabetes, and as a result, an increased life expectancy (Bach-Faig et al., 2011a). As these are all chronic diseases that are plaguing societies worldwide in the present day, it is no wonder that the Mediterranean diet has been brought to the forefront of the nutrition conversation. In fact, in the *U.S. News and World Report* "Best Diet Ranking of 2021," 25 nutrition scientists ranked 41 diets and selected the Mediterranean Diet as the "Best Diet Overall," the "Best Diet for Diabetes," the "Easiest Diet to Follow" and the "Best Plant-Based Diet"; and #2 for the "Best Diet for Healthy Eating," and the "Best Diet for Heart-Health" (Best Diets Overall).

GEOGRAPHIC ORIGINS

Links between the Mediterranean diet and health were first noted in the landmark *Seven Countries Study*, a longitudinal study launched by Ancel Keys and colleagues in 1947 with results first published in 1970 (Seven Countries Study, 2019). The study looked at dietary and lifestyle habits of individuals in Finland, the Netherlands, Italy, the former Yugoslavia, Greece, Japan and the United States. Within these countries, there were four Mediterranean cohorts that were studied: Crete and Corfu in Greece, Dalmatia in Croatia, and Montegiorgio in Italy.

One key finding from this study was that all of the Mediterranean cohorts had lower mortality rates from coronary heart disease than cohorts from the other countries. Researchers also found that a Mediterranean-style diet combined with a high level of physical activity, not smoking, and moderate alcohol consumption were all associated with a very low risk of coronary heart disease and cardiovascular disease. Interestingly, there was still variation in dietary patterns among these Mediterranean cohorts. The Greek diet had the highest content of olive oil and was also high in fruit, while the Dalmatian diet was highest in fish and the Italian diet was highest in vegetables. Data collection from this study is ongoing and results on the relationship between the Mediterranean diet and health outcomes continue to be published.

SECTION 1: DEFINING THE MEDITERRANEAN DIET

The Mediterranean diet is not a strict regimen, but rather a way of eating. The table below describes the overall recommendations (without serving suggestions) for each food group.

Table 1: Overview of Food and Beverages on the Mediterranean Diet

	Vegetable	Daily, as the foundation of most meals
	Fruit	Daily
	Grain	Daily, as the foundation of most meals, with a focus on whole grains
	Dairy	Frequent consumption (weekly or daily) but in small amounts, with a focus on fermented dairy (Greek yogurt, artisan cheese)
	Protein	Nuts: Daily Pulses/Legumes: Daily Red meat: Rarely (a few times per month, at most) Poultry: Weekly Fish: at least 2 times per week
	Fats/Oils	Focus on olive oil Fried fast food: Rarely, due to a focus on home-cooked meals Butter/margarine: not included
	Sweets	Rarely (weekly or monthly), as fruits and fruit-based dishes are the typical daily "dessert"
	Sodium	Typically, less than 2,300 mg per day. The focus is on herbs, spices, and fresh citrus to flavor cooking before adding salt
	Other	Wine: 5 ounces per day for women or up to 10 ounces per day for men is optional

121

As results from the *Seven Countries Study* show, there is not a single, prescriptive definition of the Mediterranean diet. There are 18 distinct countries that border the Mediterranean Sea, and they all differ dramatically in geography, customs, health, lifestyle and diet. The term "Mediterranean diet" then refers to the traditional way of eating among the generally poor rural communities in this area prior to the 1960s before globalization began to influence diet and lifestyle (Trichopoulou et al., 2014). The diet does not contain any magical "superfoods" or secrets, but rather it is a habitual way of eating with emphasis placed on certain foods and food groups. The Mediterranean diet is also marked by a certain way of life. There is moderation in eating as serving sizes were traditionally based on frugality and scarcity.

Unfortunately, in today's world that is becoming increasingly globalized and Westernized, the current dietary pattern in Mediterranean countries has deviated from what was traditionally consumed in those regions (Miguel Ángel Martínez-González et al., 2017a). Younger individuals in the region associate being poor with the Mediterranean diet and when given the chance economically, they purchase and consume more meat and processed food.

SECTION 2: COMPONENTS OF A MEDITERRANEAN DIET

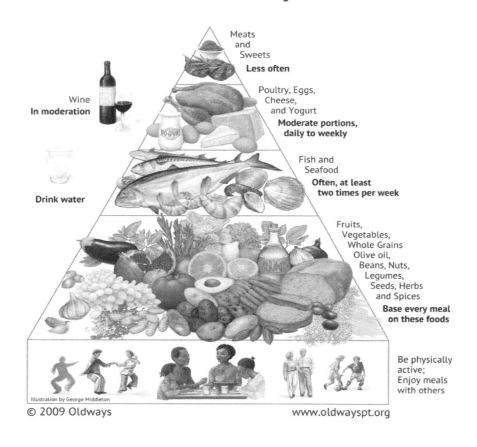

As shown in the Mediterranean diet pyramid a traditional Mediterranean diet is characterized by a high consumption of plant-based foods such as vegetables, fruits, nuts, legumes and minimally-processed grains (Miguel Ángel Martínez-González et al., 2017a). A square meal on a traditional Mediterranean table will include at least two servings of vegetables and oftentimes one to two servings of fruit as well (Bach-Faig et al., 2011a). Additionally, fruit is frequently served as a dessert at the end of the meal. Fruits and vegetables are low in caloric value but rich in healthful fiber, micronutrients, and antioxidants, allowing for greater intake of foods in this group (Miguel Ángel Martínez-González et al., 2017a).

Whole grains are also a main component of Mediterranean meals, and nuts and legumes are included in the diet multiple times each week. Whole grains (as opposed to refined grains) are an important source of fiber and several key nutrients including phosphorus, copper manganese, magnesium and B vitamins; some are also good sources of iron. Legumes, also frequently referred to as beans or pulses, provide a source of protein and are also a good source of fiber, carbohydrates, B vitamins, and minerals such as iron, copper, and zinc (Polak et al., 2015).

Similarly, nuts and seeds contain a plethora of micronutrients and are a good source of healthful fats that are the flagship of the Mediterranean diet. A serving of just 1 to 1.5 ounces of nuts or seeds each day has been associated with beneficial health outcomes including lowered LDL cholesterol and reduced markers of cardiovascular disease and metabolic disorders (Hernández-Alonso et al., 2017; Kalita et al., 2018; McKay et al., 2018). The frequency of nut consumption has also been found to be inversely associated with total and cause-specific mortality in both men and women (Bao et al., 2013).

Animal products do still appear in the Mediterranean diet, but they are typically not the main feature of a meal and instead are added to dishes for flavor (Bach-Faig et al., 2011a). A traditional Mediterranean diet will include a moderate to high consumption of fish and shellfish – usually three to four servings per week – as well as a moderate consumption of fermented dairy products, such as cheese and yogurt (Martinez-Gonzalez & Martin-Calvo, 2016a). This diet is also characterized by a low consumption of other meat and meat products, such as poultry and eggs, and a general avoidance of red and processed meats (Buckland & Gonzalez, 2015).

A key difference between the Mediterranean diet and other healthful diets, such as the Dietary Approaches to Stop Hypertension (DASH) diet or the Dietary Guidelines for Americans, is that the Mediterranean diet allows for an abundant intake of fat, sometimes up to 40% of total calories consumed (Martinez-Gonzalez & Martin-Calvo, 2016a; Trichopoulou et al., 2014). What makes the fat content of the Mediterranean diet health-promoting is that there is a high ratio of beneficial unsaturated fats to nonbeneficial saturated fats. These unsaturated fats can come from fatty fish, nuts, and seeds, but the primary source of fat in the Mediterranean diet is extra virgin olive oil, which may provide between 10% to 15% of total calories consumed just on its own (Martinez-Gonzalez & Martin-Calvo, 2016a).

For centuries, olive oil has been recognized for its health benefits, and within the last several decades we have learned this is due to its high monounsaturated fatty acid content and the numerous phytochemicals and phenolic compounds it contains, which have anti-inflammatory and antioxidant properties (Buckland & Gonzalez, 2015). These properties play a large role in the Mediterranean diet's association with a reduced risk of coronary heart disease, some cancers, and cognitive decline (Owen et al., 2000). For more specific details on olive oil and its health benefits, refer to the chapter on Fats & Oils.

Another key difference between the Mediterranean diet and other health-promoting dietary patterns is the inclusion of alcohol in daily life (Trichopoulou et al., 2014). However, it is important to recognize that within the traditional Mediterranean region, alcohol was almost always in the form of red wine and it was most often consumed with meals (Martinez-Gonzalez & Martin-Calvo, 2016a). Red wine consumption has been linked with several health benefits, and moderate red wine drinkers were found to have a reduced risk of metabolic syndrome, an abnormal waist circumference, low HDL cholesterol levels, high blood pressure, and high fasting plasma glucose compared to nondrinkers (Tresserra-Rimbau et al., 2015). Moderate alcohol consumption is defined as up to one drink daily for women and up to two drinks daily for men. A standard drink is considered to be 1.5 ounces of distilled spirits, 12 ounces of beer, or, in the case of a Mediterranean-style diet, 5 ounces of wine.

Herbs and spices are the primary source of added flavor in the Mediterranean diet, reducing the need for added salt or saturated fats. In addition to displacing salt and fat, many herbs and spices carry with them health benefits of their own. Many spices contain micronutrients, phytochemicals, and antioxidants, and some even convey anti-inflammatory and antimicrobial properties (Opara & Chohan, 2014). Refer to the chapter on Herbs and Spices for more information on the health benefits of these flavor enhancers.

While the Mediterranean diet is inclusive of many foods and food groups, there are some foods that are commonly avoided. Notably absent are the highly processed foods that make up a typically Western diet, such as soda and fruit juice, candies, packaged baked goods, French fries and other fast food or convenience items. Foods rich in sugars and unhealthful fats are reserved only for very special occasions, and fruits and hard cheeses are the typical choice for an after meal dessert (Bach-Faig et al., 2011a). Refined grains — another staple of a Western diet — take a back seat to whole grain varieties in the Mediterranean diet. Red and processed meats are also rarely seen in this dietary pattern.

Much of the avoidance of red meat and processed foods can be traced back to the lifestyle and habits within traditional Mediterranean culture. Red meat was much more expensive than it is today, so it was reserved only for special occasions and religious ceremonies. In fact, a religion-based abstinence of meat throughout much of the year was not uncommon. Similarly, refined white flour and sugar were commodities reserved only for the wealthy as the processing of these foods was expensive. Thus, everyday people consumed courser whole grains and natural sugar by way of fruit.

SECTION 3: LIFESTYLE FACTORS

The foods in a traditional Mediterranean diet are known to convey health benefits, but some of the health benefits may also come from the way daily life was experienced in that region. In addition to a Mediterranean diet, a Mediterranean lifestyle must be considered when assessing health effects (Trichopoulou et al., 2014). In this traditional culture, food represented much more than just nourishment — eating was a social phenomenon. Value was placed on socialization during family or communal meals, and many members of a family or group would be involved in culinary activities and food production as it was important that culinary traditions be passed down through generations (Bach-Faig et al., 2011b; Martinez-Gonzalez & Martin-Calvo, 2016b). These tendencies led to an affirming and renewing of family and group identity (Georgousopoulou et al., 2017).

The way that food was acquired was also a unique part of the Mediterranean lifestyle. People in this region traditionally lived in poor rural settings, so much of their food was grown, raised, or gathered (Bach-Faig et al., 2011b). This type of lifestyle promotes physical activity through activities of daily living. It also promotes a greater focus on local, seasonal, and traditional foods (Martinez-Gonzalez & Martin-Calvo, 2016b). However, while there was typically a lot of physical activity and manual labor in day-to-day life, there was also an importance placed on adequate rest (Bach-Faig et al., 2011b).

The health effects of these lifestyle factors are not nearly as well studied and documented as the health effects of foods in the Mediterranean diet, but it is suspected that psychological, social, and physical behaviors within the Mediterranean lifestyle may have protective effects from chronic disease, too (Georgousopoulou et al., 2017). For example, research shows that frequent socializing with friends is inversely associated with the presence of hypertension in adults, and more frequent family dinners are associated with a more healthful dietary intake in youth (Georgousopoulou et al., 2017; Walton et al., 2018). Some researchers even suggest that alcohol in the Mediterranean diet may positively impact socialization as it helps foster merriment and relaxation at family and community gatherings, leading to strong social ties.

The benefits of family or communal meals are also well established. For adults, those who follow a regular meal pattern versus random snacking throughout the day have lower energy intake and lower LDL cholesterol levels (Farshchi et al., 2005). In children, the frequency of family meals is positively associated with the intake of fruits, vegetables, grains and calcium-rich foods, and those who eat dinner with their families consume less soda and fried foods (Neumark-Sztainer et al., 2003; Toschke et al., 2007). Additionally, the prevalence of overweight among young teenagers is reduced by 15% among those who eat a family dinner on "most days" or "every day" compared to those who eat a family dinner "never or some days" (Taveras et al., 2005).

SECTION 4: RESEARCH SUPPORTING THE MEDITERRANEAN DIET

The Mediterranean diet is one of the most researched "diets" in the world with over 6,500 scientific studies published to date. Some of the most often cited clinical trials are described below followed by a section identifying the many health benefits associated with following a Mediterranean diet.

MEDITERRANEAN DIET SCORES

There are several scoring systems set up to measure compliance to the Mediterranean diet. For the first, the *Mediterranean Diet Score*, participants can receive a score between zero and nine based on how well their diet adheres to a Mediterranean diet pattern. Zero represents the poorest adherence and nine is the best adherence (Martinez-Gonzalez & Martin-Calvo, 2016a). Participants receive one point if consumption was **at or above** the sex-specific median for vegetables, fruits and nuts, legumes, fish, cereals and monounsaturated /saturated fat ratio; and one point if consumption **was below** sex-specific median for meat/meat products and dairy products. In addition, one point was allocated for moderate alcohol intake, defined as 5 g per day to 25 g per day for women and 10 g per day to 50 g per day for men.

Table 2: Nutrients in the *Mediterranean Diet Score*

Positively weighted items	Negatively weighted Items
Vegetables	Meat, meat products
Fruits and nuts	Dairy products
Legumes	
Fish	
Cereals	

Monounsaturated/ saturated fat ratio	
Moderate alcohol intake: 5g/day to 25g/day for women, 10g/day to 50 g/day for men	

A large limitation of the *Mediterranean Diet Score* is that it uses study-specific medians as cutoff points, so an individual's score is highly dependent on the characteristics of the sample (Trichopoulou et al., 2014). This will limit overall generalizability as well as between-study comparisons.

To address these limitations, other dietary scoring systems have been created. The researchers in the *PREDIMED* group developed their own dietary scoring system — the *PREDIMED Screener Score*. This index gives participants a score from zero to 14 based on how well they adhere to predetermined levels of intake (Martinez-Gonzalez & Martin-Calvo, 2016a). There is also a *Mediterranean-Style Dietary Pattern Score* (MSDPS), which was developed to assess the conformity to a traditional Mediterranean-style diet among non-Mediterranean populations. The MSDPS assigns a score between zero and 100 based on one's intake of 13 food groups (Rumawas, Dwyer, et al., 2009). Other indices include the *Mediterranean Adequacy Index*, the *Alternative Mediterranean Diet Index*, and many others (Alberti-Fidanza & Fidanza, 2004; Fung et al., 2005; Zaragoza-Martí et al., 2018).

Table 3: The *PREDIMED Screener Score*

PREDIMED Screener Score (0-14 Points)
1 point given for each of the following:
Olive oil as main culinary fat
>= 4 T/day olive oil
>= 2 servings/day vegetables
>= 3 servings/day fruits

>= 3 servings/week legumes
>= 3 servings/week fish
>= 3 servings/week nuts
>= 2 servings/day olive oil sauce with tomato, garlic, and onion (sofrito)
Preference for poultry > red meats
<1 serving/day red/processed meats
<1 serving/day butter/margarine/cream
<1 serving/day carbonated/sugared sodas
<2 servings/week commercial bakery, cakes, biscuits or pastries
>= 7 glasses/week wine

There are limitations in the use of such scoring indices to describe complex dietary patterns. However, on the positive side, these numerical scores allow researchers to rank the quality of participants' diets and compare that numeric quality with health outcomes.

LANDMARK CLINICAL TRIALS

Much of what we know about the associations between the Mediterranean diet and health are through observational studies, but by nature these studies are only able to comment on associations. They cannot determine cause-and-effect relationships. Intervention trials are needed to help draw these conclusions. There are a few landmark intervention trials that support the evidence found in observational studies, and they are discussed below.

The *PREDIMED* Study

The largest dietary intervention trial to date is known as the *PREDMIED* study, which stands for Prevención con Dieta Mediterránea, or Prevention with Mediterranean Diet, when translated (Ramón Estruch et al., 2018). This study comes from a research group in Spain who first published their results in 2013.

The trial included almost 7,500 Spanish patients, both men and women, with high cardiovascular disease risk but no active cardiovascular disease at the time of enrollment. Participants were then randomized to one of three diets: (1) a Mediterranean diet supplemented with extra virgin olive oil, (2) a Mediterranean diet supplemented with mixed nuts, or (3) a control diet where participants were given advice to reduce dietary fat. Participants were followed for an average of 4.8 years.

The primary outcomes of interest were myocardial infarction, stroke, or cardiovascular death, and researchers found that there was a statistically significant reduction in these outcomes in both Mediterranean diet groups compared to the control group. More specifically, there was a 30% reduction in the incidence of major cardiovascular disease events in the Mediterranean diet groups compared to the control group.

In 2018, the original *PREDIMED* study was retracted due to several issues with the randomization process used at several of the study sites. The authors ran their analyses a second time omitting the 1,558 participants that were randomized improperly and published their results, and the results were the same: the incidence of major cardiovascular events was about 30% lower in both Mediterranean diet groups than the control group (Ramón Estruch et al., 2018).

The *PREDIMED* study remains the largest Mediterranean diet intervention trial to date, and results and associations continue to be published by this group. Many of them will be discussed throughout this chapter.

The *Lyon Diet Heart Study*

Another important Mediterranean diet intervention trial that predates the *PREDIMED* study is the *Lyon Diet Heart Study*, first published in 1996 with final results published in 1999 (De Lorgeril et al., 1996; de Lorgeril Michel et al., 1999). This was a secondary prevention trial in that it included individuals who had already experienced one myocardial infarction and was looking to see if a Mediterranean diet could prevent a second myocardial infarction or other cardiovascular complications.

The study included 605 patients from France, and patients were randomized to either a Mediterranean dietary intervention or a control diet, which was to follow the prudent dietary advice given by their attending physician. The planned follow-up was 5 years, but the trial was stopped early due to clinically statistically significant findings. After 27 months of follow-up, those on a Mediterranean diet showed a 76% reduced risk of a second myocardial infarction or other clinical endpoints (unstable angina, stroke, heart failure and embolisms). It then became unethical to withhold the treatment, the Mediterranean Diet, from the control group.

The *Lyon Diet Heart Study* demonstrates that not only is a Mediterranean-style diet important in preventing cardiovascular disease and other related outcomes, but it can also be an important part of treatment in those who have cardiovascular disease.

HEALTH BENEFITS OF THE MEDITERRANEAN DIET

In the last half-century, many observational studies have shown an association between a Mediterranean-style diet and reduced rates of several chronic diseases. In fact, an umbrella review that included meta-analyses of both observational studies and randomized trials found that **greater adherence to a Mediterranean diet was associated with a reduced risk of overall mortality, cardiovascular disease, coronary heart disease, myocardial infarction, overall cancer incidence, neurodegenerative diseases and diabetes** (Dinu et al., 2018). There are many mechanisms at play within diet and lifestyle that lead to these outcomes, and many of them have to do with improvements in lipid profiles, oxidative stress, inflammation status, glucose metabolism and vascular integrity as well as effects on hormone status and gut microbiota-related metabolic health (Franquesa et al., 2019). A deeper look into how this dietary pattern relates to specific chronic diseases follows.

Cardiovascular Health

Some of the strongest evidence about the health impacts of the Mediterranean diet is in how it relates to cardiovascular health. Across numerous epidemiological studies, a Mediterranean diet has been associated with a reduced risk of cardiovascular disease among both men and women and across several diverse racial and ethnic groups. For example, in prospective cohort study of more than 40,000 Spaniards, those in the highest quintile of adherence to a Mediterranean diet had a 27% decreased risk of coronary heart disease compared with the lowest quintile of intake (Guallar-Castillón et al., 2012). Similarly, among U.S. adults in the *Northern Manhattan Study*, greater adherence to a Mediterranean diet was associated with a decreased risk of death from vascular events, such as myocardial infarction or stroke (Gardener et al., 2011).

Similar results have been seen in a large cohort of women. Among almost 75,000 U.S. women in the *Nurses' Health Study*, those with greater adherence to a Mediterranean diet were at a lower risk for both coronary heart disease and stroke compared to those with poor adherence to the diet (Fung et al., 2009). In women specifically, a Mediterranean diet has also been associated with lower mortality from cardiovascular disease, a reduced risk of heart failure, a lower risk of stroke and a greater reduction in markers of inflammation (Ahmad et al., 2018; Fung et al., 2009; Paterson Katherine E. et al., 2018; Tektonidis et al., 2015).

Systematic reviews and meta-analyses have also shown that greater adherence to a Mediterranean diet reduces cardiovascular disease incidence, including coronary heart disease, myocardial infarction, and overall mortality (Franquesa et al., 2019; Grosso et al., 2017; Martinez-Gonzalez & Martin-Calvo, 2016a). A recent Cochrane review — one of the leading databases for systematic reviews in health care — reviewed 30 randomized control trials and seven ongoing trials and found that there is still some uncertainty regarding the exact effects of a Mediterranean diet on cardiovascular risk factors, but research to date still seems to suggest a cardiovascular benefit, and ongoing studies may provide more certainty in the future (Rees et al., 2019).

The health benefits of a Mediterranean diet on cardiovascular disease risk aren't limited to just the Mediterranean region. In a study of Swedish men, greater adherence to the diet was associated with a lower risk of heart failure and a lower risk of mortality from heart failure (Tektonidis et al., 2016). In a large prospective cohort study of adults with stable coronary heart disease from 29 different countries, greater adherence to a Mediterranean diet was associated with a lower risk of subsequent major cardiovascular events (Stewart et al., 2016).

The Mediterranean diet is not only beneficial in preventing cardiovascular disease, but it can be beneficial in limiting disease progression. For example, among American adults, a Mediterranean-style diet was associated with a reduced recurrence of cardiovascular disease by 50% to 70% (Carter et al., 2010). Similarly, a European study found that those who followed a Mediterranean diet for three years had a 50% to 70% reduced risk of heart attack and a 56% lower risk of dying from any cause (de Lorgeril & Salen, 2006).

The results of the *PREDIMED* trial put even more strength behind this association when it showed that a Mediterranean diet intervention was successful in improving cardiovascular biomarkers. A sub-study within the *PREDIMED* clinical trial showed that adherence to a Mediterranean diet is associated with a lower level of inflammation (Ruiz-Canela et al., 2015).

Obesity, Weight Management, and Metabolic Syndrome

Adherence to a Mediterranean diet has proven to be beneficial in preventing obesity and metabolic syndrome, and it is also beneficial in promoting weight loss and improving symptoms in those who are overweight or obese. Observational studies have shown that adherence to a Mediterranean diet helps with weight management and can prevent overweight and obesity. A prospective cohort study of over 350,000 adults from 10 different European countries found that individuals who had a high adherence to a Mediterranean diet were 10% less likely to develop overweight or obesity than individuals with a low adherence (Romaguera et al., 2010). Research has also shown that a Mediterranean diet may result in greater weight loss than a low-fat diet (Ramon Estruch et al., 2019; Mancini et al., 2016).

Systematic reviews have shown that adherence to **a Mediterranean diet can reduce weight, waist circumference and abdominal adiposity, thereby reducing BMI and thus obesity** (Franquesa et al., 2019; Goulet et al., 2003). Studies have also found that a Mediterranean diet has **favorable effects on triglycerides, blood glucose, HDL cholesterol levels, systolic blood pressure and diastolic blood pressure**, and the benefits may be greater the longer one adheres to the diet (Garcia et al., 2016; Kastorini et al., 2011; Rumawas, Meigs, et al., 2009).

Metabolic syndrome is a cluster of physiological and biochemical abnormalities that are associated with the development of several chronic diseases. These abnormalities include abdominal obesity, atherogenic dyslipidemia, elevated blood pressure, insulin resistance with or without glucose intolerance, a proinflammatory state and a prothrombotic state (Grundy et al., 2004). Individuals with a high adherence to the Mediterranean diet are found to have fewer components of metabolic syndrome and a 28% lower risk of developing metabolic syndrome than those with lower adherence (Steffen et al., 2014). In a trial with Spanish adults who already had metabolic syndrome, those who participated in a program that included a Mediterranean diet and regular exercise saw significant changes in waist circumference, blood pressure, and HDL cholesterol levels compared to adults receiving usual care (Gomez-Huelgas et al., 2015).

Cognition and Longevity

The Mediterranean diet contains many components that are neuroprotective including antioxidants, unsaturated fatty acids, and phytochemicals, and research has shown that a Mediterranean lifestyle may be associated with healthful aging and positive cognitive outcomes. Greater adherence to a Mediterranean diet during adulthood has been associated with better cognitive performance and improvements in cognitive function (McEvoy et al., 2019; Valls-Pedret et al., 2015). In fact, data from an ongoing cohort study in Greece showed that each unit increase in a Mediterranean dietary score was associated with a 10% decrease in the odds of dementia, and adherence to a Mediterranean diet was also associated with better performance in memory, language, and visuospatial perception (Anastasiou et al., 2017). Adhering to a Mediterranean diet may also yield some protection against depression and Parkinson's disease and is associated with a longer life in elderly individuals (Bonaccio et al., 2018; Lassale et al., 2019; Maraki et al., 2019).

Diabetes

Since the Mediterranean diet is beneficial for cardiovascular disease, obesity and metabolic syndrome, it should come as no surprise that there are benefits in the area of diabetes as well. Numerous studies have found that greater **adherence to a Mediterranean diet reduces the risk of developing type 2 diabetes mellitus in healthy individuals** (Franquesa et al., 2019; Georgoulis et al., 2014; Schwingshackl et al., 2015). In a study of Spanish university graduates, a two point increase in *Mediterranean Diet Score* was associated with a 35% risk reduction in type 2 diabetes development (M Á Martínez-González et al., 2008).

Following a Mediterranean diet can also be beneficial for individuals who have already been diagnosed with diabetes. Studies have shown that a Mediterranean diet is associated with favorable changes in plasma glucose and insulin levels, better glycemic control and improved HbAlc levels in patients with diabetes (Esposito et al., 2015; Shai et al., 2008; Sleiman et al., 2015). Interestingly, a systematic review of dietary management of type 2 diabetes showed that a Mediterranean diet demonstrated a greater reduction in body weight, better HgAlc control, and a delayed need for medication compared to other diets, including low carbohydrate, low fat, vegetarian, vegan and intermittent fasting (Papamichou et al., 2019).

Cancer

The role of the Mediterranean diet in cancer prevention is less clear than for other chronic diseases, but there is still some evidence that this dietary pattern can be protective. In a meta-analysis that comprised over 1,700,000 subjects, the highest adherence score to the Mediterranean diet was associated with a significantly lower risk of all-cause cancer mortality, colorectal cancer, breast cancer, gastric cancer, prostate cancer, liver cancer, head and neck cancer, pancreatic cancer and respiratory cancer (Schwingshackl & Hoffmann, 2015). In other studies, in addition to a reduction in breast cancer risk, the diet has also been associated with reductions in cancers of the digestive tract, and colorectal cancer (Barak & Fridman, 2017; Jones et al., 2017; Toledo et al., 2015).

PROPOSED MECHANISMS OF ACTION

The exact mechanisms by which a Mediterranean-style pattern leads to beneficial health outcomes is still largely unknown, however there are several different factors that are hypothesized to play a role in working synergistically to reduce the risk of the chronic diseases mentioned above (Tosti et al., 2018). It is thought that the foods in a Mediterranean diet together create a diet that is **rich in antioxidants** and other bioactive elements that have **anti-inflammatory effects** (Miguel Ángel Martínez-González et al., 2017b).

A reduced risk of cardiovascular disease is one of the most well-known benefits of a Mediterranean diet, and the diet may achieve this in part through its **lipid lowering effects**. Elevated cholesterol is one of the key factors in the development of atherosclerosis, and atherosclerosis is one of the leading causes of other cardiovascular complications such as myocardial infarction, stroke, and heart disease. Elevated cholesterol levels are associated with diets high in saturated fats and refined carbohydrates. In contrast, unsaturated fats may help lower cholesterol levels. Because the Mediterranean diet is low in meat, milk, and butter (all main sources of saturated fat in the Western diet) and high in olive oil, fatty fish, and nuts (all sources of unsaturated fat) the diet has a **cholesterol-lowering effect**, which helps to minimize the development of atherosclerosis. Dietary fiber, particularly soluble fiber, is also known to play a role in lowering cholesterol levels, and as the Mediterranean diet is rich in vegetables, fruits, and whole grains, it contains sufficient dietary fiber as well.

Another key element in fruits, vegetables, and whole grains as well as legumes, nuts, seeds and extra virgin olive oil are important micronutrients and bioactive elements. These foods are rich in antioxidant vitamins such as beta carotene, vitamin C, and vitamin E; natural folate; phytochemicals such as flavonoids; and minerals like selenium. All of these dietary elements help to decrease oxidative stress and inflammation throughout the body. Oxidative stress and inflammation have been implicated in the development of cardiovascular disease, cancer, and other chronic conditions, including dementia (Tosti et al., 2018). A diet rich in antioxidants and phytochemicals can help to minimize oxidative stress and thus reduce the risk of developing certain chronic diseases.

Foods like vegetables and whole grains that are common in the Mediterranean diet share a common quality. They are **low on the glycemic index**, which may in part explain why the Mediterranean diet has been shown to be beneficial in the prevention and management of type 2 diabetes (Miguel Ángel Martínez-González et al., 2017b). Foods with a high glycemic index such as sweets and refined grains cause large fluctuations in serum glucose levels, leading to difficult glycemic control in diabetic patients. In contrast, foods with a lower glycemic index cause more gradual changes in serum glucose levels and help to keep these levels consistent throughout the day, leading to better health outcomes.

There is a known synergistic effect with some of the foods common in the Mediterranean diet that can lead to greater nutrient absorption when certain foods are eaten together than when eaten separately. For example, the absorption of lycopene, a carotenoid found in greatest concentrations in tomatoes, is increased in the presence of olive oil (Arranz et al., 2015). Lycopene is known to have cardiovascular benefits. Phytonutrients in onion and garlic may also help to increase the absorption of lycopene. A recent study found that a single serving of sofrito — a sauce made of tomatoes, onions, garlic, and olive oil — resulted in decreased levels of inflammatory markers in the blood (Hurtado-Barroso et al., 2019). The presence of unsaturated fats like olive oil also help aid in the absorption of fat-soluble vitamins — vitamins A, D, E and K. All are important micronutrients, and vitamin E is especially known for its antioxidant properties.

A final mechanism by which the Mediterranean diet may impact chronic disease risk is through the gut microbiota. It is well established that diet has a major impact on the gut microbiome, however the specific physiological effects of these changes are not yet well understood. It has been observed that the gut flora of individuals on a Mediterranean diet differs significantly from the gut flora of individuals on a more Westernized diet, and this difference may play a role in the differing rates of obesity and type 2 diabetes between these two dietary patterns (Haro et al., 2016; Mitsou et al., 2017; Tindall et al., 2018). Studies have also shown that among adults with existing metabolic syndrome, a Mediterranean diet intervention can restore potentially beneficial members of the gut microbiota that were previously reduced due to a Western diet (Haro et al., 2016).

SECTION 5: CULINARY COMPETENCIES

In addition to following the culinary competencies for Fruit, Vegetables, Grains, Dairy, Fats & Oils, Protein and Sodium, individuals who wish to follow a Mediterranean diet will do well if they can:

1. Describe the Mediterranean diet, including food groups included and amounts recommended
2. List the health benefits of following the Mediterranean diet
3. Model consumption of the Mediterranean diet
4. Choose fruit for dessert
5. Cook and consume fish at least twice weekly
6. Limit red meat and avoid processed meat
7. Choose unsaturated fats like olive oil in cooking and preparing dishes
8. Select herbs and spices to flavor food instead of relying on salt
9. Prepare recipes with legumes, nuts, and seeds
10. Consume appropriate portions of meat, poultry, and fermented dairy
11. Design a weekly menu that aligns with the Mediterranean diet
12. Eat with others

SECTION 6: AT THE STORE

Think whole foods when shopping for foods that are typical in the Mediterranean diet.

Many foods consumed today are more akin to a Western diet than a traditionally Mediterranean one and may not be considered heart healthy. Some common misconceptions about the traditional Mediterranean diet include the following:

- The traditional Mediterranean diet is not a vegetarian diet. While it is primarily plant-based, it does include some animal products, primarily in the form of fish, seafood and fermented dairy products.
- American-style pizza is not a traditional Mediterranean food and should be considered a type of fast food and not in accordance with the Mediterranean dietary pattern.
- While moderate alcohol consumption is included in the Mediterranean diet, it is likely the pattern of consumption, not the mere amount of ethanol, that is associated with health benefits. Alcohol in the Mediterranean diet is primarily red wine with meals and there is little to no room for liquor consumption.
- Some foods misclassified as being Mediterranean include avocado, quinoa, potatoes and tofu. While these foods may confer health benefits, they were not included in a traditional Mediterranean diet.

Table 4: Foods Common in the Traditional Mediterranean Diet

Grains	Vegetables	Fruits	Legumes	Herbs/Spices	Fish/Seafood	Nuts/Seeds
Bulgur	Artichokes	Apples	Black beans	Anise	Clams	Almonds
Barley	Arugula	Apricots	Black-eyed peas	Basil	Flounder	Cashews
Farro	Beets	Avocados	Fava beans	Bay Leaf	Lobster	Hazelnuts
Brown, black, or red rice	Broccoli	Cherries	Garbanzo beans	Chiles	Mackerel	Walnuts
	Brussels sprouts	Clementine	Great northern beans	Cloves	Mussels	Pine nuts
	Cabbage	Dates	Kidney beans	Cumin	Octopus	Pistachios
	Carrots	Figs	Lentils	Fennel	Oysters	Sesame seeds
	Celery	Grapefruits	Lima beans	Garlic	Sardines	
	Eggplant	Grapes	Navy beans	Marjoram	Shrimp	
	Cucumbers	Melons	Peanuts	Mint	Tilapia	
	Leeks	Nectarines	Pinto beans	Oregano	Tuna	
	Mushrooms	Olives		Parsley		
	Pumpkin	Oranges	Split peas	Pepper		
	Turnips	Peaches		Rosemary		
	Zucchini	Pears		Sage		
		Pomegranate		Savory		

		Strawberries		Tarragon		
		Tangerines		Thyme		
		Tomatoes				

(Oldways Preservation & Exchange Trust, 2009)

Oldways provides a grocery list to make shopping easier. As the traditional Mediterranean diet was eaten by those with limited resources, following it doesn't need to be expensive. Here are some shopping tips:

1. Buy grains in bulk and cook in large batches. Refrigerate or freeze cooked grains for later use.
2. Legumes will be eaten often so buy them dried as they are much cheaper that way. Using dried legumes will take some planning as they need to be soaked before cooking.
3. Buy nuts and seeds in bulk.
4. Grow your own herbs or buy what is available locally.
5. Look for fish in the freezer section.

In addition to the tips listed above, follow shopping tips in the chapters for FRUITS, VEGETABLES, DAIRY, PROTEIN SODIUM, GRAINS and FATS.

SECTION 7: IN THE KITCHEN

If there was a star of the show in cooking a Mediterranean diet, olive oil would take center stage. Flavor is also the name of the game with an abundance of herbs and spices and fresh food. Learning how to cook the Mediterranean way will allow for a mastery in techniques that build flavor without reaching for sugar, salt, and saturated fat.

Is it safe to cook with olive oil?

Some chefs and home cooks may approach cooking with extra virgin olive oil with hesitancy as olive oil has a lower smoke point than other cooking oils such as canola oil, peanut oil, or even butter. An oil's smoke point is correlated with its safety and stability under heat, and at temperatures above the smoke point an oil can begin to break down and produce several by-products, such as free fatty acids, secondary products of oxidation, and polar compounds (De Alzaa, 2018). It is thought that some of these by-products may have adverse effects on health, which make's extra virgin olive oil's low smoke point concerning.

A recent study looked at the by-products of various cooking oils after they had been heated for several hours (De Alzaa, 2018). Researchers found that extra virgin olive oil yielded low levels of polar compounds and oxidative by-products, while other common cooking oils such as canola oil yielded high levels of oxidative by-products. It is hypothesized that extra virgin olive oil's unique fatty acid profile and high antioxidant content allow it to remain stable when heated. Thus, olive oil is a safe and healthful oil to cook with despite its lower smoke point.

Cooking with extra virgin olive oil has also been shown to increase the antioxidant content of vegetables. When compared with boiling in water or a water-oil combination, deep frying or sautéing in extra virgin olive oil led to increased fat content and total phenols, a type of phytonutrient (Ramirez-Anaya, 2015). Interestingly, all cooking methods led to increased antioxidant capacity in the vegetables tested, which included potatoes, tomatoes, eggplant and pumpkin.

(De Alzaa F, Guillaume C* and Ravetti L, 2018) (Ramírez-Anaya et al., 2019)

Plan a week's worth of dinners by focusing first on the protein source. Below is just one example, but the options and combinations are endless:
- 2+ nights of fish
- 1 night of lean meat (every other week)
- 1 night of poultry
- 3 nights of vegetable sources of protein – legumes, nuts, and seeds – and/or fermented dairy products

To get started, a <u>4-Week Menu Plan by Oldways</u> lists ideas of what to have for each meal for a month (there is a cost). Build your meal around the protein, but remember that the largest portion of the plate will contain vegetables (at least two servings), fruit (two servings with one usually as dessert), and a smaller portion of grains. Nuts, seeds, legumes, herbs and spices are also usually at most meal. Any type of meat present will be in a smaller portion (2 to 3 ounces) and is often used to flavor the dish.

In cooking and meal preparation, try these tips:
- Substitute red and processed meat in dishes with seafood, legumes, and nuts
- Use whole grains when you can, including whole grain pasta, brown rice, or less common grains such as bulgur or farro
- Use olive oil instead of butter or margarine
- Add more beans, peas, and lentils to your meals
- Make vegetable and/or bean dishes the focus of your meals instead of meat products
- Experiment with flavor by adding different Mediterranean herbs and spices to cooking, such as cinnamon, coriander, cumin or oregano
- Use yogurt in appetizer dips, and offer hard cheeses as an appetizer or with fruit at the end of a meal

Knowing how to expand and enhance flavor while limiting salt, sugar, and saturated fat is the key to cooking a delicious meal on the Mediterranean diet. Additinoal information on cooking and preparing food commonly found in the Mediterranean diet can be found in the following chapters – Fruits, Protein, Vegetables, Grains, Fats and Oils, Dairy, Herbs and Spice.

SECTION 8: AT THE TABLE

Making mealtime a social occasion is part of the Mediterranean diet's charm, and being together in and of itself confers health benefits. It is not necessary to plan a party for each meal but creating a space and a time where all distractions fall away and allowing the focus to be on eating is important.

Transitioning to a Mediterranean-style eating pattern does not have to be challenging, and small steps can be taken to start moving in that direction. Choose one topic at a time, become successful, and make it a habit before moving on to the next change. In day-to-day life, try these steps (Miguel Ángel Martínez-González et al., 2017b):

- Replace bagged processed snacks with more healthful options, such as mixed nuts, fruits, or vegetables
- Replace soda and juice with water and red wine at mealtimes (only for adults without a substance use disorder or history)
- Reduce snacking in between meals
- Make fruit your first choice for dessert and reserve sweets, ice creams, and baked goods for celebratory occasions

SECTION 9: RESOURCES

Shopping and Tasting the Mediterranean Diet: Cooking Demos is a good place to start.

Oldways provide menu ideas, challenges, and lots of information on the Mediterranean diet.

Download Oldways' list of **Common Foods and Flavors in the Mediterranean Diet**

SUMMARY

The Mediterranean diet has far reaching effects on one's health, all while being delicious and inexpensive. It is full of antioxidants and foods that are anti-inflammatory. The Mediterranean diet has been shown to reduce the risk of heart disease and stroke, type 2 diabetes, cognitive decline, and some types of cancer as well as help aid in weight loss and weight maintenance.

Rather than being considered a "diet," which connotes restrictions and effort, the Mediterranean way of eating should be considered more of a lifestyle. It is the way people with limited incomes ate and continue to eat along the Mediterranean basin. They enjoy meals full of fruits, vegetables, whole grains, nuts, beans and seeds. At least a couple of times a week fish is served with meat making the occasional appearance. Food is prepared full of flavor from herbs, spices, and extra virgin olive oil, which means individuals can follow this way of eating happily as healthful food is turned into delicious and cravable dishes.

REFERENCES

Ahmad, S., Moorthy, M. V., Demler, O. V., Hu, F. B., Ridker, P. M., Chasman, D. I., & Mora, S. (2018). Assessment of Risk Factors and Biomarkers Associated With Risk of Cardiovascular Disease Among Women Consuming a Mediterranean Diet. *JAMA Network Open*, *1*(8), e185708–e185708. https://doi.org/10.1001/jamanetworkopen.2018.5708

Alberti-Fidanza, A., & Fidanza, F. (2004). Mediterranean Adequacy Index of Italian diets. *Public Health Nutrition*, *7*(7), 937–941. https://doi.org/10.1079/phn2004557

Anastasiou, C. A., Yannakoulia, M., Kosmidis, M. H., Dardiotis, E., Hadjigeorgiou, G. M., Sakka, P., Arampatzi, X., Bougea, A., Labropoulos, I., & Scarmeas, N. (2017). Mediterranean diet and cognitive health: Initial results from the Hellenic Longitudinal Investigation of Ageing and Diet. *PloS One*, *12*(8), e0182048. https://doi.org/10.1371/journal.pone.0182048

Arranz, S., Martínez-Huélamo, M., Vallverdu-Queralt, A., Valderas-Martinez, P., Illán, M., Sacanella, E., Escribano, E., Estruch, R., & Lamuela-Raventos, R. M. (2015). Influence of olive oil on carotenoid absorption from tomato juice and effects on postprandial lipemia. *Food Chemistry*, *168*, 203–210. https://doi.org/10.1016/j.foodchem.2014.07.053

Bach-Faig, A., Berry, E. M., Lairon, D., Reguant, J., Trichopoulou, A., Dernini, S., Medina, F. X., Battino, M., Belahsen, R., Miranda, G., Serra-Majem, L., & Mediterranean Diet Foundation Expert Group. (2011a). Mediterranean diet pyramid today. Science and cultural updates. *Public Health Nutrition*, *14*(12A), 2274–2284. https://doi.org/10.1017/S1368980011002515

Bach-Faig, A., Berry, E. M., Lairon, D., Reguant, J., Trichopoulou, A., Dernini, S., Medina, F. X., Battino, M., Belahsen, R., Miranda, G., Serra-Majem, L., & Mediterranean Diet Foundation Expert Group. (2011b). Mediterranean diet pyramid today. Science and cultural updates. *Public Health Nutrition*, *14*(12A), 2274–2284. https://doi.org/10.1017/S1368980011002515

Bao, Y., Han, J., Hu, F. B., Giovannucci, E. L., Stampfer, M. J., Willett, W. C., & Fuchs, C. S. (2013). Association of Nut Consumption with Total and Cause-Specific Mortality. *New England Journal of Medicine*, *369*(21), 2001–2011. https://doi.org/10.1056/NEJMoa1307352

Barak, Y., & Fridman, D. (2017). Impact of Mediterranean Diet on Cancer: Focused Literature Review. *Cancer Genomics & Proteomics*, *14*(6), 403–408. https://doi.org/10.21873/cgp.20050

Bonaccio, M., Di Castelnuovo, A., Costanzo, S., Gialluisi, A., Persichillo, M., Cerletti, C., Donati, M. B., de Gaetano, G., & Iacoviello, L. (2018). Mediterranean diet and mortality in the elderly: A prospective cohort study and a meta-analysis. *The British Journal of Nutrition, 120*(8), 841–854. https://doi.org/10.1017/S0007114518002179

Buckland, G., & Gonzalez, C. A. (2015). The role of olive oil in disease prevention: A focus on the recent epidemiological evidence from cohort studies and dietary intervention trials. *The British Journal of Nutrition, 113 Suppl 2*, S94-101.   https://doi.org/10.1017/S0007114514003936

Carter, S. J., Roberts, M. B., Salter, J., & Eaton, C. B. (2010). Relationship between Mediterranean Diet Score and atherothrombotic risk: Findings from the Third National Health and Nutrition Examination Survey (NHANES III), 1988-1994. *Atherosclerosis, 210*(2), 630–636. https://doi.org/10.1016/j.atherosclerosis.2009.12.035

De Alzaa F, Guillaume C* and Ravetti L. (2018). Evaluation of Chemical and Physical Changes in Different Commercial Oils during Heating. *Acta Scientific Nutritional Health, 2*(6), 2–11.

de Lorgeril, M., & Salen, P. (2006). The Mediterranean diet in secondary prevention of coronary heart disease. *Clinical and Investigative Medicine. Medecine Clinique Et Experimentale, 29*(3), 154–158.

De Lorgeril, M., Salen, P., Martin, J. L., Mamelle, N., Monjaud, I., Touboul, P., & Delaye, J. (1996). Effect of a mediterranean type of diet on the rate of cardiovascular complications in patients with coronary artery disease. Insights into the cardioprotective effect of certain nutriments. *Journal of the American College of Cardiology, 28*(5), 1103–1108. https://doi.org/10.1016/S0735-1097(96)00280-X

de Lorgeril Michel, Salen Patricia, Martin Jean-Louis, Monjaud Isabelle, Delaye Jacques, & Mamelle Nicole. (1999). Mediterranean Diet, Traditional Risk Factors, and the Rate of Cardiovascular Complications After Myocardial Infarction. *Circulation, 99*(6), 779–785. https://doi.org/10.1161/01.CIR.99.6.779

Dinu, M., Pagliai, G., Casini, A., & Sofi, F. (2018). Mediterranean diet and multiple health outcomes: An umbrella review of meta-analyses of observational studies and randomised trials. *European Journal of Clinical Nutrition, 72*(1), 30–43. https://doi.org/10.1038/ejcn.2017.58

Esposito, K., Maiorino, M. I., Bellastella, G., Chiodini, P., Panagiotakos, D., & Giugliano, D. (2015). A journey into a Mediterranean diet and type 2 diabetes: A systematic review with meta-analyses. *BMJ Open, 5*(8). https://doi.org/10.1136/bmjopen-2015-008222

Estruch, Ramon, Martínez-González, M. A., Corella, D., Salas-Salvadó, J., Fitó, M., Chiva-Blanch, G., Fiol, M., Gómez-Gracia, E., Arós, F., Lapetra, J., Serra-

Majem, L., Pintó, X., Buil-Cosiales, P., Sorlí, J. V., Muñoz, M. A., Basora-Gallisá, J., Lamuela-Raventós, R. M., Serra-Mir, M., Ros, E., & PREDIMED Study Investigators. (2019). Effect of a high-fat Mediterranean diet on bodyweight and waist circumference: A prespecified secondary outcomes analysis of the PREDIMED randomised controlled trial. *The Lancet. Diabetes & Endocrinology*, *7*(5), e6–e17. https://doi.org/10.1016/S2213-8587(19)30074-9

Estruch, Ramón, Ros, E., Salas-Salvadó, J., Covas, M.-I., Corella, D., Arós, F., Gómez-Gracia, E., Ruiz-Gutiérrez, V., Fiol, M., Lapetra, J., Lamuela-Raventos, R. M., Serra-Majem, L., Pintó, X., Basora, J., Muñoz, M. A., Sorlí, J. V., Martínez, J. A., Fitó, M., Gea, A., … PREDIMED Study Investigators. (2018). Primary Prevention of Cardiovascular Disease with a Mediterranean Diet Supplemented with Extra-Virgin Olive Oil or Nuts. *The New England Journal of Medicine*, *378*(25), e34. https://doi.org/10.1056/NEJMoa1800389

Farshchi, H. R., Taylor, M. A., & Macdonald, I. A. (2005). Beneficial metabolic effects of regular meal frequency on dietary thermogenesis, insulin sensitivity, and fasting lipid profiles in healthy obese women. *The American Journal of Clinical Nutrition*, *81*(1), 16–24. https://doi.org/10.1093/ajcn/81.1.16

Franquesa, M., Pujol-Busquets, G., García-Fernández, E., Rico, L., Shamirian-Pulido, L., Aguilar-Martínez, A., Medina, F. X., Serra-Majem, L., & Bach-Faig, A. (2019). Mediterranean Diet and Cardiodiabesity: A Systematic Review through Evidence-Based Answers to Key Clinical Questions. *Nutrients*, *11*(3). https://doi.org/10.3390/nu11030655

Fung, T. T., McCullough, M. L., Newby, P. K., Manson, J. E., Meigs, J. B., Rifai, N., Willett, W. C., & Hu, F. B. (2005). Diet-quality scores and plasma concentrations of markers of inflammation and endothelial dysfunction. *The American Journal of Clinical Nutrition*, *82*(1), 163–173. https://doi.org/10.1093/ajcn.82.1.163

Fung, T. T., Rexrode, K. M., Mantzoros, C. S., Manson, J. E., Willett, W. C., & Hu, F. B. (2009). Mediterranean diet and incidence of and mortality from coronary heart disease and stroke in women. *Circulation*, *119*(8), 1093–1100. https://doi.org/10.1161/CIRCULATIONAHA.108.816736

Garcia, M., Bihuniak, J. D., Shook, J., Kenny, A., Kerstetter, J., & Huedo-Medina, T. B. (2016). The Effect of the Traditional Mediterranean-Style Diet on Metabolic Risk Factors: A Meta-Analysis. *Nutrients*, *8*(3), 168. https://doi.org/10.3390/nu8030168

Gardener, H., Wright, C. B., Gu, Y., Demmer, R. T., Boden-Albala, B., Elkind, M. S. V., Sacco, R. L., & Scarmeas, N. (2011). Mediterranean-style diet and risk of ischemic stroke, myocardial infarction, and vascular death: The Northern

Manhattan Study. *The American Journal of Clinical Nutrition*, *94*(6), 1458–1464. https://doi.org/10.3945/ajcn.111.012799

Georgoulis, M., Kontogianni, M. D., & Yiannakouris, N. (2014). Mediterranean Diet and Diabetes: Prevention and Treatment. *Nutrients*, *6*(4), 1406–1423. https://doi.org/10.3390/nu6041406

Georgousopoulou, E. N., Mellor, D. D., Naumovski, N., Polychronopoulos, E., Tyrovolas, S., Piscopo, S., Valacchi, G., Anastasiou, F., Zeimbekis, A., Bountziouka, V., Gotsis, E., Metallinos, G., Tyrovola, D., Foscolou, A., Tur, J.-A., Matalas, A.-L., Lionis, C., Sidossis, L., Panagiotakos, D., & MEDIS study group. (2017). Mediterranean lifestyle and cardiovascular disease prevention. *Cardiovascular Diagnosis and Therapy*, *7*(Suppl 1), S39–S47. https://doi.org/10.21037/cdt.2017.03.11

Gomez-Huelgas, R., Jansen-Chaparro, S., Baca-Osorio, A. J., Mancera-Romero, J., Tinahones, F. J., & Bernal-López, M. R. (2015). Effects of a long-term lifestyle intervention program with Mediterranean diet and exercise for the management of patients with metabolic syndrome in a primary care setting. *European Journal of Internal Medicine*, *26*(5), 317–323. https://doi.org/10.1016/j.ejim.2015.04.007

Goulet, J., Lamarche, B., Nadeau, G., & Lemieux, S. (2003). Effect of a nutritional intervention promoting the Mediterranean food pattern on plasma lipids, lipoproteins and body weight in healthy French-Canadian women. *Atherosclerosis*, *170*(1), 115–124. https://doi.org/10.1016/s0021-9150(03)00243-0

Grosso, G., Marventano, S., Yang, J., Micek, A., Pajak, A., Scalfi, L., Galvano, F., & Kales, S. N. (2017). A comprehensive meta-analysis on evidence of Mediterranean diet and cardiovascular disease: Are individual components equal? *Critical Reviews in Food Science and Nutrition*, *57*(15), 3218–3232. https://doi.org/10.1080/10408398.2015.1107021

Grundy, S. M., Brewer, H. B., Cleeman, J. I., Smith, S. C., Lenfant, C., National Heart, Lung, and Blood Institute, & American Heart Association. (2004). Definition of metabolic syndrome: Report of the National Heart, Lung, and Blood Institute/American Heart Association conference on scientific issues related to definition. *Arteriosclerosis, Thrombosis, and Vascular Biology*, *24*(2), e13-18. https://doi.org/10.1161/01.ATV.0000111245.75752.C6

Guallar-Castillón, P., Rodríguez-Artalejo, F., Tormo, M. J., Sánchez, M. J., Rodríguez, L., Quirós, J. R., Navarro, C., Molina, E., Martínez, C., Marín, P., Lopez-Garcia, E., Larrañaga, N., Huerta, J. M., Dorronsoro, M., Chirlaque, M. D., Buckland, G., Barricarte, A., Banegas, J. R., Arriola, L., … Moreno-Iribas, C. (2012). Major dietary patterns and risk of coronary heart disease in middle-aged persons from a Mediterranean country: The EPIC-Spain cohort study. *Nutrition,*

Metabolism, and Cardiovascular Diseases: NMCD, 22(3), 192–199.
https://doi.org/10.1016/j.numecd.2010.06.004

Haro, C., Montes-Borrego, M., Rangel-Zúñiga, O. A., Alcalá-Díaz, J. F., Gómez-Delgado, F., Pérez-Martínez, P., Delgado-Lista, J., Quintana-Navarro, G. M., Tinahones, F. J., Landa, B. B., López-Miranda, J., Camargo, A., & Pérez-Jiménez, F. (2016). Two Healthy Diets Modulate Gut Microbial Community Improving Insulin Sensitivity in a Human Obese Population. *The Journal of Clinical Endocrinology and Metabolism, 101*(1), 233–242. https://doi.org/10.1210/jc.2015-3351

Hernández-Alonso, P., Giardina, S., Salas-Salvadó, J., Arcelin, P., & Bulló, M. (2017). Chronic pistachio intake modulates circulating microRNAs related to glucose metabolism and insulin resistance in prediabetic subjects. *European Journal of Nutrition, 56*(6), 2181–2191. https://doi.org/10.1007/s00394-016-1262-5

Hurtado-Barroso, S., Martínez-Huélamo, M., Rinaldi de Alvarenga, J. F., Quifer-Rada, P., Vallverdú-Queralt, A., Pérez-Fernández, S., & Lamuela-Raventós, R. M. (2019). Acute Effect of a Single Dose of Tomato Sofrito on Plasmatic Inflammatory Biomarkers in Healthy Men. *Nutrients, 11*(4). https://doi.org/10.3390/nu11040851

Jones, P., Cade, J. E., Evans, C. E. L., Hancock, N., & Greenwood, D. C. (2017). The Mediterranean diet and risk of colorectal cancer in the UK Women's Cohort Study. *International Journal of Epidemiology, 46*(6), 1786–1796. https://doi.org/10.1093/ije/dyx155

Kalita, S., Khandelwal, S., Madan, J., Pandya, H., Sesikeran, B., & Krishnaswamy, K. (2018). Almonds and Cardiovascular Health: A Review. *Nutrients, 10*(4). https://doi.org/10.3390/nu10040468

Kastorini, C.-M., Milionis, H. J., Esposito, K., Giugliano, D., Goudevenos, J. A., & Panagiotakos, D. B. (2011). The effect of Mediterranean diet on metabolic syndrome and its components: A meta-analysis of 50 studies and 534,906 individuals. *Journal of the American College of Cardiology, 57*(11), 1299–1313. https://doi.org/10.1016/j.jacc.2010.09.073

Lassale, C., Batty, G. D., Baghdadli, A., Jacka, F., Sánchez-Villegas, A., Kivimäki, M., & Akbaraly, T. (2019). Correction: Healthy dietary indices and risk of depressive outcomes: a systematic review and meta-analysis of observational studies. *Molecular Psychiatry, 24*(7), 1094. https://doi.org/10.1038/s41380-018-0299-7

Mancini, J. G., Filion, K. B., Atallah, R., & Eisenberg, M. J. (2016). Systematic Review of the Mediterranean Diet for Long-Term Weight Loss. *The American Journal of Medicine, 129*(4), 407-415.e4. https://doi.org/10.1016/j.amjmed.2015.11.028

Maraki, M. I., Yannakoulia, M., Stamelou, M., Stefanis, L., Xiromerisiou, G., Kosmidis, M. H., Dardiotis, E., Hadjigeorgiou, G. M., Sakka, P., Anastasiou, C. A., Simopoulou, E., & Scarmeas, N. (2019). Mediterranean diet adherence is related to reduced probability of prodromal Parkinson's disease. *Movement Disorders: Official Journal of the Movement Disorder Society*, *34*(1), 48–57. https://doi.org/10.1002/mds.27489

Martínez-González, M Á, de la Fuente-Arrillaga, C., Nunez-Cordoba, J. M., Basterra-Gortari, F. J., Beunza, J. J., Vazquez, Z., Benito, S., Tortosa, A., & Bes-Rastrollo, M. (2008). Adherence to Mediterranean diet and risk of developing diabetes: Prospective cohort study. *BMJ : British Medical Journal*, *336*(7657), 1348–1351.
https://doi.org/10.1136/bmj.39561.501007.BE

Martinez-Gonzalez, M. A., & Martin-Calvo, N. (2016a). Mediterranean diet and life expectancy; beyond olive oil, fruits, and vegetables. *Current Opinion in Clinical Nutrition and Metabolic Care*, *19*(6), 401–407. https://doi.org/10.1097/MCO.0000000000000316

Martinez-Gonzalez, M. A., & Martin-Calvo, N. (2016b). Mediterranean diet and life expectancy; beyond olive oil, fruits, and vegetables. *Current Opinion in Clinical Nutrition and Metabolic Care*, *19*(6), 401–407. https://doi.org/10.1097/MCO.0000000000000316

Martínez-González, Miguel Ángel, Hershey, M. S., Zazpe, I., & Trichopoulou, A. (2017a). Transferability of the Mediterranean Diet to Non-Mediterranean Countries. What Is and What Is Not the Mediterranean Diet. *Nutrients*, *9*(11). https://doi.org/10.3390/nu9111226

Martínez-González, Miguel Ángel, Hershey, M. S., Zazpe, I., & Trichopoulou, A. (2017b). Transferability of the Mediterranean Diet to Non-Mediterranean Countries. What Is and What Is Not the Mediterranean Diet. *Nutrients*, *9*(11). https://doi.org/10.3390/nu9111226

McEvoy, C. T., Hoang, T., Sidney, S., Steffen, L. M., Jacobs, D. R., Shikany, J. M., Wilkins, J. T., & Yaffe, K. (2019). Dietary patterns during adulthood and cognitive performance in midlife: The CARDIA study. *Neurology*, *92*(14), e1589–e1599. https://doi.org/10.1212/WNL.0000000000007243

McKay, D. L., Eliasziw, M., Chen, C. Y. O., & Blumberg, J. B. (2018). A Pecan-Rich Diet Improves Cardiometabolic Risk Factors in Overweight and Obese Adults: A Randomized Controlled Trial. *Nutrients*, *10*(3). https://doi.org/10.3390/nu10030339

Mitsou, E. K., Kakali, A., Antonopoulou, S., Mountzouris, K. C., Yannakoulia, M., Panagiotakos, D. B., & Kyriacou, A. (2017). Adherence to the Mediterranean diet is associated with the gut microbiota pattern and gastrointestinal characteristics in an adult population. *The British Journal of Nutrition*, *117*(12), 1645–1655. https://doi.org/10.1017/S0007114517001593

Neumark-Sztainer, D., Hannan, P. J., Story, M., Croll, J., & Perry, C. (2003). Family meal patterns: Associations with sociodemographic characteristics and improved dietary intake among adolescents. *Journal of the American Dietetic Association*, *103*(3), 317–322. https://doi.org/10.1053/jada.2003.50048

Opara, E. I., & Chohan, M. (2014). Culinary herbs and spices: Their bioactive properties, the contribution of polyphenols and the challenges in deducing their true health benefits. *International Journal of Molecular Sciences*, *15*(10), 19183–19202. https://doi.org/10.3390/ijms151019183

Owen, R. W., Giacosa, A., Hull, W. E., Haubner, R., Würtele, G., Spiegelhalder, B., & Bartsch, H. (2000). Olive-oil consumption and health: The possible role of antioxidants. *The Lancet. Oncology*, *1*, 107–112. https://doi.org/10.1016/s1470-2045(00)00015-2

Papamichou, D., Panagiotakos, D. B., & Itsiopoulos, C. (2019). Dietary patterns and management of type 2 diabetes: A systematic review of randomised clinical trials. *Nutrition, Metabolism, and Cardiovascular Diseases: NMCD*, *29*(6), 531–543. https://doi.org/10.1016/j.numecd.2019.02.004

Paterson Katherine E., Myint Phyo K., Jennings Amy, Bain Lucy K.M., Lentjes Marleen A.H., Khaw Kay-Tee, & Welch Ailsa A. (2018). Mediterranean Diet Reduces Risk of Incident Stroke in a Population With Varying Cardiovascular Disease Risk Profiles. *Stroke*, *0*(0), 2415–2420. https://doi.org/10.1161/STROKEAHA.117.020258

Polak, R., Phillips, E. M., & Campbell, A. (2015). Legumes: Health Benefits and Culinary Approaches to Increase Intake. *Clinical Diabetes : A Publication of the American Diabetes Association*, *33*(4), 198–205. https://doi.org/10.2337/diaclin.33.4.198

Ramírez-Anaya, J. del P., Castañeda-Saucedo, Ma. C., Olalla-Herrera, M., Villalón-Mir, M., de la Serrana, H. L.-G., & Samaniego-Sánchez, C. (2019). Changes in the Antioxidant Properties of Extra Virgin Olive Oil after Cooking Typical Mediterranean Vegetables. *Antioxidants*, *8*(8). https://doi.org/10.3390/antiox8080246

Rees, K., Takeda, A., Martin, N., Ellis, L., Wijesekara, D., Vepa, A., Das, A., Hartley, L., & Stranges, S. (2019). Mediterranean-style diet for the primary and secondary prevention of cardiovascular disease. *The Cochrane Database of Systematic Reviews*, *3*, CD009825. https://doi.org/10.1002/14651858.CD009825.pub3

Romaguera, D., Norat, T., Vergnaud, A.-C., Mouw, T., May, A. M., Agudo, A., Buckland, G., Slimani, N., Rinaldi, S., Couto, E., Clavel-Chapelon, F., Boutron-Ruault, M.-C., Cottet, V., Rohrmann, S., Teucher, B., Bergmann, M., Boeing, H.,

Tjønneland, A., Halkjaer, J., … Peeters, P. H. (2010). Mediterranean dietary patterns and prospective weight change in participants of the EPIC-PANACEA project. *The American Journal of Clinical Nutrition, 92*(4), 912–921. https://doi.org/10.3945/ajcn.2010.29482

Ruiz-Canela, M., Zazpe, I., Shivappa, N., Hébert, J. R., Sánchez-Tainta, A., Corella, D., Salas-Salvadó, J., Fitó, M., Lamuela-Raventós, R. M., Rekondo, J., Fernández-Crehuet, J., Fiol, M., Santos-Lozano, J. M., Serra-Majem, L., Pinto, X., Martínez, J. A., Ros, E., Estruch, R., & Martínez-González, M. A. (2015). Dietary inflammatory index and anthropometric measures of obesity in a population sample at high cardiovascular risk from the PREDIMED (PREvención con DIeta MEDiterránea) trial. *The British Journal of Nutrition, 113*(6), 984–995. https://doi.org/10.1017/S0007114514004401

Rumawas, M. E., Dwyer, J. T., Mckeown, N. M., Meigs, J. B., Rogers, G., & Jacques, P. F. (2009). The Development of the Mediterranean-Style Dietary Pattern Score and Its Application to the American Diet in the Framingham Offspring Cohort. *The Journal of Nutrition, 139*(6), 1150–1156. https://doi.org/10.3945/jn.109.103424

Rumawas, M. E., Meigs, J. B., Dwyer, J. T., McKeown, N. M., & Jacques, P. F. (2009). Mediterranean-style dietary pattern, reduced risk of metabolic syndrome traits, and incidence in the Framingham Offspring Cohort. *The American Journal of Clinical Nutrition, 90*(6), 1608–1614. https://doi.org/10.3945/ajcn.2009.27908

Schwingshackl, L., & Hoffmann, G. (2015). Adherence to Mediterranean diet and risk of cancer: An updated systematic review and meta-analysis of observational studies. *Cancer Medicine, 4*(12), 1933–1947. https://doi.org/10.1002/cam4.539

Schwingshackl, L., Missbach, B., König, J., & Hoffmann, G. (2015). Adherence to a Mediterranean diet and risk of diabetes: A systematic review and meta-analysis. *Public Health Nutrition, 18*(7), 1292–1299. https://doi.org/10.1017/S1368980014001542

Seven Countries Study | The first study to relate diet with cardiovascular disease. - The Seven Countries Study (SCS for short) is the first major study to look at dietary components and patterns and lifestyle as risk factors for cardiovascular disease, over multiple countries and extended periods of time. (n.d.). Seven Countries Study | The First Study to Relate Diet with Cardiovascular Disease. Retrieved January 28, 2020, from https://www.sevencountriesstudy.com/

Shai, I., Schwarzfuchs, D., Henkin, Y., Shahar, D. R., Witkow, S., Greenberg, I., Golan, R., Fraser, D., Bolotin, A., Vardi, H., Tangi-Rozental, O., Zuk-Ramot, R., Sarusi, B., Brickner, D., Schwartz, Z., Sheiner, E., Marko, R., Katorza, E., Thiery, J., …

Stampfer, M. J. (2008). Weight Loss with a Low-Carbohydrate, Mediterranean, or Low-Fat Diet. *New England Journal of Medicine*, *359*(3), 229–241. https://doi.org/10.1056/NEJMoa0708681

Sleiman, D., Al-Badri, M. R., & Azar, S. T. (2015). Effect of mediterranean diet in diabetes control and cardiovascular risk modification: A systematic review. *Frontiers in Public Health*, *3*, 69. https://doi.org/10.3389/fpubh.2015.00069

Steffen, L. M., Van Horn, L., Daviglus, M. L., Zhou, X., Reis, J. P., Loria, C. M., Jacobs, D. R., & Duffey, K. J. (2014). A modified Mediterranean diet score is associated with a lower risk of incident metabolic syndrome over 25 years among young adults: The CARDIA (Coronary Artery Risk Development in Young Adults) study. *The British Journal of Nutrition*, *112*(10), 1654–1661. https://doi.org/10.1017/S0007114514002633

Stewart, R. A. H., Wallentin, L., Benatar, J., Danchin, N., Hagström, E., Held, C., Husted, S., Lonn, E., Stebbins, A., Chiswell, K., Vedin, O., Watson, D., White, H. D., & STABILITY Investigators. (2016). Dietary patterns and the risk of major adverse cardiovascular events in a global study of high-risk patients with stable coronary heart disease. *European Heart Journal*, *37*(25), 1993–2001. https://doi.org/10.1093/eurheartj/ehw125

Taveras, E. M., Rifas-Shiman, S. L., Berkey, C. S., Rockett, H. R. H., Field, A. E., Frazier, A. L., Colditz, G. A., & Gillman, M. W. (2005). Family dinner and adolescent overweight. *Obesity Research*, *13*(5), 900–906. https://doi.org/10.1038/oby.2005.104

Tektonidis, T. G., Åkesson, A., Gigante, B., Wolk, A., & Larsson, S. C. (2015). A Mediterranean diet and risk of myocardial infarction, heart failure and stroke: A population-based cohort study. *Atherosclerosis*, *243*(1), 93–98. https://doi.org/10.1016/j.atherosclerosis.2015.08.039

Tektonidis, T. G., Åkesson, A., Gigante, B., Wolk, A., & Larsson, S. C. (2016). Adherence to a Mediterranean diet is associated with reduced risk of heart failure in men. *European Journal of Heart Failure*, *18*(3), 253–259. https://doi.org/10.1002/ejhf.481

Tindall, A. M., Petersen, K. S., & Kris-Etherton, P. M. (2018). Dietary Patterns Affect the Gut Microbiome-The Link to Risk of Cardiometabolic Diseases. *The Journal of Nutrition*, *148*(9), 1402–1407. https://doi.org/10.1093/jn/nxy141

Toledo, E., Salas-Salvadó, J., Donat-Vargas, C., Buil-Cosiales, P., Estruch, R., Ros, E., Corella, D., Fitó, M., Hu, F. B., Arós, F., Gómez-Gracia, E., Romaguera, D., Ortega-Calvo, M., Serra-Majem, L., Pintó, X., Schröder, H., Basora, J., Sorlí, J. V., Bulló, M., … Martínez-González, M. A. (2015). Mediterranean Diet and Invasive Breast Cancer Risk Among Women at High Cardiovascular Risk in the PREDIMED Trial: A Randomized Clinical Trial. *JAMA Internal Medicine*, *175*(11), 1752–1760. https://doi.org/10.1001/jamainternmed.2015.4838

Toschke, A. M., Rückinger, S., Böhler, E., & Von Kries, R. (2007). Adjusted population attributable fractions and preventable potential of risk factors for childhood obesity. *Public Health Nutrition*, *10*(9), 902–906. https://doi.org/10.1017/S136898000725846X

Tosti, V., Bertozzi, B., & Fontana, L. (2018). Health Benefits of the Mediterranean Diet: Metabolic and Molecular Mechanisms. *The Journals of Gerontology. Series A, Biological Sciences and Medical Sciences*, *73*(3), 318–326. https://doi.org/10.1093/gerona/glx227

Tresserra-Rimbau, A., Medina-Remón, A., Lamuela-Raventós, R. M., Bulló, M., Salas-Salvadó, J., Corella, D., Fitó, M., Gea, A., Gómez-Gracia, E., Lapetra, J., Arós, F., Fiol, M., Ros, E., Serra-Majem, L., Pintó, X., Muñoz, M. A., Estruch, R., & PREDIMED Study Investigators. (2015). Moderate red wine consumption is associated with a lower prevalence of the metabolic syndrome in the PREDIMED population. *The British Journal of Nutrition*, *113 Suppl 2*, S121-130. https://doi.org/10.1017/S0007114514003262

Trichopoulou, A., Martínez-González, M. A., Tong, T. Y., Forouhi, N. G., Khandelwal, S., Prabhakaran, D., Mozaffarian, D., & de Lorgeril, M. (2014). Definitions and potential health benefits of the Mediterranean diet: Views from experts around the world. *BMC Medicine*, *12*(1), 112. https://doi.org/10.1186/1741-7015-12-112

Valls-Pedret, C., Sala-Vila, A., Serra-Mir, M., Corella, D., de la Torre, R., Martínez-González, M. Á., Martínez-Lapiscina, E. H., Fitó, M., Pérez-Heras, A., Salas-Salvadó, J., Estruch, R., & Ros, E. (2015). Mediterranean Diet and Age-Related Cognitive Decline: A Randomized Clinical Trial. *JAMA Internal Medicine*, *175*(7), 1094–1103. https://doi.org/10.1001/jamainternmed.2015.1668

Walton, K., Horton, N. J., Rifas-Shiman, S. L., Field, A. E., Austin, S. B., Haycraft, E., Breen, A., & Haines, J. (2018). Exploring the Role of Family Functioning in the Association Between Frequency of Family Dinners and Dietary Intake Among Adolescents and Young Adults. *JAMA Network Open*, *1*(7), e185217–e185217. https://doi.org/10.1001/jamanetworkopen.2018.5217

Zaragoza-Martí, A., Cabañero-Martínez, M. J., Hurtado-Sánchez, J. A., Laguna-Pérez, A., & Ferrer-Cascales, R. (2018). Evaluation of Mediterranean diet adherence scores: A systematic review. *BMJ Open*, *8*(2), e019033. https://doi.org/10.1136/bmjopen-2017-019033

THE VEGETARIAN DIET

By Jasna Robinson-Wright, MSc, RD, CDE, CIEC
and Gita Patel, MS, RDN, LD, CLT

"To eat is a necessity, but to eat intelligently is an art."
Quote by François La Rochefoucauld, *Maxims*, 1665

The earliest records of plant-based eating came from India and Greece in the fifth century BCE (Before Common Era). Plant-based eating was popular with some of the great figures of the ancient world, most notably Pythagoras (580 BCE), whose ideas mirrored, in part, the traditions of much earlier civilizations including the Babylonians and ancient Egyptians. The vegetarian ideology was practiced among religious groups in Egypt around 3200 BCE, with abstinence from flesh and the wearing of animal-derived clothing based upon karmic beliefs in reincarnation (Narayan; Sayeed, 2014).

The history of plant-based eating in India can be traced to the Vedic period, an era that dawned sometime between 4000 and 1500 BCE. The Vedas were the sacred texts that formed the bedrock of the early Hindu spiritual thought. In subsequent ancient texts, including the Upanishads, the idea of "rebirth" emerged as a central point. All creatures harbored the Divine, so that rather than being fixed in time, life was considered fluid. Therefore, the idea of having meat that once lived in a different form made it less edible (Narayan; Sayeed, 2014).

The great Indian sages, or rishis as they are called in India, laid a tradition of plant-based eating by living harmlessly to attain salvation. They promoted a healthful and cruelty-free lifestyle and established the importance of existence of all living beings and their interrelations. They subsisted on fruits, nuts, and roots, which could be equated with the eating habits of the current day raw foodies, fruitarians, or vegan-organic eaters (Narayan; Sayeed, 2014).

Plant-based eating was closely connected with the principle of "ahimsa," or nonviolence, and was promoted across history by many religious leaders and philosophers. Thus, abstention from consumption of meat was central not only to ancient religions like Hinduism, Buddhism, and Jainism that originated in India but also to later religions like Zoroastrianism or the Parsis. Mahatma Gandhi sought to draw a close association between the practice of plant-based eating and the observance of nonviolence (Narayan; Sayeed, 2014).

Since the International Vegetarian Union (IVU) was formed in 1908 at its first Congress at Dresden in Germany, India has participated in and contributed to the organized Worldwide Vegetarian Movement in many ways. India has organized five of the 38 IVU World Vegetarian Congresses and the 11th International Vegan Festival in 2007 (Narayan; Sayeed, 2014).

Today in the United States and most developed countries the reasons for following a vegetarian or vegan diet are many: environmental issues, religious or spiritual beliefs, family influence, preference, ethical reasons, medical reasons and concern for one's health.

Table 1: Vegetarian Eating Plan: Servings for a 2,000-Calorie-Level Eating Plan

	Food Group	Recommended Servings	Serving Size
	Vegetable	Ad-lib, as long as intake does not replace adequate intake of other food groups 2 to 3/day of leafy greens	1 serving = 1 cup raw or ½ cup cooked leafy greens; ½ cup all other vegetables
	Fruit	2 to 4/day	1 serving = ½ cup
	Grain	6 to 11/day	1 serving = ½ cup cooked rice, pasta, other grains

			or 1 slice bread, ¾ cup cooked oats, or ½ cup cold cereal
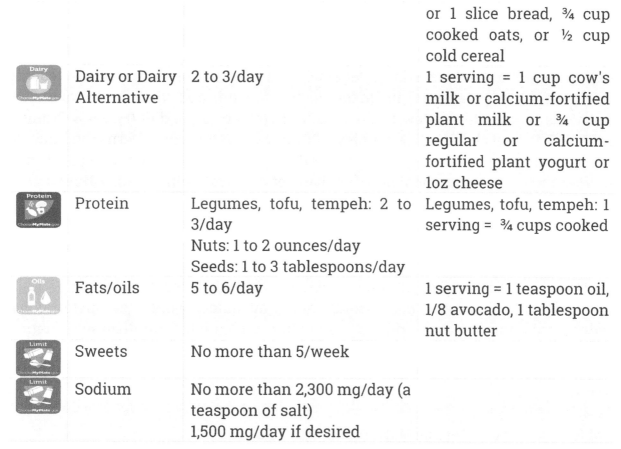	Dairy or Dairy Alternative	2 to 3/day	1 serving = 1 cup cow's milk or calcium-fortified plant milk or ¾ cup regular or calcium-fortified plant yogurt or 1oz cheese
	Protein	Legumes, tofu, tempeh: 2 to 3/day Nuts: 1 to 2 ounces/day Seeds: 1 to 3 tablespoons/day	Legumes, tofu, tempeh: 1 serving = ¾ cups cooked
	Fats/oils	5 to 6/day	1 serving = 1 teaspoon oil, 1/8 avocado, 1 tablespoon nut butter
	Sweets	No more than 5/week	
	Sodium	No more than 2,300 mg/day (a teaspoon of salt) 1,500 mg/day if desired	

SECTION 1: DEFINING A VEGETARIAN DIET

A whole food, plant-based vegetarian diet consists of vegetables, fruits, legumes, whole grains, nuts, seeds, herbs and spices (Hever & Cronise, 2017). Eating patterns that include a wide variety of plant foods are associated with health benefits including lower rates of heart disease, diabetes, and cancer, among other conditions (Locke et al., 2018; Lozano et al., 2012; Slavin & Lloyd, 2012; Wallace et al., 2020). According to the United States Department of Agriculture, the American Heart Association, Health Canada and the American Institute for Cancer Research, half of the plate should consist of vegetables and fruits in order to ensure adequate intake of fiber, potassium, magnesium, folate, iron, and vitamins A and C – nutrients that tend to be low in the standard Western-style diet (Hever & Cronise, 2017; R. C. Post et al., 2011; Slavin & Lloyd, 2012). Even in dietary patterns that include animal-based foods, a large portion of the diet should ideally come from plants due to their important nutritional benefits (Ivers et al., 2019; Melina et al., 2016).

Plant foods are the only foods that contain two critical nutrients: **fiber and phytonutrients**. Fiber (soluble, insoluble, and resistant), found in all intact plant foods, offers powerful protection in the gastrointestinal, cardiovascular, and immune systems, while phytonutrients, a class of thousands of compounds including glucosinolates, carotenoids, and flavonoids, work synergistically to reduce inflammation and oxidation, providing protection from disease initiation and progression (Aune et al., 2012; Hartley et al., 2016; Hever & Cronise, 2017; Locke et al., 2018; Pereira et al., 2004). The chapter on Vegetables goes into this in more depth.

Table 2: Sources of Notable Nutrients in Plant Foods

Nutrient	Food Source
Protein	Legumes (beans, lentils, peas, peanuts), nuts, seeds, soy foods (tempeh, tofu)
Fiber	Vegetables, fruits (especially berries, papayas, pears, dried fruits), avocados, legumes (beans, lentils, peas), nuts, seeds, whole grains
Calcium	Low-oxalate leafy greens (bok choy, broccoli, cabbage, collard, dandelion, watercress), calcium-set tofu, almonds and almond butter, fortified plant milks, sesame seeds, tahini, figs, blackstrap molasses, fortified fruit juices
Iodine	Sea vegetables (e.g., arame, dulse, nori, wame)
Iron	Legumes (beans, lentils, peas, peanuts), leafy greens, soybeans and soy foods, quinoa, potatoes, dried fruit, dark chocolate, tahini, seeds (pumpkin, sesame, sunflower), sea vegetables (dulse, nori), blackstrap molasses, enriched cereals, Marmite
Choline	Legumes (beans, lentils, peas, peanuts), bananas, broccoli, oats, oranges, quinoa, soy foods

Folate	Leafy green vegetables, almonds, asparagus, avocado, beets, enriched grains (breads, pasta, rice), oranges, quinoa, nutritional yeast
Vitamin K	Leafy green vegetables, sea vegetables, asparagus, avocado, broccoli, Brussels sprouts, cauliflower, lentils, peas, natto (a traditional Japanese food made from fermented soybeans)
Vitamin D	Fortified plant milks, fortified margarines, fortified fruit juices
Vitamin C	Fruits (especially berries, citrus, cantaloupe, kiwifruit, mango, papaya, pineapple), leafy green vegetables, potatoes, peas, bell peppers, chili peppers, tomatoes
Vitamin B_{12}	Fortified foods (nutritional yeast, plant milks)
Zinc	Legumes (beans, lentils, peas, peanuts), soy foods, nuts, seeds, oats
Omega-3 fatty acids	Alpha-linolenic acid (ALA) is found in nuts and seeds (walnuts, flaxseeds, chia seeds, hemp seeds) Eicosapentaenoic acid (EPA) and docosahexaenoic acid (DHA) are found in algae oil and algae-based omega-3 supplements
Probiotics	Fermented foods (sauerkraut, kimchi, kombucha, fermented soy products such as tempeh), plant-based yogurt with probiotics

It is recommended that the term *plant-forward* is used and not *plant-based,* as it takes into account that not everyone follows a strictly vegan diet.

Many individuals are interested in reducing their meat intake for personal health benefits as well as for environmental sustainability (Hopwood et al., 2020; Miki et al., 2020; Ruby, 2012), and for many individuals, giving up meat entirely comes with its share of challenges and inconveniences. Therefore, trying a "plant-forward" or "plant-centric" diet in which individuals cut back on meat and increase their intake of vegetables and plant proteins can be an acceptable compromise.

A study published in Public Health Nutrition found that **two-thirds of American adults are trying to reduce their meat intake**, particularly red meat and processed meat (Neff et al., 2018). Several studies have shown similar results with 30% to 40% of American adults reporting decreasing intake of animal-based foods and increasing plant-based foods (Anon, 2012; Dibb & Fitzpatrick, 2014; *Eat Less Meat, We're Told. But Americans' Habits Are Slow To Change*, n.d.; Latvala et al., 2012; Neff et al., 2018). Another study found that 36% of Americans are now eating at least one vegetarian meal per week (*How Often Do Americans Eat Vegetarian Meals?/ Vegetarian Journal / Vegetarian Resource Group*, 2015) (Song et al., 2016).

> **Every change counts:** Substituting only 3% of calories from animal protein (red meat and processed meat) with vegetable protein lowered a person's risk of all-cause mortality (Song et al., 2016).

SECTION 2: TYPES OF VEGETARIAN DIETS

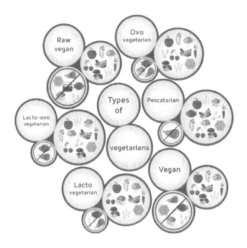

There are various types of vegetarian diets, with "vegan" being the strictest. Most people who follow a vegetarian diet don't eat meat, fish, or poultry. Other variations involve the inclusion or exclusion of eggs, dairy, and other animal products. Below is a description of the various types of vegetarian diets (Melina et al., 2016):

- **Vegetarian diet:** May or may not include egg or dairy products
- **Lacto-ovo-vegetarian diet:** Eliminates meat, fish, and poultry but includes eggs and dairy products
- **Lacto-vegetarian diet:** Eliminates meat, fish, poultry and eggs but allows dairy products
- **Ovo-vegetarian diet:** Eliminates meat, fish, poultry and dairy products but allows eggs
- **Vegan diet:** Eliminates meat, fish, poultry, eggs and dairy products, as well as other animal-derived products, such as honey and other bee products
- **Raw vegan:** Based on vegetables, fruit, nuts and seeds, legumes and sprouted grains. The amount of uncooked food varies from 75% to 100%
- **Pescatarian diet:** Eliminates meat and poultry but allows fish
- **Flexitarian diet:** A mostly vegetarian diet that incorporates occasional meat, fish, or poultry
- **Fruitarian diet:** Based on fruits, nuts, honey, vegetables and vegetable oils

Table 3: Foods Included in Various Types of Vegetarian Diets

Type of Food	Vegan	Pesca	Lacto-Veg	Ovo	Flexitarian
Fruit	Yes	Yes	Yes	Yes	Yes
Vegetable	Yes	Yes	Yes	Yes	Yes
Grains	Yes	Yes	Yes	Yes	Yes
Fats/oils	Yes	Yes	Yes	Yes	Yes
Vegetable protein	Yes	Yes	Yes	Yes	Yes
Animal protein	No	Fish	No meat, only dairy	Only eggs	Occasional animal
Sweets	Yes	Yes	Yes	Yes	Yes
Beverages	Plant-based	Yes	Yes	Plant-based	Yes
Dairy and plant-based dairy alternatives	Dairy alternatives	Occasional dairy	Dairy	Dairy alternatives	Yes
Sodium	Yes	Yes	Yes	Yes	Yes
Herbs and spices	Yes	Yes	Yes	Yes	Yes

Interest in following a vegan diet in the United States rose 300% between 2004 and 2019 according to Google search data (Kirkwood, 2020). According to a 2018 Gallup poll, **5% of adults in the United States consider themselves to be a vegetarian, and 3% vegan** (Hrynowski, 2019). Data from the Gallup poll found that individuals with the following characteristics are more likely to be vegetarian (Hrynowski, 2019; Reinhart, 2018):

- Being a political liberal
- Earning less than $30,000 per year
- Being under the age of 50
- Women are more likely to be vegetarian than men
- Non-whites (9%) were more likely to be a vegetarian than whites (3%)

SECTION 3: NUTRIENTS OF CONCERN FOR VEGETARIANS

Nutrients of concern for vegetarians and vegans include: **omega-3 fatty acids such as eicosapentaenoic acid (EPA) and docosahexaenoic acid (DHA), iron, zinc, iodine, calcium, vitamin D, vitamin B$_{12}$, choline and chromium.** Individuals who are vegan or vegetarian may need to take supplemental vitamin B$_{12}$ and vitamin D$_3$ if they are

not getting adequate amounts from fortified plant foods, and from sunshine in the case of vitamin D. Vitamin B$_{12}$ is primarily found in animal foods such as meat, poultry, fish, eggs and dairy and is available in only a few vegan foods, so supplementation is usually recommended for those not consuming any animal-based foods (Markle, 1996).

Supplemental long-chain omega-3 fatty acids in the form of algae-based supplements may also be beneficial as the conversion of alpha-linolenic acid (ALA) from nuts and seeds to EPA and DHA is low (Lane et al., 2014; Peltomaa et al., 2018). Most of the other nutrients can be obtained from a well-balanced plant food diet.

Vegetarians may absorb less calcium than omnivores due to the higher plant food content of the diet, which provides more oxalic and phytic acids that inhibit calcium absorption (Institute of Medicine (U.S.) Committee to Review Dietary Reference Intakes for Vitamin D and Calcium, 2011). Studies have found that lacto-ovo vegetarians have similar calcium intakes to omnivores; however, vegans and vegetarians who avoid milk products tend to have lower dietary calcium intakes (American Dietetic Association & Dietitians of Canada, 2003; Janelle & Barr, 1995; A. G. Marsh et al., 1980; Reed et al., 1994). The European Prospective Investigation into Cancer and Nutrition study found that vegetarians, pescatarians, and omnivores had similar bone fracture risks, but vegans had higher bone fracture risk, likely due to lower calcium intake (Appleby et al., 2007). Since the content of an individual's diet varies greatly from person to person, the need for supplemental calcium should be assessed on a case-by-case basis with a certified nutritionist or registered dietitian.

Table 4: Nutrients of Concern When Following a Vegan or Vegetarian Diet

Nutrient	Vegan Sources	Guidance
High Concern		
Vitamin B$_{12}$	Fortified dairy alternatives and meat alternatives such as veggie burgers, nutritional yeast, Marmite	The Vegetarian Nutrition Dietetic Practice Group recommends (Palmer, 2018): • All vegetarians, regardless of type, should periodically be screened for vitamin B$_{12}$ deficiency, using either methylmalonic acid (MMA) or TCII (transcobalamin) assessment. • All women considering pregnancy and those already pregnant should take at least 250 µg per day of a vitamin B$_{12}$ supplement. (This amount is about 100 times higher than the recommended daily allowance (RDA) to account for the absorption rate of supplemental B$_{12}$ of only 1%.) • All vegans should take at least 250 µg per day of a vitamin B$_{12}$ supplement. • All lacto-ovo vegetarians should consider taking at least 250 µg per day of a B$_{12}$ supplement a few times per week.
Vitamin D$_3$	Sun, fortified plant milks, fortified margarines, fortified fruit juices	• Consider recommending a supplement of 400 to 1,000 IU (10 to 25 µg) of vitamin D per day for people living in Canada and the Northern United States to ensure adequacy (Health Canada, 2007)
Moderate Concern		
Calcium	Fortified plant milks such as soy milk, low-oxalate leafy greens (bok choy, broccoli, cabbage, collard, dandelion, watercress), calcium-set tofu, almonds, almond	• As long as the diet contains at least three servings per day of high-calcium foods, including at least one cup per day of calcium-fortified plant milk and a wide variety of other calcium-containing foods and there is an absence of signs of inadequacy (osteoporosis/osteomalacia/low bone mineral density, fractures, etc.), routine calcium supplementation is not

	butter, fortified plant milks, sesame seeds, tahini, figs, blackstrap molasses, fortified fruit juices	recommended. The need for calcium supplementation should be assessed on a case-by-case basis. Calcium absorption is best in doses of no more than 500 mg at a time; therefore if 1,000 mg of calcium is prescribed, splitting the dose is advised (NIH, 2020).
Choline	Legumes (beans, lentils, peas, peanuts), bananas, broccoli, oats, oranges, quinoa, soy foods, nuts, seeds	• Eggs are a good source of choline; most vegetarians who include eggs do not require supplementation. Vegans and those who do not consume eggs but are consuming a variety of foods are unlikely to become choline deficient unless they are in a life stage requiring increased choline (such as pregnancy and lactation).
Chromium	Fruit and vegetable juices, brewer's yeast, apples, green beans, bananas, tomato, peanut butter, beer, wine	• Chromium deficiency is rare in healthy populations and routine chromium supplementation is not necessary. Oxalate in plant foods inhibits chromium absorption; however, chromium deficiency in people consuming a variety of foods is unlikely. Those consuming very restrictive diets may be at risk of chromium deficiency and should be assessed on a case-by-case basis.
Iodine	Sea vegetables (arame, dulse, nori, wame), iodized salt, bread made with iodate dough conditioner	• Supplementation is not necessary if consuming iodized salt. Vegans with very restrictive diets who do not use iodized salt may be at risk of iodine deficiency (iodine is found in milk products, eggs, and seafood, so lacto-ovo vegetarians and pescatarians are at low risk of iodine deficiency). Supplementation is required if signs of deficiency are present (goiter) (NIH, 2020).
Iron	Legumes (beans, lentils, peas,	• The need for iron supplementation should be considered on a case-by-case

	peanuts), leafy greens, soybeans and soy foods, quinoa, potatoes, dried fruit, dark chocolate, tahini, seeds (pumpkin, sesame, sunflower), sea vegetables (dulse, nori), blackstrap molasses, enriched cereals, Marmite	basis. Women who are menstruating, pregnant women, athletes, infants, young children and those with more restrictive diets may be at risk for iron deficiency. • The iron present in plant foods is in the non-heme form, which is less well absorbed. • Supplementation is not necessary unless signs of iron deficiency (low serum ferritin, anemia) are present.
Omega-3 fatty acids	Alpha-linolenic acid (ALA) is found in nuts and seeds (walnuts, flaxseeds, chia seeds, hemp seeds) Eicosapentaenoic acid (EPA) and docosahexaenoic acid (DHA) are found in algae oil and algae-based omega-3 supplements (Peltomaa et al., 2017; Lane et al., 2014)	• Lower intakes of omega-3 fatty acids are common in the North American diet, and many people may benefit from higher intakes to help reduce inflammation and improve heart health. • Symptoms of low intakes of essential fatty acids such as omega-3 and omega-6 include dry skin and dry eyes. • Algae-based omega-3 supplements are available and are one of the few available vegan options for long-chain EPA and DHA. • Omega-3 supplementation may be beneficial for those who do not consume fatty fish, for pregnant and breastfeeding women, for those with inflammatory conditions (such as arthritis and allergic conditions) and for those with cardiovascular disease (NIH, 2020; Peltomaa et al., 2017; Lane et al., 2014).
Zinc	Legumes (beans, lentils, peas, peanuts), soy foods, nuts (cashews, almonds), seeds	• People who do not consume animal products require 50% more zinc from the diet due to lower bioavailability of zinc from plant foods. Phytates in foods such as legumes and whole grains bind to zinc and inhibit its absorption;

(pumpkin), oats, leavened bread	however, a balanced, varied diet can provide adequate zinc.
	• Soaking and sprouting seeds, grains, and legumes increases zinc bioavailability, and leavened bread products have better zinc bioavailability than unleavened bread.
	• People consuming very restrictive diets are at increased risk for zinc deficiency and those with signs of poor wound healing, poor growth, or impaired immune response should be assessed for the need for zinc supplementation.

SECTION 4: PROTEIN SOURCES IN A VEGETARIAN DIET

One does not need to eat meat products to consume enough protein in their diet. There are plenty of plant-based protein sources like those listed below:

- Nuts and seeds
- Legumes and beans
- Tofu and tempeh
- Grains
- Some vegetables

In the past, it was thought that in order to get enough high-quality protein, individuals needed to combine certain plant proteins in a single meal. However, this has been shown to be false. While some plant foods contain relatively low proportions of some amino acids such as lysine, eating a diet that contains a wide variety of plant foods provides adequate amino acids, and it is not necessary to combine certain foods together in a specific meal (such as rice and beans) to create "complementary" or "complete" proteins for amino acid adequacy or protein adequacy, as was previously hypothesized. The human body maintains free pools of amino acids and therefore can do the "complementing" or combining of amino acids supplied from several meals in order to create the needed proteins to keep the body functioning optimally (Boye et al., 2012; Gardner et al., 2019; Mariotti, 2017; Mariotti & Gardner, 2019; Melina et al., 2016).

A study by Rizzo et al. (2013) compared the total protein intake of vegetarians, vegans, and omnivores and found that the overall protein intake of each of these groups was very similar, and all groups had relatively high protein intakes compared to the minimal requirements for their life stages (Rizzo et al., 2013). These findings are in line with those of other studies and reviews examining the protein adequacy of populations consuming vegetarian and vegan diets compared to those consuming omnivorous diets (Clarys et al., 2014; Halkjaer et al., 2009; Millward & Garnett, 2010).

The overall daily protein recommendation for vegetarians and vegans is the same as that for all non-vegetarians (Ivers et al., 2019; Melina et al., 2016):
- Healthy adults need at lesat 0.8 grams of protein per kilogram of body weight
- Toddlers 1 to 3 years need at least 1.2 grams of protein per kilogram of body weight
- Children 4 to 6 years need at least 1.1 grams of protein per kilogram of body weight
- Children 7 to 14 years need at least 1 gram of protein per kilogram of body weight

- Children 15 to 18-plus years need at least 0.8 grams of protein per kilogram of body weight
- Seniors (older adults ages 65-plus) need at least 1 gram of protein per kilogram of body weight
- Athletes need at least 1.2 to 2 grams of protein per kilogram of body weight

The typical amount of protein needed in grams for:
- **Adult male**: A minimum of 55 to 70 grams protein per day. This could be obtained from one cup of beans, ½ cup of tempeh, two tablespoons of peanut butter, one ounce of nuts/seeds, one cup of soy milk, one cup of pasta, one cup of quinoa, two slices of bread
- **Adult female**: A minimum of 45 to 55 grams protein per day. This could be obtained from one cup of lentils, ½ cup of tofu, one ounce of nuts/seeds, one cup of soy milk, ¾ cup of oatmeal, two slices of bread, one cup of quinoa
- **Child**: A minimum of 20 to 40 grams protein per day. This could be obtained from ½ cup of beans, one tablespoon of peanut butter, one cup of soy milk, one slice of bread, ½ cup of noodles, ¼ cup of peas

Table 5: Amount of Protein From Plant Sources

Food	Calories (Kcals)	Protein (grams)
Tofu (½ cup)	94	10
Tempeh (½ cup)	160	16
Peanut butter (2 tablespoons)	188	7
Almonds (1 ounce)	163	6
Quinoa (½ cup)	111	4
Lentils (½ cup)	101	9
Chickpeas (½ cup)	134	7
Black beans (½ cup)	114	8
Pinto beans (½ cup)	123	8
Red kidney beans (½ cup)	112	8
Black-eyed peas (½ cup)	100	7
Soy milk (1 cup)	130	8
Almond milk (1 cup)	60	1

Cereal (½ cup)	100	4
Pasta (½ cup)	75	3
Bread (1 slice)	70	2
Spinach (1 cup raw)	41	3
Peas (½ cup)	60	4

SECTION 5: FIBER AND THE MICROBIOME

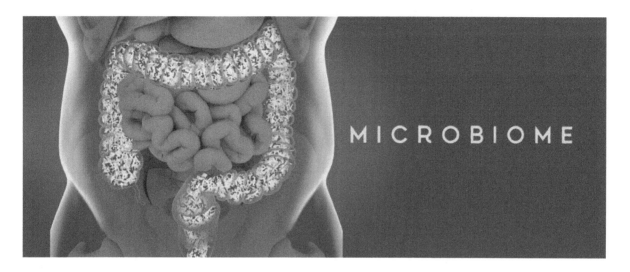

Despite the recent popularity of high-fat/high-protein low-carbohydrate diets, these types of diets tend to produce metabolic profiles that appear to be detrimental to intestinal and overall health (Hu et al., 2018; Morrison & Preston, 2016; Russell et al., 2011). Most health organizations — including the American Heart Association, American Institute of Cancer Research, American Academy of Nutrition and Dietetics, American Diabetes Association, Dietitians of Canada, Diabetes Canada, Health Canada and the USDA — recommend increasing the intake of fiber from plant foods.

There are three different kinds of fiber: soluble fiber, insoluble fiber, and resistant starch.

- **Soluble fiber** feeds the intestinal bacteria, which can break down soluble fiber to produce short-chain fatty acids (SCFA). SCFAs have a number of positive effects on the body as they nourish the cells of the large intestine and have been implicated in modulating chronic disease risk (Flint et al., 2015; Miller & Wolin, 1996; Morrison & Preston, 2016; J. Tan et al., 2014). Soluble fiber helps lower blood cholesterol (Brown et al., 1999; Gunness & Gidley, 2010; McRorie & McKeown, 2017; Surampudi et al., 2016) and slows gut transit time. It is helpful in improving both diarrhea and constipation through its stool-bulking action (Erdogan et al., 2016; Homann et al., 1994; Leib, 2000; McRorie & McKeown, 2017; *Treatments for Constipation*, 2014). It is found in oatmeal, barley, and rye; beans, peas, and lentils; fresh and dried fruits such as apples, peaches, plums and berries; and many vegetables such as broccoli, asparagus, squashes and sweet potatoes.

- **Insoluble fiber** aids in digestion by trapping water in the colon and speeding gut transit time, thus moving bacteria through the intestine for excretion (McRorie & McKeown, 2017; K.-Y. Tan & Seow-Choen, 2007). Insoluble fiber helps prevent and treat constipation (Erdogan et al., 2016; McRorie & McKeown, 2017; K.-Y. Tan & Seow-Choen, 2007). It is present in the skins and seeds of fruits and vegetables, wheat bran, whole grains, nuts, seeds and legumes.

- **Resistant starches** are starches that escape digestion in the small intestine. Natural resistant starch is insoluble, is fermented in the large intestine, and is a prebiotic fiber, providing some of the health benefits of both soluble and insoluble fiber, plus some unique advantages of its own. Colonic fermentation of indigestible carbohydrates may have the potential to regulate a patient's postprandial responses (DeMartino & Cockburn, 2020; Raigond et al., 2015; Zaman & Sarbini, 2016). Resistant starch is found in whole grains, seeds, legumes and underripe fruit, and is especially prevalent in cooked starches that have been cooled, such as pasta salad, potato salad, sushi rice and high-amylose corn.

DIGESTIVE TRACT SUPPORT: THE MICROBIOME

Over the past 15 years, the scientific community has recognized the important role of the microbiome as a regulator of human health. The term "microbiome" refers to the trillions of microorganisms that naturally reside throughout the body, particularly the gut. Variations in the diversity of the gut microbiota have been linked to numerous diseases and conditions, ranging from obesity, diabetes, and cancer to depression and overall immune function (Cresci & Bawden, 2015; Mohajeri et al., 2018; Peirce & Alviña, 2019; Shi et al., 2017; Sidhu & van der Poorten, 2017; Winter et al., 2018).

Emerging evidence indicates that diet composition exerts a powerful influence on the diversity of microbial species in the gut, carrying significant implications for health and disease. Several studies have shown certain healthful eating patterns, such as diets rich in whole plant foods, plant fibers, and phytonutrients, support a balanced gut microbiota and health maintenance throughout the life span (DeMartino & Cockburn, 2020; Raigond et al., 2015; Zaman & Sarbini, 2016).

Nourishing the gut microbiome requires eating fiber-rich foods such as legumes, vegetables, fruits, nuts, seeds and whole grains, as well as a variety of herbs and spices.

The gut microbiota benefits humans via short-chain fatty acid (SCFA) production from carbohydrate fermentation, and deficiency in SCFA production is associated with type 2 diabetes mellitus (T2DM) (Zhao et al., 2018). Several studies have shown that people with diabetes who consume higher intakes of fiber from plant foods have better diabetes management (Aune et al., 2013; R. E. Post et al., 2012; Reynolds et al., 2020; F. M. Silva et al., 2013; Yu et al., 2014). However, the benefit was generally previously attributed to resistant starch and other fibers that lower the glycemic index of the carbohydrates eaten.

In a more recent study, it was shown that a high-fiber diet favored the growth of bacteria that produce short-chain fatty acids (SCFAs), especially bacteria that produce butyric acid. The authors found the increased SCFA production was inversely correlated with HbA1c (Davis & Schor, 2018). Thus, a diet based on plant foods may help lower the risk of type 2 diabetes as well as aid in its management. This study suggests that glycemic control can be improved by shifting bacterial populations in the intestinal microbiome. It provides an explanation for why a diet high in vegetables (which provide fiber) and fruits may have anti-amylase action, which is useful in treating type 2 diabetes: The gut biome shifts to increase SCFA production. Individuals with diabetes are sometimes cautioned against eating fruit, but this advice may actually be counterproductive. Sugar-sweetened fruit juices are significantly associated with the risk of developing type 2 diabetes, but whole fruits and 100% fruit juices are not (Davis and Schor, 2018).

The gut microbiota is considered important for cardiovascular health, and abnormal bacterial communities have been associated with hypertension and atherosclerosis (Battson et al., 2018; Brial et al., 2018; Hever & Cronise, 2017; Kazemian et al., 2020; Locke et al., 2018; Pereira et al., 2004; Sanchez-Rodriguez et al., 2020; Tang et al., 2017; Wang & Zhao, 2018). A study by Bartolomaeus et al. (2019) shows that propionate, a short-chain fatty acid produced by intestinal bacteria, has profound beneficial anti-inflammatory properties limiting cardiovascular disease progression (Bartolomaeus et al., 2019). Recent data suggests a direct effect of SCFAs on renin release and vasomotor function leading to blood pressure reduction (Bartolomaeus et al., 2019).

SECTION 6: RESEARCH SUPPORTING A VEGETARIAN DIET

At least four of the 10 leading causes of death in the U.S. — diabetes, heart disease, stroke and cancer — are directly related to the diet (*Leading Cause of Death*, 2021). Vegetarians and vegans are at reduced risk of certain health conditions, including ischemic heart disease, type 2 diabetes, hypertension, certain types of cancer and obesity (Hemler & Hu, 2019; Melina et al., 2016; Singh et al., 2014). Phytonutrients and fiber found in plant food play a major role in promoting health. Vegetarians tend to have lower cholesterol levels and blood pressure and lower rates of hypertension and type 2 diabetes, plus lower weights and lower overall cancer rates, according to the Academy of Nutrition and Dietetics.

Nutrients in whole, unprocessed plant foods are involved in many functions in the body and are the source of health. Foods contain various proportions of the macronutrients (carbohydrate, fat, and protein), water, various amounts of the well-known micronutrients (vitamins, minerals, fiber and electrolytes), as well as several hundred naturally occurring substances in plant foods called **phytochemicals**.

> Evidence suggests that antioxidant supplements do not work as well as naturally-occurring antioxidants in whole, unprocessed foods such as fruits, vegetables, beans, legumes, nuts, seeds, whole grains, herbs and spices.

These benefits are likely the result of both the consistent consumption of health-promoting compounds found in whole plant foods and the reduction of exposure to harmful substances found in animal products and highly processed foods. While animal-source foods contain many beneficial nutrients such as easily absorbable iron, vitamin B_{12}, calcium, zinc and protein, among other nutrients, they can also contain potentially harmful substances. Meat (including processed, red, and white), fish, dairy, and eggs may contain health-damaging saturated fats (detrimental to blood lipids and heart health), heme iron (increases risk of gastrointestinal cancers at high intakes), N-glycolylneuraminic acid (Neu5Gc), carnitine and chemical contaminants formed when flesh is cooked, such as polycyclic aromatic hydrocarbons, heterocyclic amines, and advanced glycation end products. These substances in animal foods can contribute to inflammation, oxidation, and carcinogenesis, promoting disease (Hever & Cronise, 2017; Lila, 2007).

CARDIOVASCULAR DISEASE

Cardiovascular disease (CVD) remains the world's leading cause of death (WHO, 2020). In the United States, heart disease accounts for over 659,000 deaths per year (CDC, 2021). A review article by Kahleova et al. (2018) found that plant-based eating reduces CVD mortality and the risk of coronary heart disease (CHD) by 40%. Lifestyle choices and nutrition may reduce the risk of myocardial infarction by more than 80% (Kahleova et al., 2018).

There is evidence that suggests benefits of plant-based eating in both the prevention and treatment of heart failure and cerebrovascular disease. Plant-based eating is associated with lower blood pressure, lower blood lipids, and lower body weights, which have implications for cardiovascular disease risk (Hever & Cronise, 2017; Kahleova et al., 2018; Schulze et al., 2004).

A systematic review of trials by Wang et al. (2015) assessing the effects of vegetarian diets on blood lipids over an average of 24 weeks found that compared to on omnivorous diet, vegetarian diets reduced LDL cholesterol and total cholesterol. However, there were also relative reductions in HDL and no change in triglycerides, but these were off-set by the significant improvements in LDL in terms of overall cardiovascular risk (Wang et al., 2015). The estimated reduction in coronary heart disease risk across the 10 reviewed trials was approximately 22%. The trials also found that vegetarians had lower weights than those following an omnivorous diet. Both the lower lipids and lower overall weights may be mechanisms by which cardiovascular health is improved among those who follow a vegetarian diet.

A meta-analysis of randomized controlled trials has similarly found that people following vegetarian diets have lower body weights than those who consume an omnivorous diet (Huang et al., 2015). Furthermore, a study by Jenkins et al. (2011) showed that plant-based diets improve lipid profiles and blood pressure, independent of their effect on weight (Jenkins et al., 2011). A meta-analysis by Yokoyama et al. (2014) has also shown that vegetarian diets produce lower blood pressures compared to non-vegetarian diets (Yokoyama, Nishimura, et al., 2014). Another systematic review and meta-analysis by Huang et al. (2012) shownned similar findings that a vegetarian diet (compared to a non-vegetarian diet) reduced the risk of ischemic heart disease by about 30% (T. Huang et al., 2012). A meta-analysis of over 120,000 vegetarians found that following a vegetarian diet reduced ischemic heart disease risk by 25% (Dinu et al., 2017).

The cardiometabolic benefits of vegetarian diets are not only due to the reduced intake of red meat and high saturated fat sources but also due to the relative increase in the intake of beneficial plant foods including whole grains, legumes, nuts, seeds, vegetables and fruits – foods that are high in potassium, fiber, and antioxidants, which are cardioprotective (Fraser, 2009; Ha Vanessa & de Souza Russell J., n.d.; McDonough et al., 2017; Sievenpiper & Dworatzek, 2013). Higher fiber intakes from plant-based foods have been associated with lower rates of cardiovascular disease in several studies (Aune et al., 2012; Hartley et al., 2016; Pereira et al., 2004). Soluble fiber helps lower low-density lipoprotein (LDL), which helps lower the risk of ischemic heart disease (Brown et al., 1999; Gunness & Gidley, 2010; McRorie & McKeown, 2017; Surampudi et al., 2016).

Researchers at the University of Southern California found that increasing dietary potassium is as important to improving the risk factors for cardiovascular and kidney disease as limiting dietary sodium. Higher intake and excretion of potassium has also been found to slow the progression of kidney and heart disease (McDonough et al., 2017). Plant-based foods are a significant dietary source of potassium.

Pulses are the edible dried seeds of legumes such as chickpeas, lentils, beans and peas. Dietary pulses are high in fiber, protein, and various micronutrients and low in fat and low on the glycemic index (GI) (Ivers et al., 2019). They are increasingly recognized for their benefits in the prevention and management of type 2 diabetes and cardiovascular diseases (CVDs) across various chronic disease guidelines. The American Heart Association, Canadian Cardiovascular Society, and European Society for Cardiology encourage dietary patterns that emphasize intake of legumes (which include dietary pulses, soybeans, peanuts, fresh peas and fresh beans) for lowering LDL cholesterol and blood pressure, dietary pulses for lowering LDL cholesterol, and legumes for lowering LDL cholesterol and improving the overall lipoprotein profile, respectively (Viguiliouk et al., 2019).

TYPE 2 DIABETES

Diabetes is a chronic, progressive illness that requires continuing medical care and patient self-management to prevent acute complications and reduce the risk of long-term complications, such as cardiovascular disease, retinopathy, neuropathy and nephropathy. What we eat has a big influence in both prevention and management of type 2 diabetes (Ivers et al., 2019).

Type 2 diabetes is a metabolic disorder characterized by hyperglycemia and insulin resistance. In addition to genetic risk factors, some of the main risk factors are lifestyle-related and include an energy-dense diet, high BMI, and physical inactivity. Making changes to lifestyle such as shifting toward an eating pattern that is lower in fat and higher in fiber and including regular moderate physical activity has been shown to help reduce the risk of type 2 diabetes (Ivers et al., 2019; Knowler et al., 2002; Tuomilehto et al., 2001).

Diabetes Canada and the American Diabetes Association recommend a plant-based eating pattern (e.g., a vegetarian or vegan diet) as one of the evidence-based medical nutrition therapies for managing diabetes (American Diabetes Association, 2017; Ivers et al., 2019). In a 74-week randomized controlled trial, following a vegan diet was shown to help improve hemoglobin A1c, a marker for diabetes management (Barnard et al., 2009). A review article by Kahleova et al. (2018) found similar findings of reduced A1c among people with type 2 diabetes following vegetarian diets compared to those consuming omnivorous diets. Similarly, a systematic review and meta-analysis by Yokoyama et al. (2014) showed that people living with diabetes who follow vegetarian diets have better glycemic control compared to those consuming omnivorous diets (Yokoyama, Barnard, et al., 2014). Furthermore, several systematic reviews and meta-analyses have found that people living with type 2 diabetes who consume a vegetarian diet have less cardiovascular complications, lower weights, and better overall health outcomes compared to those consuming an omnivorous diet (Barnard et al., 2015; Dinu et al., 2017; Wang et al., 2015).

A systematic review by Esposito et al. (2010) found that consuming a low-calorie vegetarian diet was more effective at decreasing the risk of type 2 diabetes as well as improving management and outcomes of type 2 diabetes compared to conventional recommendations (Esposito et al., 2010). Notably, far more vegetarians in the study were able to maintain good glycemic control while reducing their use of antihyperglycemic medications compared to those following conventional diabetes nutrition guidelines (43% vs. 5%). Higher intakes of fiber from plant foods are associated with lower incidence of type 2 diabetes (Schulze et al., 2004). However, another possible reason for the improved prevention and management of diabetes that is provided by a vegetarian diet is that a plant-based diet tends to be high in antioxidants, which help reduce oxidative stress in the body that contributes to insulin resistance, inflammation, and increased risk of diabetes complications such as cardiovascular disease (Federico et al., 2012; Mancini et al., 2018; Pugazhenthi et al., 2017; Shukla et al., 2011; Yazıcı & Sezer, 2017).

There is evidence that suggests oxidative stress may contribute to the pathogenesis of type 2 diabetes. Plant foods, and especially fruits, vegetables, wine, coffee and tea, contain a variety of phytochemicals with antioxidant activity, which may have cumulative/synergistic antioxidant effects. Mancini et al. (2018) suggest that the total antioxidant capacity may play an important role in reducing the risk of type 2 diabetes in middle-aged women (Mancini et al., 2018). More studies are needed to better understand this association.

The inclusion of nutrient-dense and low glycemic index foods such as legumes, which are prevalent in the vegetarian diet, likely also plays a role in the observed reduction in diabetes risk and improved diabetes management among vegetarians. Systematic reviews and meta-analyses of randomized controlled trials have found that people with diabetes who consume diets high in legumes or pulses had lower fasting blood glucose and hemoglobin A1c, as well as improvements in other risk factors for diabetes complications including LDL cholesterol, blood pressure, and weight (Ha et al., 2014; Jayalath et al., 2014; Kim et al., 2016; Sievenpiper et al., 2009). Diabetes Canada recommends that individuals with diabetes consume dietary pulses to help manage glycemic control, blood pressure, and body weight (Federico et al., 2012; Mancini et al., 2018; Pugazhenthi et al., 2017; Shukla et al., 2011; Yazıcı & Sezer, 2017). Diabetes Canada and the American Diabetes Association recommend various dietary patterns that include dietary pulses as acceptable for the management of diabetes (American Dietetic Association & Dietitians of Canada, 2003; Ivers et al., 2019).

Professor David Jenkins and his team at the University of Toronto investigated the effects of exchanging carbohydrates for mixed nuts — a source of unsaturated fats — on critical risk factors for cardiovascular disease, such as low-density lipoprotein particle size and apolipoprotein B levels. Nut intake as a replacement for carbohydrate consumption improved glycemic control and lipid risk factors in individuals with type 2 diabetes (Ananthakrishnan et al., 2013). Other studies have similarly found that nut consumption is associated with lower fasting blood glucose, A1c, and blood lipids among people with diabetes (Blanco Mejia et al., 2014; Sabaté, 2010; Viguiliouk et al., 2014). A systematic review and meta-analysis of 12 randomized controlled trials found that an average of 56 grams of nuts per day caused a significant reduction in A1c and fasting blood glucose (Viguiliouk et al., 2014).

GASTROINTESTINAL HEALTH

Constipation

High-fiber foods reduce constipation and contribute to regular, smooth bowel movements. Soluble fiber from foods such as beans, oats, barley, berries, squash, potatoes, broccoli and apples draw water to the colon, making stools soft and easy to pass, and supports healthy gut bacteria (Erdogan et al., 2016; Homann et al., 1994; McRorie & McKeown, 2017; Slavin, 1987; *Treatments for Constipation*, 2014). Movement of stool is further enhanced with insoluble fiber found in the more sturdy parts of plant foods, such as fruit peels, bran, seeds, nuts and many vegetables (Erdogan et al., 2016; McRorie & McKeown, 2017; Slavin, 1987; K.-Y. Tan & Seow-Choen, 2007). As a result, vegetarian diets, which tend to be higher in plant foods and total fiber content, also reduce the risk of diverticulosis and its complications (Gear et al., 1981; Melina et al., 2016; Nair & Mayberry, 1994). In a 12-week trial where teachers and students switched from an omnivorous diet to a vegetarian diet, there was a reduction in functional constipation among both adults and children (Lee et al., 2016). More studies are needed to examine whether a vegetarian dietary pattern can be used as a treatment for constipation.

Inflammatory Bowel Disease/Irritable Bowel Syndrome

Some of the risk factors for inflammatory bowel disease (IBD) such as Crohn's disease and ulcerative colitis include dietary factors. High intakes of sugar, animal fat, and linoleic acid (omega-6) are risk factors for developing IBD, whereas a high-fiber diet and consuming citrus fruits appear to be protective against IBD (Amre et al., 2007; Owczarek et al., 2016; RD(USA)(SA), 2012; Reif et al., 1997; Sakamoto et al., 2005; Ananthakrishnan et al., 2013). During flare-ups of IBD, most patients are advised to follow a low-fiber diet to provide the bowels with rest (Owczarek et al., 2016), whereas a high-fiber diet and lower intake of sulfur-containing foods (such as meat, eggs, nuts and cheese) during remission periods have been shown to reduce the risk of further flare-ups (Jowett et al., 2004).

Other studies have similarly found that high fiber intakes help prolong remission of IBS (Brotherton et al., 2014; Fernández-Bañares et al., 1999; Hallert et al., 1991; Wedlake et al., 2014). A study by Chiba et al. (2010) found that a semi-vegetarian diet was highly effective at maintaining IBD remission (100% of the 16 participants maintained remission at one year and 92% maintained remission at two years) (Chiba et al., 2010). A vegetarian diet tends to be higher in fiber and lower in sulfur-containing foods and animal fat, and thus a nutritious and well-planned plant-based diet may be helpful in reducing the risk of IBD and in maintaining remission in those who have IBD (Jantchou et al., 2010; Tomasello et al., 2016). More studies to examine this are warranted, as there has also been conflicting evidence in regards to diet for remission of IBD. A study by Schreiner et al. (2019) found that patients with IBD following a vegetarian diet did not have an improved disease course for their IBD (Schreiner et al., 2019).

Probiotic supplements and omega-3 fatty acids may also help maintain remission from IBD flare-ups (Hsieh et al., 2020; Owczarek et al., 2016). Chronic inflammation in IBD and the use of medications such as steroids can increase the risk of several nutrient deficiencies, including iron, calcium, vitamin D, vitamin B12, folic acid, zinc, vitamin A and magnesium; therefore, a carefully planned nutrient-dense diet is critical for those with IBD (Jørgensen et al., 2013; National Clinical Guideline Centre (U.K.), 2012; Owczarek et al., 2016; A. F. da Silva et al., 2011; Zhang & Li, 2014).

WEIGHT

Higher weights have been associated with a range of chronic conditions in numerous research studies. Eating patterns that promote reduced risk of hyperlipidemia, hypertension, coronary artery disease and diabetes also tend to be associated with preventing weight gain and promoting lower weights. Vegetarian and vegan diets are nutrient-dense and not calorie-dense like the typical Western omnivorous diets. Plant-based eating, vegetarianism, and veganism are associated with lower weights partially due to the high fiber content, which may approach 40 to 50 grams per day, substantially more than typical omnivorous diets (Slavin, 1987).

This fiber content delays hunger and increases satiety via multiple mechanisms, including delays in gastric emptying and intestinal transit, thus regulating appetite and reducing caloric intake (Howarth et al., 2001; Wanders et al., 2011). Additionally, soluble fiber, found in plant foods such as legumes, oats, barley and some fruits and vegetables (apples, pears, peaches, plums, broccoli, squashes, potatoes, asparagus, etc.), provides a fermentable substrate for beneficial species in the gut microbiome (Erdogan et al., 2016; Homann et al., 1994; McRorie & McKeown, 2017; Slavin, 1987; *Treatments for Constipation*, 2014). Adverse alterations in the microbiome are now believed to play key roles in hormone expression that favors weight gain, while the microbiome profiles of people consuming high-fiber and plant-based diets tend to favor hormone expression that promotes lower weights (Hernández et al., 2019; Melina et al., 2016; Menni et al., 2017; O'Grady et al., 2019).

A systematic review and meta-analysis of trials by Huang et al. (2015) found that those who follow vegetarian diets have significantly lower body weights than those consuming omnivorous diets. Another meta-analysis by Huang et al. (2016) found similar results (R.-Y. Huang et al., 2016). This review of 12 randomized controlled trials with an average duration of 18 weeks found that those following a vegetarian eating pattern had lower weights than those following an omnivorous diet. Furthermore, those following vegan diets had lower weights compared to those eating lacto-ovo vegetarian diets. A systematic review of trials by Barnard et al. (2015) also found similar results that people following vegetarian diets had decreased weights compared to non-vegetarians (Barnard et al., 2015).

CHRONIC KIDNEY FAILURE

Diabetes and hypertension significantly increase the risk for chronic kidney disease (CKD). Vegetarian diets are associated with reduced blood glucose and blood pressure, which can help prevent and slow progression of CKD (Ivers et al., 2019; McDonough et al., 2017; Viguiliouk et al., 2019; Yokoyama, Nishimura, et al., 2014). The results of small studies suggest that a plant-based diet can delay the progression of CKD, protect the endothelium, reduce blood pressure, and decrease proteinuria, which in turn decreases the risk of complications (Azadbakht et al., 2008; Elliott et al., 2006; Kontessis et al., 1990).

The lower protein content and replacement of animal protein with plant protein as well as lower sodium content typical of vegetarian diets also limits further damage and may slow disease progression in early CKD (Aparicio et al., 2000; Barsotti et al.,

1996; Jibani et al., 1991; Melina et al., 2016; Mitch & Remuzzi, 2016; Spencer et al., 2003). Higher intake and excretion of potassium among vegetarians has also been found to slow the progression of chronic kidney disease (McDonough et al., 2017).

A study by Anderson et al. (1998) showed that vegetarian diets are associated with higher estimated glomerular filtration rates (eGFR), a marker for kidney function, among people with type 2 diabetes (Anderson et al., 1998). This finding was also seen by Lohsiriwat (2013). A study by Kontessi et al. (1990) similarly found that people on higher-protein diets had better eGFRs when the protein source was plant-based (soy) versus animal-based or even animal-based with supplemental fiber (Kontessis et al., 1990). Ensuring adequate protein intake without excess protein and energy intake improves disease progression in CKD (Gluba-Brzózka et al., 2017).

As CKD progresses, dietary phosphorus needs to be restricted since the ability of the kidneys to excrete phosphorus continues to decline. Hyperphosphatemia is a risk factor for mortality in patients with later stages of CKD. Maintaining a diet low in phosphorus can be challenging for patients who consume typical Western diets, as animal-based proteins such as dairy products and meats tend to be high in phosphorus, and many fast foods and processed foods contain phosphorus as additives (Kestenbaum et al., 2005; Moe et al., 2011; Nagano et al., 2006; Sullivan et al., 2009). Plant-based proteins are typically higher in phosphorus than animal proteins; however, plant proteins have a lower bioavailability due to phytates that bind phosphorus. Plant protein phosphorus is typically absorbed at a rate of 30% to 50%, while animal protein phosphorus is typically absorbed at 70% to 80% (Pagenkemper, 1995). A study by Moe et al. (2011) showed that vegetarians had lower serum phosphorus than those consuming an omnivorous diet (Moe et al., 2011).

Several studies have shown that consuming a vegetarian diet is safe in CKD and may help in primary prevention of CKD as well as delay progression for those who have the disease (Chauveau et al., 2019; Kramer, 2019; Liu et al., 2019; Rocha et al., 2019). Further studies are needed to examine the use of a plant-based diet as a treatment in CKD.

CANCER

Cancer is one of the leading causes of death in the United States, and dietary factors account for about 30% of all cancers (Tantamango-Bartley et al., 2013). Nutrition guidelines for cancer recovery issued by national and worldwide authorities share a focus with prevention-oriented strategies: plenty of whole grains, beans, fruits and vegetables, and significant limits on red and processed meats, although patient awareness and compliance is limited at best. There is a building body of observational research that supports the benefits of following a vegetarian diet as it pertains to cancer incidence and mortality, but more studies, including clinical trials, are needed to confirm the benefits.

The 2016 position of the Academy of Nutrition and Dietetics is that vegetarians have a lower overall risk of cancer compared to non-vegetarians (Melina et al., 2016). A systematic review of 12 studies by Parker and Vadiveloo (2019) found that overall diet quality was significantly higher among vegetarian diets compared to non-vegetarian diets, with higher intakes of several nutrients and lower intakes of animal proteins/animal fats and sodium — and this is proposed as a possible mechanism for the observed reduced incidence of cancer among vegetarians (Parker & Vadiveloo, 2019).

A meta-analysis of over 120,000 vegetarians showed an 8% reduction in the risk of cancer among those who followed a vegetarian diet compared to those following an omnivorous diet. Among those consuming a vegan diet, the risk of cancer was reduced by 15% (Dinu et al., 2017). Authors of a 2017 systematic review exploring the relationship between vegetarian diets and risk of breast, colorectal, and prostate cancer risk over five to 20 years found that there was a lower risk of colorectal cancer among pesca-vegetarians compared to non-vegetarians, and that there was a decreased risk of prostate cancer among vegetarians compared to non-vegetarians (Federico et al., 2012; Godos et al., 2017; Mancini et al., 2018; Pugazhenthi et al., 2017; Shukla et al., 2011; Yazıcı & Sezer, 2017). A study examining the results of the Adventist Health Study 2 found that the vegan diet was associated with a lower risk for overall and female-specific cancers and that a lacto-ovo vegetarian diet was associated with a lower risk of gastrointestinal cancers (Tantamango-Bartley et al., 2013). Further studies are needed to more closely examine the relationship between plant-based dietary patterns and the protective effect against specific types of cancers.

Soy and Breast Cancer

Soy is a source of isoflavones, and concerns about isoflavone safety are based almost exclusively on *in vitro* and animal research. One of the potential concerns about soy and isoflavones is the potential risk to estrogen-sensitive breast cancer patients and women at risk of developing breast cancer (Hemler & Hu, 2019; Melina et al., 2016; Singh et al., 2014). In the United States, the average isoflavone consumption is 1 to 2 mg/day, while in Asian countries, isoflavone intake ranges from 25 to 50 mg/day (Klein et al., 2010; National Toxicology Program (NTP) Center for the Evaluation of Risks to Human Reproduction, 2010). Soy foods consumed in Asian countries have traditionally been minimally processed and often fermented (examples: boiled soybeans, tofu, miso soup, natto and soy milk), whereas soy consumed in Western countries tends to be more processed (soy flour, textured vegetable protein, isolated soy protein). The isoflavones in the Asian diet are mainly in the aglycone form, while those in the Western diet are mainly in the glycoside form (Klein et al., 2010). The form and processing of soy may alter the isoflavone profile and the potential safety of soy and its impact on cancer risk (Erdman et al., 2004; Hilakivi-Clarke et al., 2010; Velentzis et al., 2008).

In addition to isoflavones, lignans are another contributor (and the main contributor in Western diets) to phytoestrogen intake (Balk et al., 2005; Diamanti-Kandarakis et al., 2009; Klein et al., 2010; Messina, 2010; National Toxicology Program (NTP) Center for the Evaluation of Risks to Human Reproduction, 2010, p. 2010). Lignans are found in flax, fruits, vegetables and beverages such as coffee and orange juice. Foods such as cereals, breads, eggs, dairy products, meat, fish, nuts and vegetables also contribute some non-soy isoflavones in a typical diet.

Isoflavones are structurally similar to estrogen, can bind and activate estrogen receptors (with a preference for beta receptors), and can exert estrogen-like effects under experimental conditions *in vitro* and *in vivo* (Hamilton-Reeves et al., 2010; Messina, 2010; Messina & Redmond, 2006; Xiao, 2008). Excessive tissue proliferation tends to lead to the development of malignant degeneration and is associated with cancer development. The beta estrogen receptor inhibits estrogen-dependent cell growth (Cheng et al., 2010; Wuttke et al., 2007; Xiao, 2008). Therefore, while soy intake may increase breast tissue growth through binding alpha estrogen receptors, it preferentially binds to the beta receptor, which inhibits breast tissue growth, potentially lowering the risk of breast cancer.

Aiming for up to two to three servings per day of minimally processed soy foods (tofu, miso, natto, fermented soybeans, soybean paste, soy milk, tofu and edamame) has been suggested to be safe and potentially beneficial in preventing breast cancer and other endocrine cancers (Dietitians of Canada, 2020). This amount would provide about 15 to 20 grams of soy protein and 50 to 75 grams of isoflavones daily, which is the amount typically found in an Asian diet, where rates of breast and other endocrine cancers are low (Dietitians of Canada, 2020). Soy consumption from whole soy foods (but not soy supplements) has been found to help reduce the risk of breast cancer in people who have never had cancer (Chen et al., 2014; Cheng et al., 2010; Dietitians of Canada, 2020; Qiu & Jiang, 2019; Takagi et al., 2015; Touillaud et al., 2019; Wuttke et al., 2007; Xiao, 2008). Several studies and meta-analyses have found that this level of soy intake from whole, minimally processed foods is associated with a decreased risk of breast cancer and that earlier exposure to soy (e.g., soy intake during childhood) seems to have a stronger protective effect (Boucher et al., 2008; Dong & Qin, 2011; Hilakivi-Clarke et al., 2010; Korde et al., 2009; Lee et al., 2009; Messina & Hilakivi-Clarke, 2009; Messina & Wu, 2009; Travis et al., 2008; Trock et al., 2006; Warri et al., 2008; Wei et al., 2020; A. H. Wu et al., 2008; L. Wu & Sun, 2016; Yan & Spitznagel, 2004).

For people who have previously had breast cancer, two servings of soy foods per day is suggested as a safe amount (Dietitians of Canada, 2020). Several studies have found that this level of consumption of soy foods (approximately two servings per day from whole soy foods, but not from soy supplements) has not been associated with recurrence of breast cancer and may have a potential protective effect, particularly after menopause in breast cancer survivors (Boyapati et al., 2005; Dong & Qin, 2011; Fink et al., 2007; Guha et al., 2009; Kang et al., 2010; Messina, 2010, 2016; Shu et al., 2009). Further research is needed to examine this relationship between soy and breast cancer.

Are supplements as effective as eating vegetables? Diet shapes health in complex ways. The influence of diet on health occurs not only from the subtle effects of numerous individual food components, but from whole foods and the associated interactions that occur among these components. Research suggests that whole foods offer more protection against chronic diseases than dietary fiber, antioxidant supplements, or other supplements of biologically active ingredients in foods (Jacobs and Tapsell, 2007; Position of ADA, 2007; Messina, et al., 2001).

SECTION 7: ENVIRONMENTAL SUSTAINABILITY

An increasing number of individuals are choosing plant-based eating for environmental sustainability reasons (Ruby, 2014; Miki et al., 2020; Hopwood et al., 2020). Whole foods of plant origin require less water to produce and create fewer greenhouse gases compared to animal-based foods (Aston et al., 2012; Joyce et al., 2014; *Meat Consumption, Health, and the Environment*, 2018.; Sabaté & Soret, 2014). A systematic review of 90 studies on the motives behind choosing a vegetarian or vegan diet showed that 59% consider environmental sustainability as part of this lifestyle choice; this is a similar percentage to those who consider animal welfare (58% of vegetarians/vegans) as part of their dietary choices (Miki et al., 2020).

SECTION 8: IS A VEGETARIAN DIET FOR EVERYONE?

"It is the position of the Academy of Nutrition and Dietetics that appropriately planned vegetarian, including vegan, diets are healthful, nutritionally adequate, and may provide health benefits for the prevention and treatment of certain diseases. These diets are appropriate for all stages of the life cycle, including pregnancy, lactation, infancy, childhood, adolescence, older adulthood and for athletes. Vegans need reliable sources of vitamin B_{12}, such as fortified foods or supplements" (Melina et al., 2016).

BABIES AND CHILDREN

Adequate nutrition in infancy supports the growth and development that occur during this important time. Exclusive breastfeeding is the ideal feeding pattern for infants from birth to 6 months. A well-planned vegetarian diet, including lacto-ovo, lacto, or vegan, can meet the needs of a growing infant and young child over the age of 6 months. Extremely restrictive diets such as fruitarian and raw food diets have not been studied in infants and are not recommended due to concerns about adequacy of energy and nutrients (Melina et al., 2016).

Nutrients of possible concern in a vegetarian or vegan diet for infants, toddlers, and children include iron, calcium, vitamin D, zinc, vitamin B_{12}, essential fatty acids and total calories (Melina et al., 2016; Schürmann et al., 2017). Ensuring that a variety of foods from all food groups are offered to children can help provide these essential nutrients for growth and development.
- Offer iron-rich food (legumes, tofu, nuts/seeds, nut butters, fortified cereals, dried fruit, leafy green vegetables, Marmite, etc.) along with a vitamin C source (citrus fruit, berries, kiwi, peppers, tomatoes, broccoli, etc.) at each meal
- Offer fortified plant-based milks such as soy milk (other plant-based milks are often too low in calories, protein, and fat) and water as the beverages of choice to prevent small stomachs from filling up on low-nutrient sweet beverages

- Provide a vitamin B_{12} supplement and other nutritional supplements as needed (such as an algae-based omega-3 supplement); children who do not consume any animal products will need a vitamin B_{12} supplement
- Ensure adequate fat content in meals and snacks from sources such as oils, nuts, seeds, avocado, coconut, etc.
- Offer three balanced meals per day and snacks in between and allow children to choose what and how much of each food they eat

Feeding in a responsive and pleasant environment is the best way to ensure the child develops a healthful relationship with food, including enjoying a wide variety of foods and nutrients while being at reduced risk of underweight or higher weight (Bergmeier et al., 2015; Galloway et al., 2006; Hurley et al., 2011; Johnson & Birch, 1994; Shloim et al., 2015; Ventura & Birch, 2008).

PREGNANCY AND LACTATION

In a 2015 systematic review of vegan or vegetarian diets on pregnancy outcomes, results were heterogeneous and very limited. The conclusion was that this type of diet is safe provided that attention is given to potential vitamin B_{12} and iron deficiencies (Piccoli et al., 2015). Both the American Dietetic Association and Dietitians of Canada conclude that a vegetarian/vegan diet can be healthful for both pregnant women and those breastfeeding (American Dietetic Association & Dietitians of Canada, 2003; Craig et al., 2009), whereas the German Nutrition Society does not recommend it during these times (Richter et al., 2016). It does, however, state that because of the variability in vegetarian diets that an individual dietary assessment is required to ensure that the mother is getting all the nutrients that she needs.

Vitamin B₁₂

Vitamin B_{12} is especially important for the developing embryo, and low vitamin B_{12} intake by the pregnant mother can result in birth defects such as neural tube defects (Stover, 2010; Thompson et al., 2009). Low vitamin B_{12} status during pregnancy/pre-conception increases the risk of difficulty conceiving, spontaneous abortion, low birth weight and preterm delivery (Molloy et al., 2008; Rogne et al., 2017).

During lactation, adequate vitamin B_{12} intake is essential, as vitamin B_{12} transfer into breast milk depends more on current intake than on maternal stores (Mariani et al., 2009; Roem, 2003; Weiss et al., 2004). The recommended daily allowance (RDA) for vitamin B_{12} during pregnancy is 2.6 µg/day (8% more than non-pregnant/non-breastfeeding women). The RDA for vitamin B_{12} during lactation is 2.8 µg/day (17% more than non-pregnant/non-breastfeeding women).

Vitamin B_{12} is generally included in prenatal and other multivitamin-mineral supplements. Consuming foods containing vitamin B_{12} at least two times per day or a supplement that contains at least 5 µg/day of B_{12} once per day should provide adequate vitamin B_{12} during pregnancy and lactation for mothers who follow vegetarian and vegan diets (Institute of Medicine, 1998).

Iron

Iron intake is essential in pregnancy for growth and development of the growing fetus, and iron needs rise particularly in the second and third trimesters as the fetus grows in size (Institute of Medicine, 2001). The recommended daily allowance (RDA) for iron during pregnancy is 27 mg/day, which is 50% more than for non-pregnant, non-breastfeeding women. Most pregnant women in North America have trouble getting enough iron from their diet alone (Cooper et al., 2006; Fernández-Ballart & Murphy, 2001; Hercberg et al., 2000; Institute of Medicine, 2001; Turner et al., 2003). Therefore, it is recommended that a supplement containing iron should be taken during pregnancy to ensure adequate intake.

The recommended daily allowance (RDA) for iron for women who are breastfeeding is 10 mg/day for women under 18 years and 9 mg/day for women 19 to 50 years, which is 50% less than for women who aren't pregnant or breastfeeding, due to the lack of iron losses during menses. This recommendation continues until menstruation resumes (Canada, 2009; Institute of Medicine, 2001).

Inadequate iron intake during the postpartum period has been associated with an increased risk of postpartum depression. Therefore, ensuring a good dietary iron intake and possible continuation of a prenatal or other multivitamin supplement during breastfeeding and the postpartum period is advised (Cahill, 2019; Nutrition Working Group et al., 2016).

Calcium

Calcium is another possible nutrient of concern, as this nutrient is essential for growth of the fetus and for transfer into breast milk, and a low oral intake by the mother can worsen maternal stores and bone density to provide adequate calcium to the child. The amount of calcium recommended during pregnancy and lactation is the same as the amount needed by non-pregnant/non-breastfeeding women (Institute of Medicine (U.S.) Committee to Review Dietary Reference Intakes for Vitamin D and Calcium, 2011).

Higher calcium intakes during pregnancy have been found to be protective against hypertensive disorders during pregnancy, such as preeclampsia, and thus preterm birth (Hofmeyr et al., 2014). Many plant foods contain oxalates and phytates which inhibit calcium absorption, therefore it is advised to include low oxalate/phytate sources of calcium such as fortified soy beverage or other fortified plant milks, kale, spinach, mustard greens, bok choy, Chinese cabbage, almonds, wheat and fortified cereals. A supplement that contains calcium is advised during pregnancy and lactation (Canada, 2009; Weaver et al., 1999).

Vitamin D

Vitamin D is essential for adequate calcium absorption. The recommended daily allowance (RDA) for vitamin D during pregnancy and lactation is 600 IU/day, which is 50% more than for non-pregnant and non-breastfeeding women (Canada, 2009; Institute of Medicine (U.S.) Committee to Review Dietary Reference Intakes for Vitamin D and Calcium, 2011). Good vitamin D status has also been shown to be important in reducing the risk of postpartum depression, and therefore getting adequate vitamin D through sunshine, fortified plant foods, and supplementation in Canada and Northern states is important in this life stage (Aghajafari et al., 2018; Nutrition Working Group et al., 2016; *SACN Update on Vitamin D - 2007.*) For more information on nutrition during pregnancy and lactation, see the chapters on Pregnancy and Lactation.

SENIORS

After menopause, iron requirements for women decrease and oral iron intake becomes less of a concern in older adulthood. Vitamin B_{12} intake, however, becomes more of a concern for seniors as vitamin B_{12} absorption becomes less efficient with increasing age and also with use of certain medications commonly prescribed to seniors, such as proton pump inhibitors, histamine H2 receptor antagonists, and metformin (Stover, 2010) (Andrès et al., 2008).

Vitamin B_{12}

Up to 38% of older adults have mild vitamin B_{12} deficiency (Hoey et al., 2009). Low vitamin B_{12} status in older adults can contribute to altered cellular metabolism, functional and cognitive decline, cardiovascular disease and compromised bone health (Carmel, 2008; Dror & Allen, 2008). Vitamin B_{12} supplementation for those consuming no or few animal products is recommended, and bloodwork to monitor vitamin B_{12} status may be prudent for older adults, especially for those with low intakes of vitamin B_{12} from food sources (including fortified plant foods and nutritional yeast).

Zinc

Zinc is another possible nutrient of concern during ageing, as zinc is important in wound healing and immune function. Intake of a variety of foods from all food groups, including whole grains, nuts, and seeds can help to provide adequate zinc.

Vitamin D

Vitamin D is a nutrient of concern for older adults due to reduced synthesis of vitamin D in the skin when exposed to sunshine. Low vitamin D status has been implicated in several diseases associated with ageing, including cognitive decline, depression, osteoporosis, cardiovascular disease, hypertension, type 2 diabetes and cancer (Holick, 2011; Meehan & Penckofer, 2014) (Hossein-nezhad and Holick, 2013). Studies in the United States have found that the prevalence of vitamin D deficiency among older adults ranges from 20% to 100% (Holick, 2011). Vitamin D supplementation of 400 IU per day is recommended by Health Canada for all Canadians aged 50-plus. Supplementation would also be prudent in Northern states to prevent deficiency among older adults. Consuming vitamin D-fortified plant foods such as plant-based milks is also recommended.

Calcium

Calcium requirements increase with age to protect bone health. While younger adults need 1,000 mg calcium per day, adults 50 and up require 1,200 mg calcium per day. As we age, our bone breaks down faster than it is rebuilt due to a shift in osteoclast versus osteoblast activity. Ensuring adequate calcium intake from a variety of foods such as fortified plant-based milks, tofu, nuts, seeds and certain green vegetables, as well as load-bearing or resistance activity on a regular basis, can help protect bone density through ageing.

Protein

Protein requirements increase with age. While younger adults need 0.8 g protein per kg of body weight per day, adults ages 65 and up need 1 g protein per kg of body weight per day. Consuming adequate and frequent protein sources to preserve muscle mass during ageing is challenging for older adults, particularly as energy requirements decrease with age, and so greater nutrient density is needed in the diet of seniors. Sarcopenia is an age-related loss of muscle mass and strength, which compromises functioning (Walston, 2012). We begin to degrade muscle faster than we build it starting as early as our 40s, and by our 80s can lose up to 50% of our muscle mass (Metter et al., 1997).

Sarcopenia increases the risk of disability and frailty (Dufour et al., 2013; A. P. Marsh et al., 2011; Xue et al., 2011). Sarcopenia is also associated with insulin resistance, fatigue, falls and mortality (Landi et al., 2012; Newman et al., 2006; Peng et al., 2012). Spreading protein out evenly across meals in a day can help reduce muscle breakdown due to ageing; many older adults have good protein intake at dinner but require increased protein at breakfast (and possibly also at lunch and snacks) to help meet their needs. Good plant-based protein sources should be encouraged for older adults, including soy beverage (most other plant milks are low in protein), tofu, tempeh, legumes, nuts, seeds, nut butters and whole grains. Go to the chapter on Seniors for more information on diet for seniors.

ATHLETES

The vegetarian and or vegan diet for the athlete is covered in the chapter on Athletes. To summarize the chapter, "vegetarian athletes eating a well-balanced diet can be assured of getting generous amounts of vitamins, minerals, phytonutrients, healthful fats and protein. However, those who eat poorly are at risk for deficiencies in iron, calcium, zinc, vitamins D and B₁₂, essential fats and amino acids, and excesses of compounds such as fiber, which can bind essential nutrients and decrease absorption."

SECTION 9: PALATABILITY AND ADHERENCE TO PLANT-BASED EATING

Eating habits are formed early in life. In fact, vegetarian moms-to-be often birth babies that like the taste of vegetables. Any dietary changes toward vegetarian or vegan lifestyle will require an adjustment, commitment, and gradual change for it to result in a sustainable eating pattern and optimum health benefits. Many individuals can start with a flexitarian diet or plant-centric/plant-forward diet. This helps in transitioning to cutting back on animal foods and increasing more plant foods.

Many people may not realize they are already eating plant-based meals such as peanut butter and jelly sandwiches, oatmeal with nuts and fruit, and vegetable stir-fry. They can expand these meals by increasing the fruits, vegetables, and types of whole grains and beans that they are familiar with. They can focus on adding, not taking away. Other meals can become more plant-based by simply adding more of these foods.

When changing behaviors, people often see and react to the biggest barriers, but these feelings can be made less intense by focusing on smaller barriers that are more easily overcome. They can substitute plant protein for meat protein in recipes and meals they already make. For example, lentils can replace half of the ground beef in a recipe such as shepherd's pie, and tofu can replace half of the chicken in a stir-fry. Legumes like beans, tofu, and tempeh or a plethora of "vegan meats" that mock the taste and texture of chicken, beef, or pork can be used. Cow milk can be exchanged for a plant milk such as soy, almond, oat, hemp or cashew. The first easy step could be eliminating animal foods for breakfast or from snacks. Then move on to eliminating animal foods for lunch. Then move onto one or more days of consuming no animal foods.

Many alternatives exist; individuals need to try a few of them to find ones that fit their taste preferences and nutrition needs. They can check the nutrition label for calcium, iron, and protein content, as levels vary. Ideally, including as many whole foods as possible will make for the most balanced eating pattern. A diet based on a variety of foods from all food groups will be much less likely to have micronutrient deficiencies than an eating pattern consisting largely of processed plant foods.

Individuals don't have to give up their favorite foods immediately or even ever. The most sustainable changes come when they are done over a period of time. Help them make the easiest changes first and when those no longer feel new, help them move on to the more difficult ones. Teach clients that taste buds will change over time and with it, their preferences as well.

SECTION 10: CULINARY COMPETENCIES

The culinary competencies for following a vegetarian diet include being able to cook and/or prepare fruit, vegetables, plant-based protein and whole grains. There is a chapter for each of these food groups that contain their own culinary competencies. In addition to those, here are the following culinary competencies for adhering to a vegetarian diet:

- Describe the various forms of vegetarian diets and foods groups included
- List the health benefits of following a vegetarian/vegan diet
- List nutrients of concern when following a vegetarian or vegan diet and food sources of those nutrients
- Refer to a registered dietitian if a nutritional supplement is likely warranted depending on the type of vegetarian diet being followed
- Model consumption of a vegetarian/vegan diet
- Swap plant-based protein for animal protein in meals and recipes
- Prepare plant-based meat alternatives
- Plan a vegetarian meal and snack
- Design a weekly menu that aligns with a vegetarian (various types) diet

SECTION 11: THE VEGETARIAN DIET AT THE STORE

Shopping for vegetarian items at the store means focusing on the produce aisle first and foremost. The next stop is the refrigerator section with plant-based milks, yogurt, cheeses and meat alternatives such as tofu and tempeh. Lastly, the internal aisles will have whole grain products, spices, and condiments. Health food shops, ethnic markets, and farmers markets also carry a variety of plant-based foods like plant milks, vegan meats, interesting produce, a variety of spices and an ever-growing selection of plant-based products to try.

Stock the kitchen with healthful plant-based whole foods, so that when you are pressed for time there are still plenty of healthful plant foods available to eat. Canned or prepared soup and beans and precooked grains stored in the refrigerator reduce preparation time. Food options like hummus and other bean dips with baby carrots, lightly steamed cauliflower, or apple slices can make snacking easy and healthful. The following is a list of vegan foods to stock in the pantry.

IN THE PANTRY

- Vegetable broth
- Bragg aminos
- Canned tomatoes, tomato paste
- Mushroom powder
- Kombu
- Canned coconut milk
- Dried and/or canned legumes — lentils, chickpeas, and beans
- Dried fruit
- Olives and capers
- Whole grains — quinoa, rice, amaranth, barley, oats and more. See the chapter on Grains for more information on shopping for and cooking with grains
- Whole grain pasta, bread, cereal, and crackers
- Spices — an assortment. See the chapter on Herbs & Spices for more information on shopping for and cooking with herbs and spices
- Soy sauce or tamari
- Seeds — sesame, pumpkin; plus flax and chia seeds, which are loaded with fiber, protein, and omega-3 fatty acids
- Nuts — any type, such as walnuts, almonds, Brazil nuts, pecans, peanuts and hazelnuts. (Check out a nutrient comparison chart for tree nuts.)

> **Nut butters have an astounding number of uses.** They can be added to breakfast foods or fruit or used as a base for plant-based sauces and dressings. Nuts and nut butters contain healthful fats, are nutrient-dense, and are low-cost.

Table 6: Plant-Based Meat Alternatives

Meat Alternative	Nutritional Information
Tofu • **Soft** • **Medium** • **Firm** • **Extra firm**	Good source of complete protein Good source of thiamin and the minerals iron, copper, manganese, magnesium, selenium and zinc *Note: As tofu increases in firmness water is pressed out, which causes the protein and fat content to rise too
Tempeh	Complete protein, high in calcium, fiber, phytochemicals and prebiotics Is a fermented food, making it good for the microbiome

Natto	High in protein, calcium, B vitamins, vitamin K, iron, copper, magnesium and zinc	
Seitan	High in protein, low in carbohydrates	

Table 7: Nutritional Comparison of 100 Grams of Tofu, Tempeh, Seitan and Beef

	Tofu	Tempeh	Seitan	Beef
Calories	101	190	141	179
Protein (g)	10	21	25	20.5
Carbohydrates (g)	2.5	14	6	0
Fiber (g)	1.3	7	1.2	0
Fat (g)	5	5	2	10
Sodium* (mg)	9	0	447	67
Calcium (mg)**	76	104	24	0
Iron (mg)	1.4	2.4	1.7	2.4
Potassium	316	338	100	

*Depending on the amount added, sodium can range from none to a significant amount

**Depending on if calcium was used as an additive; calcium values can vary wildly

SECTION 12: THE VEGETARIAN DIET IN THE KITCHEN

When building a vegetarian meal, it is important to stay true to the essence of this eating style, which includes a large variety of vegetables and grains and some fruit. It is also important to practice portion control, especially with nuts, seeds, plant-based meat alternatives and grains.

People may call themselves a vegetarian, but this does not necessarily mean that a lot of vegetables and grains are being consumed. In fact, it is possible to follow a vegetarian pattern of eating that is full of processed foods and saturated fat. This can often be seen in young adults, teens, and those new to vegetarianism. In today's supermarkets and restaurants, it is easy to find vegetarian options of cake, cookies, chips, ice cream, processed snacks, hot dogs and even bacon.

For example, examine the images below: **both meals are lacto-vegetarian:** One is full of plants with a touch of cheese, while the other is a processed white flour base smothered with saturated fat and topped with slices of tomato.

 **Versus**

BUILD A BREAKFAST

Starting the day with a nutrient-packed meal can be both quick and delicious once you know the formula. Start with whole grains you have made the night before or that morning, then add protein — nuts, nut butter, seeds — and fruit and milk or yogurt as depicted in Figure 1.

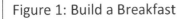

Figure 1: Build a Breakfast

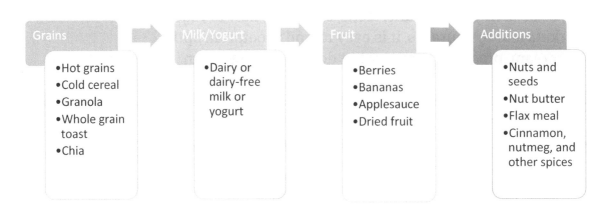

Grains	Milk/Yogurt	Fruit	Additions
• Hot grains • Cold cereal • Granola • Whole grain toast • Chia	• Dairy or dairy-free milk or yogurt	• Berries • Bananas • Applesauce • Dried fruit	• Nuts and seeds • Nut butter • Flax meal • Cinnamon, nutmeg, and other spices

Some examples of healthful breakfasts are listed below:

Whole Grain Toast

1. Start with whole grain bread that has been toasted.
2. Spread with almond, hazelnut, cashew, peanut or other nut butter. Take a walk on the wild side and try a new nut butter - you may be surprised at the different flavor profiles! You can even combine a couple of nut butters for a unique taste or make your own.
3. Top with your choice of fruit, nuts, and seeds.

Chia Bowls

For a breakfast or snack packed with protein, fiber, minerals and healthful omega-3 fats, nothing could be easier than making chia pudding. Follow the basic 3:1 ratio:

- ½ cup chia seeds
- 1 ½ cups liquid (plant-based milk)
- Optional sweetener (this can be honey or maple syrup or fruit pureed in the blender)
- Mix all ingredients together
- Wait 15 minutes and stir again
- Place chia pudding in the refrigerator for at least four hours — make it the night before for a quick breakfast option. Chia pudding can last up to four days in the refrigerator.
- Top with your choice of fruit, nuts, and seeds — the options are endless

> For a single serving — 1 tablespoon chia seeds + ¼ cup liquid (plant-based milk of your choice) + optional sweetener.

Click here for scrumptious recipes that include chai latte, dark chocolate, and banana bread at <u>Simply Quinoa.</u>

Hot Cereal

- Select one grain or several grains (make sure they have the same cooking time or mix together after they are cooked.)
- Cook for the recommended time in water, plant-based milk, or a combination of the two.
- Optional — add spices to the pot before cooking, like cinnamon, nutmeg, and/or cardamom, for example.
- Top each bowl with fresh or dried fruit or applesauce and two tablespoons nuts or seeds.

BUILD A MEAL: SALAD

Build a salad for a one-dish meal. A variety of vegetables, some beans, cooked quinoa or millet and fruit can add health-promoting phytonutrients, flavor, and appeal to any meal. Use any combination of ingredients listed below. For an unapologetically delicious salad, touch on all the taste points with a dash of crunch.

Step 1: **Select your greens.** Leafy greens vary in the amount of bitterness and sweetness they impart on the tongue. Select one or a combination depending on taste preferences. Greens also vary in terms of their texture — some leaves are delicate, while others have a heartier texture (kale).

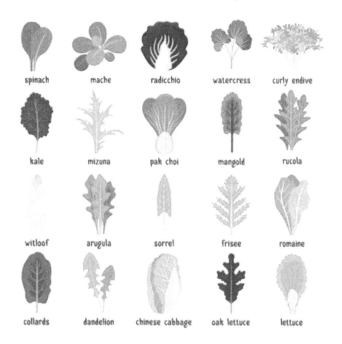

Step 2: **Add a source of protein.** Nuts, seeds, legumes, quinoa or tofu will add plenty of protein to prolong satiation.

Step 3: **Add color** with tomatoes, broccoli florets, grated carrots, green or red peppers, beets, cauliflower or edible flowers.

Step 4: **Add texture for a crunch** with toasted sesame seeds, sunflower or pumpkin seeds, almonds, pecans, pistachios, pine nuts, walnuts or peanuts.

Step 5: **Add a touch of sweetness** with fruit — pineapple, pears, orange segments, sliced strawberries, cut apples or dried fruit. A great combination is mango or grapefruit and avocado with spinach.

Step 6: **Top off with a favorite dressing** that includes a source of **acid** to brighten the salad. Vinegar, lime, or lemon juice will do the trick. See the chapter on Fats and Oils for salad dressing recipes.

COOKING WITH PLANT-BASED MEAT ALTERNATIVES

Soy-based meat alternatives include tofu and tempeh, while seitan is made from wheat gluten. Soy-based alternatives are complete proteins, making them a great vegetarian choice. On their own, there is not much flavor, but the great thing about these products is that they can easily pick up the flavor of whatever they are marinated in.

Table 8: Plant-Based Meat Alternatives

Type of Product	Made From...	Flavor and Texture	Best Used for...
Tofu	Soybeans are boiled and curdled, then pressed	Very subtle, bean-like flavor, but it absorbs others flavors very well. Texture is creamy and consistency varies from soft to extra firm.	**Soft**: Smoothies, sauces, raw desserts **Medium:** Soups **Firm**: Tofu scramble, stir-fry, baked (use when you want to retain the shape) **Extra firm**: Same as for firm, plus grilled and crumbled
Tofu – silken (Japanese tofu)	Cooked soybeans that are unpressed and not curdled or drained	Subtle taste and much more delicate than regular tofu listed above. It has	Best used in sauces, desserts, smoothies and salad dressings. It can also be used in

		a custard-like texture.	baking to replace oil, eggs, or cream
Tempeh	Soybeans are cooked, fermented, and pressed into patties	Nutty flavor with firm texture	Baked, grilled, stir-fried, barbeque, fried and in soups
Natto	Soybeans are soaked, cooked, and fermented with a rich source of probiotic	Strong fermented smell and gooey stringy texture (takes getting used to)	Can be eaten from the package with special sauce and mustard, added to grains, or topped with an egg
Seitan	Wheat gluten that has been shaped and cooked	Savory flavor and chewy texture. Its texture and protein content is close to meat.	Most like meat in texture. It can also pick up flavors very well. You can do anything with seitan that you can do with meat.

Successfully cooking with plant-based meat alternatives requires the addition of flavor, as by themselves the options have very little taste. What they lack in taste is more than made up for by their ability to absorb flavors like a sponge. You can turn the basic block of plant protein into anything. Listed below are some liquids and spices that can be used to marinate plant-based proteins, but the varieties and combinations are endless.

Table 9: Liquid Marinade Ingredients to Choose From

Sweet	Salty	Acid	Other
Orange, peach, or other fruit juice	Soy sauce	Lime juice	Heat — Sriracha
Maple syrup	Tamari	Lemon juice	Olive oil
Rice vinegar	Liquid aminos	Rice vinegar	Spices

Build a Marinade Spice Blend

Select a spice blend to add to the liquid(s) chosen from Table 9, which can transport the eater anywhere they want to go in the world. The basics are soy sauce, garlic powder, and onion powder. Feel free to experiment with the spices listed in Figure 2 or other favorites.

Figure 2: Spice Blends

Carribean	Taco	Thai	Italian
• Smoked paprika • Cinnamon • Nutmeg • Thyme • Garlic • Allspice • Ginger • Red pepper flakes • Black pepper	• Chili powder • Cumin • Sweet paprika • Red pepper flakes • Onion • Garlic • Oregano (Mexican) • Black pepper	• Turmeric • Cumin • Ginger • Dry mustard • Coriander • Cayenne • Fenugreek • Black pepper	• Sage • Basil • Thyme • Oregano (Italian) • Garlic • Black pepper

- For delicious spice blends, read <u>Ottolenghi's Flavor Cookbook.</u>
- <u>Skordo</u> has some amazing ready-made blends too.

Steps to Cooking With Tofu:

Step 1: **Press** to drain excess water from <u>firm or extra firm tofu</u> or tempeh only. This will allow it to pick up more flavors and become crispy when fried or baked. This step is optional and can be skipped when in a hurry. (Note: Tofu can also be frozen for up to three months).

- Drain the excess water
- Place tofu on a plate and wrap in a dish towel or paper towel

- Add a cutting board and add weight to it: a frying pan or other weighted object on top
- Let sit for up to 30 minutes and then it is ready to use — don't press for more than four hours

Step 2: **Marinate**. This is a critical step unless the tofu is to be eaten straight from the package, thrown in smoothies, or added to soups. When tofu will be cooked — baked, fried, grilled, stir-fried — marinate it first to pick up flavors.

- In a bowl or glass pan:
  - Add orange, lemon, or lime juice (or other liquid)
  - Add soy sauce (not much is needed)
  - Add spices
- Whisk together before adding sliced or cubed tofu or tempeh
- Let marinate for a minimum of 10 minutes; 30 minutes is better but no more than four hours

Step 3: **Select cooking method**:

- Bake at 400°F 204°C for 20 minutes on a dry baking sheet; flip halfway through
- Stir-fry in oil with vegetables
- Pan-fry with a tiny bit of oil; turn over when browned on one side. It is done when both sides are browned
- Place on a grill or BBQ and turn halfway through. Both sides should have brown grill marks
- Add to soups or stews but press first — there is no need to marinate it first as it will pick up the flavor of the soup or stew

Steps to Cooking With Tempeh:

1. **Steam** one inch cubed or sliced tempeh for 10 minutes. This helps to soften the tempeh to allow flavors from a marinade to seep in.
2. **Marinate** in liquid (see options below) for 30 minutes. Save marinade for another time or use it to add some extra sauce when the tempeh is cooked. It can also make a great sauce for stir-fry.
3. **Select your cooking method:**

    - **Bake** at 425° F for 20 minutes on parchment paper, turning over after 10 minutes
    - **Grill** on a lightly oiled grill for five to six minutes each side depending on the thickness. The steaming step can be skipped as a tougher texture is needed to hold up to grilling.
    - **Stir-fry** with vegetables in a wok lightly oiled until vegetables are crisp but tender

Steps to Cooking With Seitan:

Seitan is already cooked, and it just needs to be reheated. It has very little carbohydrate and fat unless it has been packaged in oil.

1. Open the package of pre-made seitan or make your own with vital wheat gluten (follow directions on package) and create the shape you are looking for.
    a. Crumbled to resemble hamburger meat — add a sloppy Joe sauce and it's ready to eat

b. Chunks can resemble beef stew meat and can be used in place of meat in stews and soups

    c. Lobes of seitan can be braised whole like pot roast in a mushroom-based sauce

2. It is important to keep seitan moist so that it can pick up flavors. When it dries out, its texture changes to a tough, chewy piece of meat alternative

A word on the new, highly processed, plant-based meat alternatives: *Beyond Beef* and *Beyond Meat* are made with pea protein, and the *Impossible Burger* is made with soy protein. These options are considered highly processed plant-based alternatives to beef burgers. Most are high in saturated fat (from coconut oil, a saturated fat) and contain more sodium than beef burgers. Dr. Gardner at Stanford Prevention Research Center, with support from *Beyond Meat*, conducted an eight-week trial whereby approximately 30 participants ate two servings a day of Beyond Beef or two servings a day of mostly red meat products. He and his team measured a marker for cardiovascular disease — trimethylamine N-oxide (TMAO) — and found it was lower when the participants were eating the plant-based meat product. Levels of LDL cholesterol were also lower in this group.

Our experts (mostly) agree — using plant-based processed alternatives can be a step in the right direction toward eating a whole food plant-based diet. There is concern about the absence of phytochemicals that a whole vegetable-made burger can provide versus these options made with a protein isolate derived from pea or soy. One of our experts reminded us that mock meat products have been used in Asia for centuries and are a part of their cuisine. For a great opinion piece, read Dr. Hu's opinion on Harvard's Nutrition Source.

BUILD A VEGETARIAN MEAL

The key to building a vegetarian meal is to combine whole grains, plant-based protein, and vegetables.

From the basics listed above, one can create a stir-fry, salad, grain bowl, stew, soup or roasted meal. Go to the chapter on Vegetables to learn how to cook and prepare delicious vegetables.

> **For meal and snack options see Appendix A**
> **For scrumptious vegan recipes see Appendix B**

SECTION 13: TIPS AND STRATEGIES FOR EATING A PLANT-BASED DIET

With accumulating scientific evidence supporting their health advantages, whole food, plant-based diets are steadily on the rise. Moving from the meat and potatoes diet to one that features whole plants often requires restructuring and the development of new skills. With practice and the accumulation of nutrition knowledge and a repertoire of recipes, this lifestyle becomes progressively easier. Here are some things to think about as one transitions to increasing the number of vegetables into their diet or moves to a plant-based eating pattern.

1. New to vegetarianism? **Start with the swap.** Take your favorite recipes and swap out beef and chicken for tofu, tempeh, or legumes. You want to ease into a plant-based diet especially if you are not used to consuming a lot of fiber — too much fiber too soon can cause gastrointestinal upset.
2. Don't let perfectionism be the enemy of good. Add more plant-based food into your diet. If you reach a place that feels good to you, stop there. Any additional plant-based food in your diet will promote health. **You don't have to be a vegan to see benefits.**
3. **Save money** by buying in bulk, purchasing dried legumes instead of in cans, and stocking up when items go on sale. If you are planning broccoli for dinner but find that green beans are on sale, feel free to adjust your recipe.

4. **Save time by cooking in bulk.** Cook a batch of grains, which can be frozen and removed right before meal preparation, or legumes, which can be prepared ahead of time and used throughout the week. It is also totally fine to use canned legumes if you don't have the time to soak and cook them.

5. **Prepare vegetables in batches.** Take one day where you cut up hard vegetables (carrots, peppers, cauliflower, broccoli, cabbage or celery, for example) and keep them in a zip-close bag with a paper towel in the bottom. You can add this mix during the week to make a salad or stir-fry, add to soups, roast or just snack on. This tip is guaranteed to increase your consumption of vegetables.

6. **Dilute.** If you are trying to switch to vegetarianism, dilute your meat dishes with legumes and vegetables. Try adding chickpeas to pasta dishes, black beans to taco meat, or cashews and beans to chili. Increase the number of plant-based ingredients over time and decrease meat products. Before you know it, you have transitioned into a vegetarian dish. This technique works with resistant family members.

7. **Focus on nutrients of concern**, including **vitamin B$_{12}$** (fortified foods such as cereals or soy products, or take a vitamin B$_{12}$ supplement), **iron** (fortified breakfast cereals, soybeans, beans, eggs and some dark leafy greens including spinach and chard, plus eat it with vitamin C foods like orange juice, lemons, and limes to increase absorption), and **calcium** (calcium-fortified soy milk/soy beverage, tofu made with calcium sulfate, calcium-fortified breakfast cereals and orange juice, and some dark-green leafy vegetables, including collard greens, turnip greens, mustard greens and bok choy).

8. **Use different cooking methods to bring out different tastes and flavors.** Compare the taste of carrots eaten raw, roasted, and stir-fried. Each method brings with it a different texture and flavor profile.

9. **Try plant-based meat alternatives.** A variety of vegetarian products look — and may taste — like their non-vegetarian counterparts but are usually lower in saturated fat and contain no cholesterol. For breakfast, try soy-based sausage patties or links. For dinner, rather than hamburgers, try bean burgers or falafel (chickpea patties). Just like their traditional counterparts, consume them occasionally as they are a processed product and may contain high amounts of sodium.

10. **Enjoy!** It takes time to learn how to cook scrumptious plant-based meals. Share recipes, go online to find new ones, and give yourself a break if at first you don't succeed. VIsit a vegetarian restaurant to get inspired.

SECTION 14: RESOURCES

WEBSITES

The internet has thousands of free vegan and vegetarian recipes. The websites listed below have excellent free recipes:

The Physicians Committee for Responsible Nutrition has many healthful vegan recipes

The Vegetarian Resource Group has many healthful vegan recipes

The American Institute for Cancer Research website has many plant food recipes

BOOKS

Blending Science with Spices*: Tasty Recipes & Nutrition Tips for Healthy Living* by Gita Patel, MS, RDN, mostly vegan, vegetarian and gluten-free; both as hard copy and e-book

Vegan Under Pressure by Jill Nussinow, MS, RDN

The New Fast Food*: The Veggie Queen Pressure Cooks Whole Food Meals* by Jill Nussinow, MS, RDN

Nutrition Champs*: The Veggie Queen's Guide to Eating & Cooking for Optimum Health, Happiness, Energy & Vitality* by Jill Nussinow, MS, RDN

The Veggie Queen*: Vegetables Get the Royal Treatment* by Jill Nussinow, MS, RDN

The Plant-Powered Diet by Sharon Palmer, RDN

Vegan for Life by Jack Norris, RDN, and Virginia Messina, MPH, RDN

Vegetarian Planet*: 350 Big-Flavor Recipes for Out-of-This-World Food Every Day* by Didi Emmons

The Greens Cookbook*: Extraordinary Vegetarian Cuisine* by Deborah Madison with Edward Espe Brown

Spinach and Beyond*, Loving Life & Dark Green Leafy Vegetables: A Cookbook* by Linda Diane Feldt

Vegetarian Health Recipes by Patricia and Paul Bragg

The Power of Your Plate by Neal D. Barnard, MD

Greene on Greens & Grains*: Over 850 Incomparable and Inventive Recipes for the Crispiest, Freshest Greens and Most Richly Textured Grains* by Bert Greene

The Schwarzbein Principle Vegetarian Cookbook by Diana Schwarzbein, MD, Nancy Deville, and Evelyn Jacob Jaffe

The World's Healthiest Foods by George Mateljan (has many vegetarian and vegan recipes)

The Plant Power Way: Whole Food Plant-Based Recipes and Guidance for the Whole Family: A Cookbook by Rich Roll and Julie Piatt

SUMMARY

Over the last decade there has been an incredible amount of research that has supported shifting toward a plant-based eating approach due to the prevalence of many chronic diseases that are on the rise today. Many respected health institutions recommend reducing consumption of animal products, especially red meat, while increasing plant-based foods; these institutions include the American Institute of Cancer Research, the American Heart Association, the Academy of Nutrition & Dietetics and the 2015 and 2020 Dietary Guidelines Advisory Committee.

The good news is that one does not need to be a total vegan or vegetarian to confer the health benefits that come from a diet full of vegetables, whole grains, and fruit. Just moving closer to a plant-based diet is very beneficial for health, as well as prevention and management of chronic disease.

APPENDIX A: Meal and Snack Vegetarian Options

Breakfast Options

1. Serve leftovers, cold or reheated
2. Try sliced apple or banana with a dollop of nut butter such as almond, peanut, cashew, sunflower, soy, hazelnut, peanut or pistachio
3. Add mixed nuts and dried or fresh fruit to yogurt or oatmeal
4. Make smoothies in the blender out of silken tofu, milk, juice or water, fruit and ground flaxseed
5. Create a roll-up: Take a whole grain tortilla, spread with nut butter, add sliced fruit or a banana, nuts and seeds, roll and go...

Lunch Options

1. Build your salad around half a cup of beans, adding any combination of mixed mesclun greens, baby spinach, avocado, fruit, sesame or ground flaxseeds, vegetables, nuts, scallions or grated carrots. Now dress it with your favorite dressing.
2. On the weekend, roast any combination of the following vegetables: beets, carrots, eggplant, yellow and green zucchini, winter squash, Brussels sprouts, asparagus, turnips, colored peppers, cauliflower, onion, garlic, sweet potatoes, yams or green beans. Enjoy roasted vegetables with a simple olive oil and balsamic vinegar dressing, salted and peppered to taste, or topped with another favorite dressing. Add a few cooked beans from the freezer or open a can and add a sprinkle of toasted sunflower, pumpkin, poppy, sesame or ground flaxseeds.
3. Make a quick salad out of cooked chickpeas, sliced tomatoes, cilantro or parsley, lime or lemon juice, ground cumin, salt, pepper, scallions and avocado.

4. Make a quick soup, adding some tofu, fresh or frozen spinach, garlic, ginger, or any other herbs or spices to a miso-and-water broth.
5. Make another quick soup with V8 vegetable juice, cooked beans, spices and herbs.
6. Build a salad using your favorite dressing on a mixture of greens (lettuce, spinach), beans, vegetables, nuts or seeds and grilled tofu or tempeh.
7. Make grain-based salads: Sprinkle sesame or sunflower seeds, vegetables, herbs and spices on either cooked millet, barley, quinoa, couscous, bulgur or rice, and top with your favorite dressing.
8. Add cooked edamame to garden salads.
9. Make a stew — a vegetarian chili, black bean stew, mixed vegetables with beans,
   spinach-lentil or split pea stew by adding water, herbs, and spices.
10. Serve hummus sandwiches with roasted vegetables or a green salad.
11. Make black bean burritos with vegetables on the side.
12. Make soups or casseroles from mixed grains, vegetables, herbs and spices.
13. Prepare sandwiches with hummus, tempeh or marinated tofu, grilled vegetables or baby greens.
14. Mix grilled vegetables with beans, tofu, or tempeh. Serve Mexican beans in tortillas with lettuce and tomato — simple and delicious.
15. Leftovers can always be served with vegetables and fruit.
16. Top a baked or steamed potato with beans and salsa.
17. Combine edamame with pesto and serve over rice or any other grain — or add corn to the edamame with pesto and make that a lunch!
18. Serve steamed or microwaved vegetables with hummus or pesto.
19. Make vegetable stir-fry with tofu or edamame beans.
20. Make a salad with greens, vegetables, avocado, nuts, edamame or other beans, fruit or roasted beets.
21. Roasted vegetables can be served over rice or any grain or bean or in a pita pocket.
22. Ground flax or sesame seeds may be sprinkled on just about any food.

Dinner

1. Quick one-dish meal: a combination of beans, grains, vegetables and greens. Make the meal colorful and add flavor with herbs, spices, nuts and fruits.
2. Make a salad out of lightly steamed vegetables mixed with tofu cubes, a grain or pasta, and a favorite dressing.
3. Mix tomato sauce, kidney beans, corn, ground cumin, chopped cilantro and chili powder for a quick stew.

4. Top rice or any other cooked grain with cooked pinto, kidney, or black beans, chopped tomatoes, chopped cilantro or parsley, or even salsa
5. Add a tomato-based sauce to pureed beans. This will add texture and richness to a quick low-fat soup, stew, or other cooked dish.
6. Try a vegetable stir-fry: vegetables, tofu, tempeh or beans with herbs and spices served over a grain such as rice, millet, barley, corn grits, quinoa or even a baked potato.
7. Mix cold cooked Japanese soba noodles with edamame, shredded carrots, julienned pepper, and seeded cucumber strips and toss with a tasty peanut sesame dressing.
8. Fill soft tacos or taco shells with beans and vegetables.
9. Mix grains with pesto, hummus, nut butter or a favorite sauce or dressing and some
heated frozen kale or other greens.
10. Stir some pesto or a favorite sauce or dressing into thawed frozen leftover lentils
or beans.
11. A quick miso soup with tofu or tempeh — add some garlic and greens to the soup.

Snacks

1. Roasted chickpeas or nuts
2. Fruit (fresh or dried) with a few nuts
3. Serve vegetables with hummus
4. Bean dip and salsa with baked tortilla chips
5. Air-popped popcorn
6. Fruit with plain yogurt
7. Cooked or reheated edamame in the pod or shelled, hot or cold
8. Snack mix made from a combination of dried fruit, nuts, seeds and chocolate chips
9. Pack celery stalks with nut butter (peanut, sunflower, almond, cashew, etc.) and
raisins
10. Crackers with hummus or almond butter or any other nut butter
11. Pair an apple or banana with almond or peanut butter

APPENDIX B: Recipes

Tempeh Quinoa Stuffed Poblano Pepper
By Chef Russell — TheCulinaryArchitect.com

Ingredients

2 each	Pepper, poblano or pasilla
1 teaspoon	Olive oil
½ oz.	Onion, yellow, diced
¼ oz.	Garlic, minced
2 oz.	Ground tempeh
1 teaspoon	Adobo spice
2 oz.	Red quinoa
1 oz.	Zucchini, diced
½ oz.	Cherry tomatoes, cut in half
1 oz.	Avocado, peeled, diced
½ oz.	Cranberries, dried
1 teaspoon	Parsley, chopped
1 teaspoon	Cilantro, chopped
¼ teaspoon	Lemon zest
1 oz.	Vegan parmesan cheese (recipe below)

Preparation

1. Cook the quinoa by adding the grain to boiling water. Cook until white threads begin showing. Drain the quinoa and place on a tray to cool at room temperature.

2. Fire-roast the chili peppers whole. Blacken all sides of the peppers. Once the entire outer portion of the chili peppers are charred, place in a bowl, covering with plastic wrap. Allow to steam in the bowl for 10 to 15 minutes.

3. While the chilies are steaming, place the olive oil in a sauté pan over medium heat. Add the onion and garlic to the pan, cooking for approximately four minutes or until the onion becomes translucent, making sure not to burn the garlic.

4. Add the tempeh to the pan, heating the tempeh, stirring consistently, for approximately three minutes. Set aside in the pan.

5. Prepare tomato, zucchini, and avocado to recipe specifications.

6. Prepare the herbs and zest. Weigh the cranberries.

7. In a mixing bowl, place all ingredients, except the peppers, and mix well.

8. Peel the black skins from the peppers. Easier when peeling over slow running water over the sink. Make a straight incision along the top of the peppers ½ inch from the stem to ½ inch from the end. Gently open the pocket of the pepper and remove the seeds. Rinse the pocket out.

9. Stuff the pocket of the peppers with the filling.

10. Bake at 350° F/177 °C degrees for 12 to 15 minutes.

11. This can be served with a tomato sauce to lighten the heat of the chili pepper.

12. Sprinkle the grated cheese over the peppers if desired and garnish with cilantro leaves.

Vegan "parmesan cheese"

Ingredients

¼ cup	Almonds, sliced, raw, no skin
¼ cup	Cashews, raw
¼ teaspoon	Garlic granules
¼ teaspoon	Onion powder
¼ cup	Nutritional yeast
Pinch	Salt, sea or Himalayan

Preparation

1. Place the nuts into a spice grinder. Grind to a powder.

2. Place the ground nuts into a mixing bowl.

3. Add remaining ingredients. Mix well.

Southwest Grilled Tofu with Avocado Chimichurri
By Chef Russell — TheCulinaryArchitect.com

Servings: 2

Ingredients

8 oz.	Tofu, extra firm, pressed
1 teaspoon	Southwestern spice rub
¼ cup	Orange juice
1 tablespoon	Lime juice
Pinch	Zest, orange, microplaned
Pinch	Salt, Himalayan
Pinch	Pepper, black
1 ea.	Tomato, heirloom, large, sliced
4 oz.	Avocado chimichurri (component recipe)
4 oz.	Morita chili barbecue sauce (component recipe)
6 each	Cilantro, sprigs

Preparation

1. Marinate the tofu in Southwestern spice rub, juices, and zest for a minimum of four hours.
2. Preheat grill on high for 10 minutes, ensuring the grill grates are very hot.
3. Preheat oven to 350° F/177° C.
4. Once marinating is complete, remove tofu from the marinade, patting dry with a paper towel. Reserve the marinade.
5. Spray the grill and the tofu with non-stick canola spray as tofu is very low in fat and will stick to the grill.
6. Season the tofu with salt and pepper on both sides.

7. For grill marks, lay one side of the tofu on the grill to an angle so one grill grate is lined up on the top and bottom tips of the tofu. Allow the tofu to grill for approximately one minute. *See Chef's Note.*

8. With a pair of tongs, gently check to ensure the tofu is not stuck to the grates. Turn over the tofu following the same positioning on the reverse side. Allow the tofu to grill for one minute.

9. Check to ensure the tofu is not stuck to the grate, then turn the tofu over to the original side. Prior to placing on the grill, place the opposite two points on the grill grate in order to make a square grill mark. Cook for one minute ensuring you have a nice mark.

10. Follow this step on the reverse side.

11. By using the reserved marinade, brush the tofu on the completed side with the square markings.

12. After grill marks are complete on both sides, remove the tofu from the grill, placing on a non-stick pan basted side down. Brush the marinade on the other side of the tofu and place in the oven for five to seven minutes.

Chef's Note: All grills cook differently. Cooking times may vary based upon the grill temperatures. The markings should be deep in color but not charred.

Plating Guide

Place two thick slices of the tomatoes on the center of the plate. Slice the tofu in ½-inch-thick slices resting atop the tomatoes. Dress the tofu with the morita chili barbecue sauce, top with avocado chimichurri, and garnish with cilantro leaves for a fresh vibrant appearance.

Avocado Chimichurri

Ingredients (serves 8)

2 oz.	Cilantro, fresh, chopped
2 oz.	Parsley, fresh, bunch, chopped
¼ oz.	Garlic, fresh, minced
¼ teaspoon	Chili flakes, red
2 oz.	Vinegar, red wine
2 oz.	Olive oil
¼ teaspoon	Salt, sea or Himalayan
¼ teaspoon	Pepper, black, ground
2 each	Avocado, fresh, diced

Preparation

1. Combine cilantro, parsley, garlic, chili flakes and vinegar in a food processor.
2. Pulse the ingredients six times.
3. Turn on medium low; slowly add the oil until fully incorporated.
4. Transfer to a mixing bowl.
5. Add the diced avocado, salt, and pepper. Fold the avocado into the herb mixture gently until fully incorporated. Try not to mash the avocado during this process.
6. Place in an airtight container and cover the top surface of the mixture with plastic wrap to avoid oxidation; Cryovacing is best if an option. Store at 40° F or less for up to six days.

Morita Chili Barbecue Sauce
By Chef Russell — TheCulinaryArchitect.com

Ingredients

1 oz.	Olive oil
3 oz.	Shallots, chopped
1 oz.	Garlic, minced
12 oz.	Tomato sauce
6 oz.	Molasses
6 oz.	Prickly pear puree
5 oz.	Pineapple, peeled, diced
1 oz.	Mustard, yellow
2 oz.	Mustard, Dijon
4 oz.	Worcestershire sauce
½ oz.	Morita chili, ground
1 teaspoon	Oregano, dry
1 teaspoon	Thyme, leaves only
3 oz.	Apple cider vinegar
3 oz.	Water
1 teaspoon	Sea salt
1 teaspoon	Black pepper

Preparation

1. Place the oil in a preheated pot over medium high heat.
2. Add the shallots, sautéing for three minutes, stirring frequently.
3. Add the garlic, sautéing for one minute.
4. Add the tomato sauce, molasses, prickly pear puree, pineapple, mustards, Worcestershire sauce, morita chili, herbs, vinegar and water. Bring to a boil then reduce to simmer.
5. Allow to simmer for 30 minutes.
6. Blend well with an immersion blender until smooth.
7. Season with salt and black pepper.

8. Remove from heat and keep warm.

9. You can store for six days in the refrigerator if the temperature is 40°F or lower, or you can freeze up to one year.

Beet Hummus
By Chef Russell — TheCulinaryArchitect.com

Ingredients

10 oz   Roasted red beets (gold can be substituted)
15 oz   Chickpeas (garbanzo beans), drained, liquid reserved
2 tablespoons   Juice, lemon, fresh
1 teaspoon   Zest, lemon, microplaned
2 tablespoons Tahini
1 teaspoon   Garlic, fresh
¼ teaspoon   Cumin, powder
1 teaspoon   Tarragon, fresh, leaves only, chopped
½ teaspoon   Himalayan salt
¼ teaspoon   Black pepper
1 oz   Olive oil

Preparation

1. Gather all ingredients and equipment needed prior to starting the recipe.
2. Preheat oven to 375° F.
3. Wash the beets well.
4. Wrap the beets securely in foil with olive oil, salt, and pepper.
5. Roast until tender, approximately 40 minutes.
6. Allow cooling to room temperature; peel and remove stems.
7. While the beets are cooling, prepare the hummus base.
8. In a blender or food processor, place the chickpeas, lemon juice, lemon zest, tahini, garlic and cumin; blend to fully incorporate all ingredients. If the mixture is too thick to blend, add a small amount of the chickpea liquid. *Careful not to add too much as the beets will add moisture when they are added. Adding too much liquid will cause the hummus to be thin; add more at the end if needed for desired consistency.*

9. While blending on high speed, add the oil slowly until fully incorporated.
10. Once the hummus is smooth, place into a mixing bowl.
11. Chop 4 oz. of the beets and place into the blender or food processor blending until smooth. Reserve the remaining beets for the presentation.
12. Once the beets are smooth, add the tarragon, pulsing six times.
13. Pour beet mixture into the hummus, mixing well with a whisk.
14. Store the hummus up to six days under refrigeration at 40° F or lower. Do not freeze.

Individual plate presentation

3 oz.	Roasted beet hummus
3 oz.	Roasted beets, large pieces
2 oz.	Orange, segments or slices, peeled
4 each	Belgian endive
1 oz.	Watercress, red if available
1 teaspoon	Parsley, Italian, chopped fine
1 tablespoon	Olive oil
Pinch	Salt and black pepper
1 tablespoon	Pistachios, toasted, ground

Place the hummus on the plate in a circular shape; place the roasted beets in the middle of the hummus; place the oranges on top of the beets; toss the endive, watercress, and parsley with the olive oil and light dusting of salt and black pepper. Place the salad atop the beets and oranges, arranging them so all ingredients may be visible. Sprinkle the ground pistachios over the top. Enjoy!

REFERENCES

Academy of Nutrition and Dietetics. RD Resources from the Vegetarian Nutrition Dietetic practice group of the Academy of Nutrition and Dietetics.

Aghajafari F, Letourneau N, Mahinpey N, Cosic N, Giesbrecht G. Vitamin D Deficiency and Antenatal and Postpartum Depression: A Systematic Review. Nutrients. 2018 Apr 12;10(4).

American Diabetes Association. 2021. Available from: https://www.diabetes.org/

American Dietetic Association, Dietitians of Canada. Position of the American Dietetic Association and Dietitians of Canada: vegetarian diets. J Am Diet Assoc 2003;103:748-65. [PubMed abstract]

Amre DK, D'Souza S, Morgan K, Seidman G, Lambrette P, Grimard G, Israel D, Mack D, Ghadirian P, Deslandres C, et al. Imbalances in dietary consumption of fatty acids, vegetables, and fruits are associated with risk for Crohn's disease in children. Am J Gastroenterol. 2007;102:2016–2025. [PubMed] [Google Scholar]

Ananthakrishnan AN, Khalili H, Konijeti GG, Higuchi LM, de Silva P, Korzenik JR, Fuchs CS, Willett WC, Richter JM, Chan AT. A prospective study of long-term intake of dietary fiber and risk of Crohn's disease and ulcerative colitis. Gastroenterology. 2013;145:970–977. [PMC free article] [PubMed] [Google Scholar]

Anderson J.W., Blake J.E., Turner J., Smith B.M. Effects of soy protein on renal function and proteinuria in patients with type 2 diabetes. Am. J. Clin. Nutr. 1998;68:1347S–1353S. [PubMed] [Google Scholar]

Andres E, Federici L, Serraj K, Kaltenbach G. Update of nutrient-deficiency anemia in elderly patients. Eur J Intern Med. 2008;19:488–493. [PubMed] [Google Scholar]

Anon. (2012) Thomson Reuters–NPR Health Poll: Meat Consumption 2012, March 2012. https://truvenhealth.com/portals/0/NPR-Truven-Health-Poll/NPR_report_MeatConsumption_1203.pdf (accessed February 2018).

Aparicio M., Chauveau P., de Précigout V., Bouchet J.L., Lasseur C., Combe C. Nutrition and outcome on renal replacement therapy of patients with chronic renal failure treated with supplemented very low-protein diet. J. Am. Soc. Nephrol. 2000;11:708–716. [PubMed] [Google Scholar]

Appleby P, Roddam A, Allen N, Key T. Comparative fracture risk in vegetarians and nonvegetarians in EPIC-Oxford. Eur J Clin Nutr. 2007 Dec;61(12):1400-6. [PubMed abstract]

Aston LM, Smith JN, Powles JW. Impact of a reduced red and processed meat dietary pattern on disease risks and greenhouse gas emissions in the UK: a modelling study. BMJ Open. 2012;2(5):e001072 10.1136/bmjopen-2012-001072 [PMC free article] [PubMed] [CrossRef] [Google Scholar]

Aune D, Chan DS, Greenwood DC, et al. Dietary fiber and breast cancer risk: a systematic review and meta-analysis of prospective studies. *Ann Oncol.* 2012;23(6):1394–1402.

Aune D, Norat T, Romundstad P, Vatten LJ. Whole grain and refined grain consumption and the risk of type 2 diabetes: a systematic review and dose-response meta-analysis of cohort studies. Eur J Epidemiol. 2013 Nov;28(11):845-58. doi: 10.1007/s10654-013-9852-5. Epub 2013 Oct 25. PMID: 24158434.

Azadbakht L., Atabak S., Esmaillzadek A. Soy protein intake, cardiorenal indices, and C reactive protein in type II diabetes with nephropathy; a longitudinal randomized clinical trial. Diabetes Care. 2008;31:648–654. doi: 10.2337/dc07-2065. [PubMed] [CrossRef] [Google Scholar]

Barclay E & Aubrey A (2016) Eat less meat, we're told. But Americans' habits are slow to change. *The Salt*, 26 February. http://www.npr.org/sections/thesalt/2016/02/26/465431695/eat-less-meat-were-told-but-americans-habits-are-slow-to-change (accessed February 2018).

Barnard ND, Cohen J, Jenkins DJ, et al. A low-fat vegan diet and a conventional diabetes diet in the treatment of type 2 diabetes: A randomized, controlled, 74-wk clinical trial. Am J Clin Nutr 2009;89:1588s–96s.

Barnard ND, Levin SM, Yokoyama Y. A systematic review and meta-analysis of changes in body weight in clinical trials of vegetarian diets. J Acad Nutr Diet 2015;115:954–69.

Barsotti G., Morelli E., Cupisti A., Meola M., Dani L., Giovannetti S. A low-nitrogen low-phosphorous vegan diet for patients with chronic renal failure. Nephron. 1996;74:390–394. doi: 10.1159/000189341. [PubMed] [CrossRef] [Google Scholar]

Bartolomaeus H, Balogh A, Yakoub M, Homann S, Markó L, Höges S, Tsvetkov Y, Krannich A, Wundersitz S, Avery EG, Haase N, Kräker K, Hering L, Maase M, Kusche-Vihrog K, Grandoch M, Fielitz J, Kempa S, Gollasch M, Zhumadilov Z, Kozhakhmetov S, Kushugulova A, Eckardt K, Dechend R, Rump LC, Forslund SK, Müller DN, Stegbauer J, Wilck N. Circulation. 2019 Mar 12; 139(11): 1407–1421. doi: 10.1161/CIRCULATIONAHA.118.036652 ; PMCID: PMC6416008 PMID: 30586752 Short-Chain Fatty Acid Propionate Protects From Hypertensive Cardiovascular Damage.

Basson A. Nutrition management in the adult patient with Crohn's disease. S Afr J Clin Nutr. 2012;25:164–172. [Google Scholar]

Battson ML, Lee DM, Weir TL, Gentile CL. The gut microbiota as a novel regulator of cardiovascular function and disease. J Nutr Biochem. 2018 Jun;56:1-15. doi: 10.1016/j.jnutbio.2017.12.010. Epub 2017 Dec 27. PMID: 29427903.

Becerra-Tomás N, Díaz-López A, Rosique-Esteban N, Ros E, Buil-Cosiales P, Corella D, Estruch R, Fitó M, Serra-Majem Ll, Arós F, Lamuela-Raventós R.M, Fiol M, Santos-Lozano J.M, Diez-Espino J, Portoles O, Salas-Salvadó J, PREDIMED study investigators. "Legume consumption is inversely associated with type 2 diabetes incidence in adults: a prospective assessment from the PREDIMED study". Clinical Nutrition (2017). http://dx.doi.org/10.1016/j.clnu.2017.03.015.

Bergmeier H, Gkouteris H, Hetherington H. Systematic research review of observational approaches used to evaluate mother-child mealtime interactions during preschool years. Am J Clin Nutr. 2015;101:7-15. Abstract available from: https://www.ncbi.nlm.nih.gov/pubmed/25527745

Blanco Mejia S, Kendall CW, Viguiliouk E, et al. Effect of tree nuts onmetabolic syndrome criteria: A systematic reviewand meta-analysis of randomised controlled trials. BMJ Open 2014;4:e004660.

Boye J., Wijesinha-Bettoni R., Burlingame B. Protein quality evaluation twenty years after the introduction of the protein digestibility corrected amino acid score method. Br. J. Nutr. 2012;108:S183–S211. doi: 10.1017/S0007114512002309. [PubMed] [CrossRef] [Google Scholar]

Brial F, Le Lay A, Dumas ME, Gauguier D. Implication of gut microbiota metabolites in cardiovascular and metabolic diseases. Cell Mol Life Sci. 2018 Nov;75(21):3977-3990. doi: 10.1007/s00018-018-2901-1. Epub 2018 Aug 12. PMID: 30101405; PMCID: PMC6182343.

Brotherton CS, Taylor AG, Bourguignon C, Anderson JG. A high-fiber diet may improve bowel function and health-related quality of life in patients with Crohn disease. Gastroenterol Nurs. 2014;37:206–216. [PMC free article] [PubMed] [Google Scholar]

Brown L, Rosner B, Willett WW, Sacks FM. Cholesterol-lowering effects of dietary fiber: a meta-analysis. Am J Clin Nutr. 1999 Jan;69(1):30-42. doi: 10.1093/ajcn/69.1.30. PMID: 9925120.

Cahill N, PhD. Postpartum Women: A neglected population in dietetics? Presented at the Dietitians of Canada National Conference, Ottawa, Canada. 2019 June 8.

Carmel R. Nutritional anemias and the elderly. Semin Hematol. 2008;45:225–234. [PubMed] [Google Scholar]

Centers for Disease Control (CDC). Leading causes of death. 2021, January 12. Available from: https://www.cdc.gov/nchs/fastats/leading-causes-of-death.htm

Chauveau P, Koppe L, Combe C, Lasseur C, Trolonge S, Aparicio M. Vegetarian diets and chronic kidney disease. Nephrol Dial Transplant. 2019 Feb 1;34(2):199-207. doi: 10.1093/ndt/gfy164. PMID: 29982610.

Chiba M, Abe T, Tsuda H, Sugawara T, Tsuda S, Tozawa H, Fujiwara K, Imai H. Lifestyle-related disease in Crohn's disease: relapse prevention by a semi-vegetarian diet. World J Gastroenterol. 2010;16:2484–2495. [PMC free article] [PubMed] [Google Scholar]

Clarys P., Deliens T., Huybrechts I., Deriemaeker P., Vanaelst B., De Keyzer W., Hebbelinck M., Mullie P. Comparison of nutritional quality of the vegan, vegetarian, semi-vegetarian, pesco-vegetarian and omnivorous diet. Nutrients. 2014;6:1318–1332. doi: 10.3390/nu6031318. [PMC free article] [PubMed] [CrossRef] [Google Scholar]

Committee to Review Dietary Reference Intakes for Vitamin D and Calcium, Food and Nutrition Board, Institute of Medicine. Dietary Reference Intakes for Calcium and Vitamin D. Washington, DC: National Academy Press, 2010.

Cooper MJ, Cockell KA, L'Abbé MR. The iron status of Canadian adolescents and adults: Current knowledge and practical implications. Can J Diet Pract. 2006; 67(3):130-8.

Cresci GA, Bawden E. Gut Microbiome: What We Do and Don't Know. *Nutr Clin Pract.* 2015;30(6):734-746. doi:10.1177/0884533615609899

Davis M and Schor J. Fiber Feeds Bacteria to Control Type 2 Diabetes Mellitus; Investigators pit high-fiber diet against standard diet for glycemic control; August 2018 Vol. 10 Issue 81 2018 Microbiome Special Issue.

DeMartino P, Cockburn DW. Resistant starch: impact on the gut microbiome and health. Curr Opin Biotechnol. 2020 Feb;61:66-71. doi: 10.1016/j.copbio.2019.10.008. Epub 2019 Nov 22. PMID: 31765963.

Diabetes Canada Clinical Practice Guidelines Expert Committee. *Diabetes Canada 2018 Clinical Practice Guidelines for the Prevention and Management of Diabetes in Canada.* Can J Diabetes. 2018;42(Suppl 1):S1-S325.

Dibb S & Fitzpatrick I (2014) Let's Talk about Meat: Changing Dietary Behaviour for the 21st Century. UK: Eating Better. [Google Scholar]

Dinu M, Abbate R, Gensini GF, Casini A, Sofi F. Vegetarian, vegan diets and multiple health outcomes: a systematic review with meta-analysis of observational studies. Crit Rev Food Sci Nutr. 2016 [PubMed] [Google Scholar]

Dror DK, Allen LH. Effect of vitamin B12 deficiency on neurodevelopment in infants: current knowledge and possible mechanisms. Nutr Rev. 2008;66:250–255. [PubMed] [Google Scholar]

Dufour AB, Hannan MT, Murabito JM, et al. Sarcopenia definitions considering body size and fat mass are associated with mobility limitations: The Framingham Study. J Gerontol A Biol Sci Med Sci. 2012 Epub ahead of print. [PMC free article] [PubMed] [Google Scholar]

Elliott P., Stamler J., Dyer A.R., Appel L., Dennis B., Kesteloot H., Ueshima H., Okayama A., Chan Q., Garside D.B., et al. Association between Protein intake and blood pressure. Arch. Intern. Med. 2006;166:79–87. doi: 10.1001/archinte.166.1.79. [PMC free article] [PubMed] [CrossRef] [Google Scholar]

Erdogan A, Rao SS, Thiruvaiyaru D, Lee YY, Coss Adame E, Valestin J, O'Banion M. Randomised clinical trial: mixed soluble/insoluble fibre vs. psyllium for chronic constipation. Aliment Pharmacol Ther. 2016 Jul;44(1):35-44. doi: 10.1111/apt.13647. Epub 2016 Apr 29. PMID: 27125883; PMCID: PMC4891216.

Esposito K, Maiorino MI, Ceriello A, et al. Prevention and control of type 2 diabetes by Mediterranean diet: A systematic review. Diabetes Res Clin Pract 2010;89:97–102.

Fraser GE. Vegetarian diets: what do we know of their effects on common chronic diseases? Am J Clin Nutr. 2009;89:1607S–1612S. [PMC free article] [PubMed] [Google Scholar]

Federico A., Cardaioli E., Da Pozzo P., Formichi P., Gallus G.N., Radi E. Mitochondria, oxidative stress and neurodegeneration. J. Neurol. Sci. 2012 doi: 10.1016/j.jns.2012.05.030. [PubMed] [CrossRef] [Google Scholar]

Fernández-Bañares F, Hinojosa J, Sánchez-Lombraña JL, Navarro E, Martínez-Salmerón JF, García-Pugés A, González-Huix F, Riera J, González-Lara V, Domínguez-Abascal F, et al. Randomized clinical trial of Plantago ovata seeds (dietary fiber) as compared with mesalamine in maintaining remission in ulcerative colitis. Spanish Group for the Study of Crohn's Disease and Ulcerative Colitis (GETECCU) Am J Gastroenterol. 1999;94:427–433. [PubMed] [Google Scholar]

Fernández-Ballart J, Murphy MM. Preventive nutritional supplementation throughout the reproductive life cycle. Publ Health Nutr. 2001; 4(6A):1363-6.

FGI Research Inc. (2014) FGI Survey Report 2014 Monday Effect Online Panel. Durham, NC: FGI Research. [Google Scholar]

Flint HJ, Duncan SH, Scott KP, Louis P. Links between diet, gut microbiota composition and gut metabolism. Proc Nutr Soc 2015; 74:13-22; PMID:25268552; http://dx.doi.org/10.1017/S0029665114001463 [PubMed] [CrossRef] [Google Scholar]

Food and Nutrition Board, Institute of Medicine. Dietary Reference Intakes for thiamin, riboflavin, niacin, vitamin B6, folate, vitamin B12, pantothenic acid, biotin, and choline. Washington, D.C.: The National Academies Press; 1998. Available from: http://www.nap.edu/openbook.php?isbn=0309065542

Galloway AT, Fiorito LM, Francis LA, Birch LL. 'Finish your soup': counterproductive effects of pressuring children to eat on intake and affect. Appetite. 2006 May; 46(3):318-23. Epub 2006 Apr 19. Abstract available from: https://www.ncbi.nlm.nih.gov/pubmed/16626838

Gardner C.D., Hartle J.C., Garrett R.D., Offringa L.C., Wasserman A.S. Maximizing the intersection of human health and the health of the environment with regard to the amount and type of protein produced and consumed in the United States. Nutr. Rev. 2019;77:197–215. doi: 10.1093/nutrit/nuy073. [PMC free article] [PubMed] [CrossRef] [Google Scholar]

Gluba-Brzózka A, Franczyk B, Rysz J. Vegetarian Diet in Chronic Kidney Disease- A Friend or Foe. *Nutrients*. 2017;9(4):374. Published 2017 Apr 10. doi:10.3390/nu9040374

Godfray HCJ, Aveyard P, Garnett T, Hall JW, Key TJ, Lorimer J, et al. Meat consumption, health, and the environment. Science. 2018;361(6399):eaam5324 10.1126/science.aam5324 [PubMed] [CrossRef] [Google Scholar]

Godos J, Bella F, Sciacca S, Galvano F, Grosso G. Vegetarianism and breast, colorectal and prostate cancer risk: an overview and meta-analysis of cohort studies. J Hum Nutr Diet. 2017 Jun;30(3):349-59. doi: 10.1111/jhn.12426. Epub 2016 Oct 6. Abstract available from: https://www.ncbi.nlm.nih.gov/pubmed

Gear JS, Brodribb AJ, Ware A, Mann JI. Fibre and bowel transit times. Br J Nutr. 1981 Jan;45(1):77-82. doi: 10.1079/bjn19810078. PMID: 6258626.

Gunness P, Gidley MJ. Mechanisms underlying the cholesterol-lowering properties of soluble dietary fibre polysaccharides. Food Funct. 2010 Nov;1(2):149-55. doi: 10.1039/c0fo00080a. Epub 2010 Sep 30. PMID: 21776465.

Ha V, de Souza RJ. "Fleshing Out" the Benefits of Adopting a Vegetarian Diet. *J Am Heart Assoc*. 2015;4(10):e002654. Published 2015 Oct 27. doi:10.1161/JAHA.115.002654

Ha V, Sievenpiper JL, de Souza RJ, et al. Effect of dietary pulse intake on established therapeutic lipid targets for cardiovascular risk reduction: A systematic reviewandmeta-analysis of randomized controlled trials. CMAJ 2014;186:E252–62.

Haddad EH, Tanzman JS. What do vegetarians in the United States eat? Am J Clin Nutr. 2003;78:626S–632S. [PubMed] [Google Scholar]

Hallert C, Kaldma M, Petersson BG. Ispaghula husk may relieve gastrointestinal symptoms in ulcerative colitis in remission. Scand J Gastroenterol. 1991;26:747–750. [PubMed] [Google Scholar]

Halkjaer J., Olsen A., Bjerregaard L.J., Deharveng G., Tjonneland A., Welch A.A., Crowe F.L., Wirfalt E., Hellstrom V., Niravong M., et al. Intake of total, animal and plant proteins, and their food sources in 10 countries in the European prospective investigation into cancer and nutrition. Eur. J. Clin. Nutr. 2009;63:S16–S36. doi: 10.1038/ejcn.2009.73. [PubMed] [CrossRef] [Google Scholar]

Hartley L, May MD, Loveman E, Colquitt JL, Rees K. Dietary fibre for the primary prevention of cardiovascular disease. *Cochrane Database Syst Rev.* 2016;(1):CD011472.

Health Canada. Eating well with Canada's food guide. Ottawa (ON): Health Canada; 2007. Available from: https://www.canada.ca/en/health-canada/services/canada-food-guides.html

Health Canada (2019). Canada's Food Guide. Canada's Dietary Guidelines. Created January 22, 2019. Available from: https://food-guide.canada.ca/en/guidelines/

Health Canada. Dietary Reference Intakes. Reference values for vitamins. Ottawa (ON): Health Canada; 2010. Available from: https://www.canada.ca/en/health-canada/services/food-nutrition/healthy-eating/dietary-reference-intakes/tables/reference-values-vitamins-dietary-reference-intakes-tables-2005.html

Health Canada. Eating well with Canada's food guide. Ottawa (ON): Health Canada; 2007. Available from: https://www.canada.ca/en/health-canada/services/canada-food-guides.html

Health Canada. Prenatal guidelines for health professionals - iron contributes to a healthy pregnancy. 2009. Available from: https://www.canada.ca/en/health-canada/services/food-nutrition/reports-publications/nutrition-healthy-eating/prenatal-nutrition-guidelines-health-professionals-iron-contributes-healthy-pregnancy-2009.html

Hemler EC, Hu FB. Plant-Based Diets for Personal, Population, and Planetary Health. Adv Nutr. 2019 Nov 1;10(Suppl_4):S275-S283. doi: 10.1093/advances/nmy117. PMID: 31728495; PMCID: PMC6855934.

Hercberg S, Galan P, Preziosi P, Aissa M. Consequences of iron deficiency in pregnant women. Current issues. Clin Drug Invest. 2000;19suppl(1):1-7.

Hernández MAG, Canfora EE, Jocken JWE, Blaak EE. The Short-Chain Fatty Acid Acetate in Body Weight Control and Insulin Sensitivity. Nutrients. 2019 Aug 18;11(8):1943. doi: 10.3390/nu11081943. PMID: 31426593; PMCID: PMC6723943.

Hever J, Cronies RJ. Plant-based nutrition for healthcare professionals: implementing diet as a primary modality in the prevention and treatment of chronic disease. Journal of Geriatric Cardiology (2017) 14: 355-368

Hodson G, Earle M. Conservatism predicts lapses from vegetarian/vegan diets to meat consumption (through lower social justice concerns and social support). Appetite. 2018 Jan 1;120:75-81. doi: 10.1016/j.appet.2017.08.027. Epub 2017 Aug 30. PMID: 28859869.

Hoey L, Strain JJ, McNulty H. Studies of biomarker responses to intervention with vitamin B-12: a systematic review of randomized controlled trials. Am J Clin Nutr. 2009;89:1981S–1996S. [PubMed] [Google Scholar]

Hofmeyr GJ, Lawrie TA, Atallah AN, Duley L, Torloni MR. Calcium supplementation during pregnancy for preventing hypertensive disorders and related problems. Cochrane Database Syst Rev. 2014 Jun 24;(6):CD001059. doi: 10.1002/14651858.CD001059.pub4. Abstract available from: https://www.ncbi.nlm.nih.gov/pubmed/24960615

Holick MF. Vitamin D: a delightful solution for health. J Investig Med. 2011;59(6):872–80. [PMC free article] [PubMed] [Google Scholar]

Holick MF, Binkley NC, Bischoff-Ferrari HA, Gordon CM, Hanley DA, Heaney RP, et al. Evaluation, treatment, and prevention of vitamin D deficiency: an endocrine society clinical practice guideline. J Clin Endocrinol Metab. 2011;96(7):1911–30. http://dx.doi.org/10.1210/jc.2011-0385. [PubMed] [Google Scholar]

Homann HH, Kemen M, Fuessenich C, Senkal M, Zumtobel V. Reduction in diarrhea incidence by soluble fiber in patients receiving total or supplemental enteral nutrition. JPEN J Parenter Enteral Nutr. 1994 Nov-Dec;18(6):486-90. doi: 10.1177/0148607194018006486. PMID: 7602722.

Hossein-nezhad A, Holick MF. Vitamin D for health: a global perspective. Mayo Clin Proc. 2013;88(7):720–55. http://dx.doi.org/10.1016/j.mayocp.2013.05.011. [PMC free article] [PubMed] [Google Scholar]

Hopwood CJ, Bleidorn W, Schwaba T, Chen S. Health, environmental, and animal rights motives for vegetarian eating. PLoS One. 2020;15(4):e0230609. Published 2020 Apr 2. doi:10.1371/journal.pone.0230609

Howarth NC, Saltzman E, Roberts SB. Dietary fiber and weight regulation. Nutr Rev. 2001 May;59(5):129-39. doi: 10.1111/j.1753-4887.2001.tb07001.x. PMID: 11396693.

Hsieh MS, Hsu WH, Wang JW, Wang YK, Hu HM, Chang WK, Chen CY, Wu DC, Kuo FC, Su WW. Nutritional and dietary strategy in the clinical care of inflammatory bowel disease. J Formos Med Assoc. 2020 Dec;119(12):1742-1749. doi: 10.1016/j.jfma.2019.09.005. Epub 2019 Oct 14. PMID: 31624009

Hu J, Lin S, Zheng B, Cheung PCK. Short-chain fatty acids in control of energy metabolism. Crit Rev Food Sci Nutr. 2018 May 24;58(8):1243-1249. doi: 10.1080/10408398.2016.1245650. Epub 2017 Jun 12. PMID: 27786539.

Huang RY, Huang CC, Hu FB, Chavarro JE. Vegetarian Diets and Weight Reduction: a Meta-Analysis of Randomized Controlled Trials. J Gen Intern Med. 2016 Jan;31(1):109-16. doi: 10.1007/s11606-015-3390-7. PMID: 26138004; PMCID: PMC4699995.

Huang T, Yang B, Zheng J, Li G, Wahlqvist ML, Li D. Cardiovascular disease mortality and cancer incidence in vegetarians: a meta-analysis and systematic review. Ann Nutr Metab. 2012;60:233–240. [PubMed] [Google Scholar]

Huang RY, Huang CC, Hu FB, Chavarro JE. Vegetarian diets and weight reduction: a meta-analysis of randomized controlled trials. J Gen Intern Med. 2015; [Epub ahead of print]. [PMC free article] [PubMed] [Google Scholar]

Hurley KM, Cross MB, Hughes SO. A systematic review of responsive feeding and child obesity in high-income countries. J Nutr. 2011 Mar;141(3):495-50. Abstract available from: https://www.ncbi.nlm.nih.gov/pubmed/21270360

Hwang DH. Inflammation and You: How Foods From Plants Protect Us From Disease. Agricultural Research/April 2009, 6-7.

World Gastroenterology Organisation Global Guidelines. Inflammatory bowel disease: a global perspective. June. 2009. Available from: http://www.medscape.com/index/list_7515_2. [Google Scholar]

Institute of Medicine (IOM). Dietary Reference Intakes for Vitamin A, Vitamin K, Arsenic, Boron, Chromium, Copper, Iodine, Iron, Manganese, Molybdenum, Nickel, Silicon, Vanadium, and Zinc. Washington DC: National Academy Press. 2001.

Jenkins DJA, Kendall CWC, Lamarche B, Banach MS, Srichaikul K, Vidgen E, Mitchell S, Parker T, Nishi S, Bashyam B, de Souza RJ, Ireland C, Pichika SC, Beyene J, Sievenpiper JL, Josse RG. Nuts as a replacement for carbohydrates in the diabetic diet: a reanalysis of a randomised controlled trial. Diabetologia. 2018 Aug;61(8):1734-1747. doi: 10.1007/s00125-018-4628-9.

Janelle KC, Barr SI. Nutrient intakes and eating behavior scores of vegetarian and nonvegetarian women. J Am Diet Assoc 1995;95:180-6. [PubMed abstract]

Jantchou P, Morois S, Clavel-Chapelon F, et al. Animal protein intake and risk of inflammatory bowel disease: The E3N prospective study. Am J Gastroenterol 2010; 105: 2195–2201. [PubMed] [Google Scholar]

Jayalath VH, de Souza RJ, Sievenpiper JL, et al. Effect of dietary pulses on blood pressure: A systematic review and meta-analysis of controlled feeding trials. Am J Hypertens 2014;27:56–64.

Jenkins DJ, Jones PJ, Lamarche B, Kendall CW, Faulkner D, Cermakova L, Gigleux I, Ramprasath V, de Souza R, Ireland C, Patel D, Srichaikul K, Abdulnour S,

Bashyam B, Collier C, Hoshizaki S, Josse RG, Leiter LA, Connelly PW, Frohlich J. Effect of a dietary portfolio of cholesterol-lowering foods given at 2 levels of intensity of dietary advice on serum lipids in hyperlipidemia: a randomized controlled trial. JAMA. 2011;306:831–839. [PubMed] [Google Scholar]

Jibani M.M., Bloodworth L.L., Foden E., Griffiths K.D., Galpin O.P. Predominantly vegetarian diet in patients with incipient and early clinical diabetic nephropathy: Effects of albumin excretion rate and nutritional status. Diabet. Med. 1991;8:949–953. doi: 10.1111/j.1464-5491.1991.tb01535.x. [PubMed] [CrossRef] [Google Scholar]

Johnson SL, Birch LL. Parents' and children's adiposity and eating style. Pediatrics. 1994;94:653-61. Abstract available from: https://www.ncbi.nlm.nih.gov/pubmed/7936891

Jørgensen SP, Hvas CL, Agnholt J, Christensen LA, Heickendorff L, Dahlerup JF. Active Crohn's disease is associated with low vitamin D levels. J Crohns Colitis. 2013;7:e407–e413. [PubMed] [Google Scholar]

Jowett SL, Seal CJ, Pearce MS, Phillips E, Gregory W, Barton JR, Welfare MR. Influence of dietary factors on the clinical course of ulcerative colitis: a prospective cohort study. Gut. 2004;53:1479–1484. [PMC free article] [PubMed] [Google Scholar]

Joyce A, Hallett J, Hannelly T, Carey G. The impact of nutritional choices on global warming and policy implications: examining the link between dietary choices and greenhouse gas emissions. Energy Emiss Control Technol. 2014;2:33–43. [Google Scholar]

Kahleova H, Levin S, Barnard ND. Vegetarian Dietary Patterns and Cardiovascular Disease. Progress in Cardiovascular Diseases; volume 61, Issue 1, May- June 2018, Pages 54-61; https://doi.org/10.1016/j.pcad.2018.05.002

Kazemian N, Mahmoudi M, Halperin F, Wu JC, Pakpour S. Gut microbiota and cardiovascular disease: opportunities and challenges. Microbiome. 2020 Mar 14;8(1):36. doi: 10.1186/s40168-020-00821-0. PMID: 32169105; PMCID: PMC7071638.

Kestenbaum B., Sampson J.N., Rudser K.D., Patterson D.J., Seliger S.L., Young B., Sherrard D.J., Andress D.L. Serum phosphate levels and mortality risk among people with chronic kidney disease. J. Am. Soc. Nephrol. 2005;16:520–528. doi: 10.1681/ASN.2004070602. [PubMed] [CrossRef] [Google Scholar]

Kim SJ, de Souza RJ, Choo VL, et al. Effects of dietary pulse consumption on body weight: A systematic review and meta-analysis of randomized controlled trials. Am J Clin Nutr 2016;103:1213–23

Knowler WC, Barrett-Connor E, Fowler SE, et al. Reduction in the incidence of type 2 diabetes with lifestyle intervention or metformin. N Engl J Med 2002;346:393–403.

Kontessis P., Jones S., Dodds R., Trevisan R., Nosadini R., Fioretto P., Borsato M., Sacerdoti D., Viberti G. Renal, metabolic and hormonal responses to ingestions of animal and vegetable proteins. Kidney Int. 1990;8:136–144. doi: 10.1038/ki.1990.178. [PubMed] [CrossRef] [Google Scholar]

Kramer H. Diet and Chronic Kidney Disease. Adv Nutr. 2019 Nov 1;10(Suppl_4):S367-S379. doi: 10.1093/advances/nmz011. PMID: 31728497; PMCID: PMC6855949.

Landi F, Liperoti R, Russo A, et al. Sarcopenia as a risk factor for falls in elderly individuals: Results from the ilSIRENTE study. Clin Nutr. 2012 Epub ahead of print. [PubMed] [Google Scholar]

Lane K, Derbyshire E, Li W, Brennan C. Bioavailability and potential uses of vegetarian sources of omega-3 fatty acids: a review of the literature. Crit Rev Food Sci Nutr. 2014;54(5):572-9. doi: 10.1080/10408398.2011.596292. PMID: 24261532.

Latvala T, Niva M, Mäkelä J et al. (2012) Diversifying meat consumption patterns: consumers' self-reported past behaviour and intentions for change. Meat Sci 92, 71–77. [PubMed] [Google Scholar]

Lee BR, Ko YM, Cho MH, Yoon YR, Kye SH, Park YK. Effects of 12-week Vegetarian Diet on the Nutritional Status, Stress Status and Bowel Habits in Middle School Students and Teachers. Clin Nutr Res. 2016 Apr;5(2):102-11. doi: 10.7762/cnr.2016.5.2.102. Epub 2016 Apr 30. PMID: 27152300; PMCID: PMC4855038.

Leib MS. Treatment of chronic idiopathic large-bowel diarrhea in dogs with a highly digestible diet and soluble fiber: a retrospective review of 37 cases. J Vet

Intern Med. 2000 Jan-Feb;14(1):27-32. doi: 10.1892/0891-6640(2000)014<0027:tocilb>2.3.co;2. PMID: 10668813.

Lila MA. From beans to berries and beyond: teamwork between plant chemicals for protection of optimal human health, Ann N Y Acad Sci. 2007,Oct; 1114:372-80, Division of Nutritional Sciences, University of Illinois, 211 Mumford Hall MC 710, 1301 W. Gregory Drive, Urbana, IL 61801, USA.

Liu HW, Tsai WH, Liu JS, Kuo KL. Association of Vegetarian Diet with Chronic Kidney Disease. Nutrients. 2019 Jan 27;11(2):279. doi: 10.3390/nu11020279. PMID: 30691237; PMCID: PMC6412429.

Locke A, Schneiderhan J, Zick SM. Diets for Health: Goals and Guidelines. Am Fam Physician. 2018 Jun 1;97(11):721-728. PMID: 30215930.

Lohsiriwat S. Protein Diet and Estimated Glomerular Filtration Rate. Open J. Nephrol. 2013;3:97–100. doi: 10.4236/ojneph.2013.32016. [CrossRef] [Google Scholar]

Mancini R, Affret A, Dow C, Balkau B, Bonnet F, Boutron-Ruault M and Fagherazzi G. Dietary antioxidant capacity and risk of type 2 diabetes in the large prospective E3N-EPIC cohort, Published: 09 November 2017, Diabetologia; volume 61, pages 308–316 (2018)

Mariani A, Chalies S, Jeziorski E, Ludwig C, Lalande M, Rodière M. Consequences of exclusive breastfeeding in vegan mother newborn case report. Arch Pediatr. 2009 Nov;16(11):1461-3. Abstract available from: https://www.ncbi.nlm.nih.gov/pubmed/19748244

Mariotti F. Plant protein, animal protein, and protein quality. In: Mariotti F., editor. Vegetarian and Plant-Based Diets in Health and Disease Prevention. Academic Press; Cambridge, MA, USA: 2017. pp. 621–642. [CrossRef] [Google Scholar]

Mariotti F, Gardner CD. Dietary Protein and Amino Acids in Vegetarian Diets-A Review. *Nutrients.* 2019;11(11):2661. Published 2019 Nov 4. doi:10.3390/nu11112661

Markle HV. Cobalamin. Crit Rev Clin Lab Sci 1996;33:247-356. [PubMed abstract]

Marsh AG, Sanchez TV, Midkelsen O, Keiser J, Mayor G. Cortical bone density of adult lacto-ovo-vegetarian and omnivorous women. J Am Diet Assoc 1980;76:148-51. [PubMed abstract]

Marsh AP, Rejeski WJ, Espeland MA, et al. Muscle strength and BMI as predictors of major mobility disability in the Lifestyle Interventions and Independence for Elders pilot (LIFE-P) J Gerontol A Biol Sci Med Sci. 2011;66:1376–1383. This article describes how both strength and body mass are important predictors of disability in older adults. [PMC free article] [PubMed] [Google Scholar]

McDonough AA, Veiras LC, Guevara CA, and. Ralph DL. Cardiovascular benefits associated with higher dietary K vs. lower dietary Na: evidence from population and mechanistic studies; Am J Physiol Endocrinol Metab 312: E348–E356, 2017. doi:10.1152/ajpendo.00453.2016. Department of Cell and Neurobiology, Keck School of Medicine of the University of Southern California, Los Angeles, California

McRorie JW Jr, McKeown NM. Understanding the Physics of Functional Fibers in the Gastrointestinal Tract: An Evidence-Based Approach to Resolving Enduring Misconceptions about Insoluble and Soluble Fiber. J Acad Nutr Diet. 2017 Feb;117(2):251-264. doi: 10.1016/j.jand.2016.09.021. Epub 2016 Nov 15. PMID: 27863994.

Meehan M, Penckofer S. The Role of Vitamin D in the Aging Adult. J Aging Gerontol. 2014;2(2):60-71. doi:10.12974/2309-6128.2014.02.02.1

Melina V, Craig W, Levin S. Position of the Academy of Nutrition and Dietetics: Vegetarian Diets. J Acad Nutr Diet. 2016 Dec;116(12):1970-1980. doi: 10.1016/j.jand.2016.09.025. PMID: 27886704. Abstract available from: https://www.ncbi.nlm.nih.gov/pubmed/27886704

Menni C, Jackson MA, Pallister T, Steves CJ, Spector TD, Valdes AM. Gut microbiome diversity and high-fibre intake are related to lower long-term weight gain. Int J Obes (Lond). 2017 Jul;41(7):1099-1105. doi: 10.1038/ijo.2017.66. Epub 2017 Mar 13. PMID: 28286339; PMCID: PMC5500185.

Metter EJ, Conwit R, Tobin J, Fozard JL. Age-associated loss of power and strength in the upper extremities in women and men. J Gerontol A Biol Sci Med Sci. 1997;52:B267–B276. [PubMed] [Google Scholar]

Miki AJ, Livingston KA, Karlsen MC, Folta SC, McKeown NM. Using Evidence Mapping to Examine Motivations for Following Plant-Based Diets. Curr Dev Nutr. 2020;4(3):nzaa013. Published 2020 Feb 5. doi:10.1093/cdn/nzaa013

Miller TL, Wolin MJ. Pathways of acetate, propionate, and butyrate formation by the human fecal microbial flora. Appl Environ Microbiol 1996; 62:1589-92; PMID:8633856 [PMC free article] [PubMed] [Google Scholar]

Millward D.J., Garnett T. Plenary lecture 3: Food and the planet. Nutritional dilemmas of greenhouse gas emission reductions through reduced intakes of meat and dairy foods. Proc. Nutr. Soc. 2010;69:103–118. doi: 10.1017/S0029665109991868. [PubMed] [CrossRef] [Google Scholar]

Mitch W.E., Remuzzi G. Diets for patients with chronic kidney disease, should we reconsider? BMC Nephrol. 2016;17:80. doi: 10.1186/s12882-016-0283-x. [PMC free article] [PubMed] [CrossRef] [Google Scholar]

Moe S.M., Zidehsarai M.P., Chambers M.A., Jackman L.A., Radcliffe J.S., Trevino L.L., Donahue S.E., Asplin J.R. Vegetarian compared with meat dietary protein source and phosphorus homeostasis in chronic kidney disease. Clin. J. Am. Soc. Nephrol. 2011;6:257–264. doi: 10.2215/CJN.05040610. [PMC free article] [PubMed] [CrossRef] [Google Scholar]

Mohajeri MH, La Fata G, Steinert RE, Weber P. Relationship between the gut microbiome and brain function. Nutr Rev. 2018 Jul 1;76(7):481-496. doi: 10.1093/nutrit/nuy009. PMID: 29701810.

Molloy AM, Kirke PN, Brody LC, Scott JM, Mills JL. Effects of folate and vitamin B12 deficiencies during pregnancy on fetal, infant, and child development. Food Nutr Bull. 2008 Jun;29(2 Suppl):S101-11; discussion S112-5. Review.

Morrison DJ, Preston T. Formation of short chain fatty acids by the gut microbiota and their impact on human metabolism. *Gut Microbes*. 2016;7(3):189-200. doi:10.1080/19490976.2015.1134082

Nagano N., Miyata S., Abe M., Kobayashi N., Wakita S., Yamashita T., Wada M. Effect of manipulating serum phosphorus with phosphate binder on circulating PTH and FGF23 in renal failure rats. Kidney Int. 2006;69:531–537. doi: 10.1038/sj.ki.5000020. [PubMed] [CrossRef] [Google Scholar]

Nair P, Mayberry JF. Vegetarianism, dietary fibre and gastro-intestinal disease. Dig Dis. 1994 May-Jun;12(3):177-85. doi: 10.1159/000171451. PMID: 7988064.

Narayan S. Origin & History of Vegetarianism in India; Text of speech delivered by Vn.Shankar Narayan, President of Indian Vegan Society and the Regional Coordinator for India, South & West Asia for the International Vegetarian Union (IVU), UK, Congress (Centenary Congress) at the Festsaal, Kulturpalast, Dresden, Germany.

National Institute for Health and Clinical Excellence: Guidance. Crohn's disease: Management in adults, children and young people. National Clinical Guideline Centre: October; 2012. [Google Scholar]

National Institutes of Health (NIH). Calcium Fact Sheet for Health Professionals. 2020, March 26. Available from: https://ods.od.nih.gov/factsheets/Calcium-HealthProfessional/

National Institutes of Health (NIH). Choline Fact Sheet for Health Professionals. 2020, July 10. Available from: https://ods.od.nih.gov/factsheets/Choline-HealthProfessional/

National Institutes of Health (NIH). Chromium Fact Sheet for Health Professionals. 2020, October 1. Available from: https://ods.od.nih.gov/factsheets/Chromium-HealthProfessional/

National Institutes of Health (NIH). Iodine Fact Sheet for Health Professionals. 2020, September 16. Available from: https://ods.od.nih.gov/factsheets/Iodine-HealthProfessional/

National Institutes of Health (NIH). Iron Fact Sheet for Health Professionals. 2020, February 28. Available from: https://ods.od.nih.gov/factsheets/Iron-HealthProfessional/

National Institutes of Health (NIH). Nutrient Recommendations: Dietary Reference Intakes (DRIs). 2019. Available from: https://ods.od.nih.gov/Health_Information/Dietary_Reference_Intakes.aspx

National Institutes of Health (NIH). Omega-3 Fact Sheet for Health Professionals. 2020, October 1. Available from: https://ods.od.nih.gov/factsheets/Omega3FattyAcids-HealthProfessional/

National Institutes of Health (NIH). Zinc Fact Sheet for Health Professionals. 2020, July 15. Available from: https://ods.od.nih.gov/factsheets/Zinc-HealthProfessional/

Neff RA, Edwards D, Palmer A, Ramsing R, Righter A, Wolfson J. Reducing meat consumption in the USA: a nationally representative survey of attitudes and behaviours. *Public Health Nutr.* 2018;21(10):1835-1844. doi:10.1017/S1368980017004190

Newman AB, Kupelian V, Visser M, et al. Strength, but not muscle mass, is associated with mortality in the health, aging and body composition study cohort. J Gerontol A Biol Sci Med Sci. 2006;61:72–77. [PubMed] [Google Scholar]

Nutrition Working Group, O'Connor DL, Blake J, Bell R, Bowen A, Callum J, Fenton S, Gray-Donald K, et al. Canadian consensus on female nutrition: adolescence, reproduction, menopause, and beyond. J Obstet Gynaecol Can. 2016 Jun;38(6):508-54.e18. Abstract available from: https://www.ncbi.nlm.nih.gov/pubmed/27368135

O'Grady J, O'Connor EM, Shanahan F. Review article: dietary fibre in the era of microbiome science. Aliment Pharmacol Ther. 2019 Mar;49(5):506-515. doi: 10.1111/apt.15129. PMID: 30746776.

Owczarek D, Rodacki T, Domagała-Rodacka R, Cibor D, Mach T. Diet and nutritional factors in inflammatory bowel diseases. World J Gastroenterol. 2016 Jan 21;22(3):895-905. doi: 10.3748/wjg.v22.i3.895. PMID: 26811635; PMCID: PMC4716043.

Pagenkemper J. Planning a vegetarian renal diet. J. Ren. Nutr. 1995;5:234–238. doi: 10.1016/1051-2276(95)90009-8. [CrossRef] [Google Scholar]

Palmer S. Vitamin B12 and the Vegan Diet. Today's Dietitian. Vol. 20, No. 4, P 38. April 2018 Issue.

Parker HW, Vadiveloo MK. Diet quality of vegetarian diets compared with nonvegetarian diets: a systematic review. Nutr Rev. 2019 Mar 1;77(3):144-60. doi: 10.1093/nutrit/nuy067. Abstract available from: https://www.ncbi.nlm.nih.gov/pubmed/30624697

Peirce JM, Alviña K. The role of inflammation and the gut microbiome in depression and anxiety. J Neurosci Res. 2019 Oct;97(10):1223-1241. doi: 10.1002/jnr.24476. Epub 2019 May 29. PMID: 31144383.

Peltomaa E, Johnson MD, Taipale SJ. Marine Cryptophytes Are Great Sources of EPA and DHA. Mar Drugs. 2017;16(1):3. Published 2017 Dec 26. doi:10.3390/md16010003

Peng P, Hyder O, Firoozmand A, et al. Impact of sarcopenia on outcomes following resection of pancreatic adenocarcinoma. J Gastrointest Surg. 2012;16:1478–1486. [PMC free article] [PubMed] [Google Scholar]

Pereira MA, O'Reilly E, Augustsson K, et al. Dietary fiber and risk of coronary heart disease: a pooled analysis of cohort studies. *Arch Intern Med*. 2004;164(4):370–376.

Post RC, Haven J, Maniscalco S. Setting the table with a healthy plate: make half your plate fruits and vegetables. J Am Diet Assoc. 2011 Nov;111(11):1644-7. doi: 10.1016/j.jada.2011.09.040. PMID: 22027042.

Post RE, Mainous AG 3rd, King DE, Simpson KN. Dietary fiber for the treatment of type 2 diabetes mellitus: a meta-analysis. J Am Board Fam Med. 2012 Jan-Feb;25(1):16-23. doi: 10.3122/jabfm.2012.01.110148. PMID: 22218620.

Powell FC, Farrow CV, Meyer C. Food avoidance in children. The influence of maternal feeding practices and behaviours. Appetite. 2011;57:683092. Abstract available from: https://www.ncbi.nlm.nih.gov/pubmed/21896295

Prior RL. , A Daily Dose of Antioxidants? Agricultural Research/March 2008, 4-5.

Pugazhenthi S., Qin L., Reddy P.H. Common neurodegenerative pathways in obesity, diabetes, and Alzheimer's disease. Biochim. Biophys. Acta Mol. Basis Dis. 2017 doi: 10.1016/j.bbadis.2016.04.017. [PMC free article] [PubMed] [CrossRef] [Google Scholar]

Raigond P, Ezekiel R, Raigond B. Resistant starch in food: a review. J Sci Food Agric. 2015 Aug 15;95(10):1968-78. doi: 10.1002/jsfa.6966. Epub 2014 Nov 21. PMID: 25331334.

Reed JA, Anderson JJ, Tylavsky FA, Gallagher JCJ. Comparative changes in radial-bone density of elderly female lactoovovegetarians and omnivores. Am J Clin Nutr 1994;59:1197S-202S. [PubMed abstract]

Reif S, Klein I, Lubin F, Farbstein M, Hallak A, Gilat T. Pre-illness dietary factors in inflammatory bowel disease. Gut. 1997;40:754–760. [PMC free article] [PubMed] [Google Scholar]

Reynolds AN, Akerman AP, Mann J. Dietary fibre and whole grains in diabetes management: Systematic review and meta-analyses. PLoS Med. 2020 Mar 6;17(3):e1003053. doi: 10.1371/journal.pmed.1003053. PMID: 32142510; PMCID: PMC7059907.

Rizzo N.S., Jaceldo-Siegl K., Sabate J., Fraser G.E. Nutrient profiles of vegetarian and nonvegetarian dietary patterns. J. Acad. Nutr. Diet. 2013;113:1610–1619. doi: 10.1016/j.jand.2013.06.349. [PMC free article] [PubMed] [CrossRef] [Google Scholar]

Rocha JP, Laster J, Parag B, Shah NU. Multiple Health Benefits and Minimal Risks Associated with Vegetarian Diets. Curr Nutr Rep. 2019 Dec;8(4):374-381. doi: 10.1007/s13668-019-00298-w. PMID: 31705483.

Roem K. Nutritional management of multiple pregnancies. Twin Res. 2003 Dec; 6(6):514-19. Abstract available from: http://www.ncbi.nlm.nih.gov/pubmed/14965462

Rogne T, Tielemans MJ, Chong MF, Yajnik CS, Krishnaveni GV, Poston L, Jaddoe VW, Steegers EA, Joshi S, Chong YS, Godfrey KM, Yap F, Yahyaoui R, Thomas T, Hay G, Hogeveen M, Demir A, Saravanan P, Skovlund E, Martinussen MP, Jacobsen GW, Franco OH, Bracken MB, Risnes KR. Associations of Maternal Vitamin B12 Concentration in Pregnancy With the Risks of Preterm Birth and Low Birth Weight: A Systematic Review and Meta-Analysis of Individual Participant Data. Am J Epidemiol. 2017 Feb 1;185(3):212-223. doi: 10.1093/aje/kww212. Review.

Ruby MB. Vegetarianism. A blossoming field of study. Appetite. 2012;58:141–50. [PubMed] [Google Scholar]

Russell WR, Gratz SW, Duncan SH, Holtrop G, Ince J, Scobbie L, Duncan G, Johnstone AM, Lobley GE, Wallace RJ, et al.. High-protein, reduced-carbohydrate weight-loss diets promote metabolite profiles likely to be detrimental to colonic health. Am J Clin Nutr 2011; 93:1062-72; PMID:21389180; http://dx.doi.org/10.3945/ajcn.110.002188 [PubMed] [CrossRef] [Google Scholar]

Sabate J, Oda K, Ros E. Nut consumption and blood lipid levels: A pooled analysis of 25 intervention trials. Arch Intern Med 2010;170:821–7.

Sabaté J, Soret S. Sustainability of plant-based diets: back to the future. Am J Clin Nutr. 2014 Jul;100 Suppl 1:476S-82S. doi: 10.3945/ajcn.113.071522. Epub 2014 Jun 4. PMID: 24898222.

Sakamoto N, Kono S, Wakai K, Fukuda Y, Satomi M, Shimoyama T, Inaba Y, Miyake Y, Sasaki S, Okamoto K, et al. Dietary risk factors for inflammatory bowel disease: a multicenter case-control study in Japan. Inflamm Bowel Dis. 2005;11:154–163. [PubMed] [Google Scholar]

Sayeed A. The Rich History and Tradition of Vegetarianism in India; The talk was delivered on August 9, 2014 during the 9th Annual Veggie Fest held in Chicago.

Sanchez-Rodriguez E, Egea-Zorrilla A, Plaza-Díaz J, Aragón-Vela J, Muñoz-Quezada S, Tercedor-Sánchez L, Abadia-Molina F. The Gut Microbiota and Its Implication in the Development of Atherosclerosis and Related Cardiovascular Diseases. Nutrients. 2020 Feb 26;12(3):605. doi: 10.3390/nu12030605.

Schreiner P, Yilmaz B, Rossel JB, Franc Y, Misselwitz B, Scharl M, Zeitz J, Frei P, Greuter T, Vavricka SR, Pittet V, Siebenhüner A, Juillerat P, von Känel R, Macpherson AJ, Rogler G, Biedermann L; Swiss IBD Cohort Study Group. Vegetarian or gluten-free diets in patients with inflammatory bowel disease are associated with lower psychological well-being and a different gut microbiota, but no beneficial effects on the course of the disease. United European Gastroenterol J. 2019 Jul;7(6):767-781. doi: 10.1177/2050640619841249. Epub 2019 Mar 27. PMID: 31316781; PMCID: PMC6620875.

Schulze MB, Liu S, Rimm EB, Manson JE, Willett WC, Hu FB. Glycemic index, glycemic load, and dietary fiber intake and incidence of type 2 diabetes in younger and middle-aged women. *Am J Clin Nutr.* 2004;80(2):348–356.

Schürmann S, Kersting M, Alexy U. Vegetarian diets in children: a systematic review. Eur J Nutr. 2017 Aug;56(5):1797-1817. doi: 10.1007/s00394-017-1416-0. Epub 2017 Mar 15. Abstract available from: https://www.ncbi.nlm.nih.gov/pubmed/28299420

Scientific Advisory Committee on Nutrition. Update on Vitamin D: Position statement by the Scientific Advisory Committee on Nutrition. November 2007. Available from: https://www.gov.uk/government/publications/sacn-update-on-vitamin-d-2007

Shi N, Li N, Duan X, Niu H. Interaction between the gut microbiome and mucosal immune system. Mil Med Res. 2017 Apr 27;4:14. doi: 10.1186/s40779-017-0122-9. PMID: 28465831; PMCID: PMC5408367.

Shloim N, Edelson LR, Martin N, Hetherington MM. Parenting styles, feeding styles, feeding practices, and weight status in 4-12 year-old children: a systematic review of the literature. Front Psychol. 2015 Dec 14;6:1849. doi: 10.3389/fpsyg.2015.01849. eCollection 2015. Abstract available from: https://www.ncbi.nlm.nih.gov/pubmed/26696920

Shukla V., Mishra S.K., Pant H.C. Oxidative stress in neurodegeneration. Adv. Pharmacol. Sci. 2011 doi: 10.1155/2011/572634. [PMC free article] [PubMed] [CrossRef] [Google Scholar]

Sidhu M, van der Poorten D. The gut microbiome. Aust Fam Physician. 2017;46(4):206-211. PMID: 28376573.

Sievenpiper JL, Dworatzek PD. Food and dietary pattern-based recommendations: an emerging approach to clinical practice guidelines for nutrition therapy in diabetes. Can J Diabetes. 2013;37:51–57. [PubMed] [Google Scholar]

Sievenpiper JL, Kendall CW, Esfahani A, et al. Effect of non-oil-seed pulses on glycaemic control: A systematic reviewand meta-analysis of randomised controlled experimental trials in people with and without diabetes. Diabetologia2009;52:1479–95.

Silva FM, Kramer CK, de Almeida JC, Steemburgo T, Gross JL, Azevedo MJ. Fiber intake and glycemic control in patients with type 2 diabetes mellitus: a systematic review with meta-analysis of randomized controlled trials. Nutr Rev. 2013 Dec;71(12):790-801. doi: 10.1111/nure.12076. Epub 2013 Nov 1. PMID: 24180564.

Silva AFD, Schieferdecker MEM, Amarante HMBDS. Food intake in patients with inflammatory bowel disease. Arq Bras Cir Dig. 2011;24:204–209. [Google Scholar]

Singh PN, Arthur KN, Orlich MJ, James W, Purty A, Job JS, Rajaram S, Sabaté J. Global epidemiology of obesity, vegetarian dietary patterns, and noncommunicable disease in Asian Indians. Am J Clin Nutr. 2014 Jul;100 Suppl 1(1):359S-64S. doi: 10.3945/ajcn.113.071571. Epub 2014 May 21. PMID: 24847857; PMCID: PMC4144108.

Slavin JL. Dietary fiber: classification, chemical analyses, and food sources. J Am Diet Assoc. 1987 Sep;87(9):1164-71. PMID: 3040839.

Slavin JL, Lloyd B. Health benefits of fruits and vegetables. Adv Nutr. 2012 Jul 1;3(4):506-16. doi: 10.3945/an.112.002154. PMID: 22797986; PMCID: PMC3649719.

Spencer E.A., Appleby P.N., Davey G.K., Key T.J. Diet and body mass index in 38,000 EPIC-Oxford meat-eaters, fish-eaters, vegetarians and vegans. Int. J. Obes. Relat. Metab. Disord. 2003;27:728–734. doi: 10.1038/sj.ijo.0802300. [PubMed] [CrossRef] [Google Scholar]

Stahler C (2015) How often do Americans eat vegetarian meals? And how many adults in the US are vegetarian? http://www.vrg.org/journal/vj2011issue4/vj2011issue4poll.php (accessed February 2018).

Standing Committee on the Scientific Evaluation of Dietary Reference Intakes, Food and Nutrition Board, Institute of Medicine. Dietary Reference Intake for calcium, phosphorus, magnesium, vitamin D, and fluoride. Washington, D.C.: The National Academies Press; 1997. Available from: http://www.nap.edu/openbook.php?isbn=0309063507

Statistics Canada. Vitamin D blood levels of Canadians. 2015 November 27. Available from: https://www150.statcan.gc.ca/n1/pub/82-624-x/2013001/article/11727-eng.htm

Stover PJ. Vitamin B12 and older adults. Curr Opin Clin Nutr Metab Care. 2010;13(1):24-27. doi:10.1097/MCO.0b013e328333d157

Sullivan C., Sayre S.S., Leon J.B. Effect of food additives on hyperphosphatemia among patients with end-stage renal disease. A randomized controlled trial. J.

Am. Med. Assoc. 2009;301:629–635. doi: 10.1001/jama.2009.96. [PubMed] [CrossRef] [Google Scholar]

Surampudi P, Enkhmaa B, Anuurad E, Berglund L. Lipid Lowering with Soluble Dietary Fiber. Curr Atheroscler Rep. 2016 Dec;18(12):75. doi: 10.1007/s11883-016-0624-z. PMID: 27807734.

Tan J, McKenzie C, Potamitis M, Thorburn AN, Mackay CR, Macia L. The role of short-chain fatty acids in health and disease. Adv Immunol. 2014;121:91-119. doi: 10.1016/B978-0-12-800100-4.00003-9. PMID: 24388214.

Tan KY, Seow-Choen F. Fiber and colorectal diseases: separating fact from fiction. *World J Gastroenterol.* 2007;13(31):4161-4167. doi:10.3748/wjg.v13.i31.4161

Tang WH, Kitai T, Hazen SL. Gut Microbiota in Cardiovascular Health and Disease. Circ Res. 2017 Mar 31;120(7):1183-1196. doi: 10.1161/CIRCRESAHA.117.309715. PMID: 28360349; PMCID: PMC5390330.

Tantamango-Bartley Y, Jaceldo-Siegl K, Fan J, Fraser G. Vegetarian diets and the incidence of cancer in a low-risk population. Cancer Epidemiol Biomarkers Prev. 2013 Feb;22(2):286-94. doi: 10.1158/1055-9965.EPI-12-1060. Epub 2012 Nov 20. PMID: 23169929; PMCID: PMC3565018.

Thompson MD, Cole DE, Ray JG. Vitamin B-12 and neural tube defects: the Canadian experience. Am J Clin Nutr. 2009;89:697S–701S. Insights into the potential need for vitamin B12 food fortification to prevent birth defects. [PubMed] [Google Scholar]

Tomasello G, Mazzola M, Leone A, Sinagra E, Zummo G, Farina F, Damiani P, Cappello F, Gerges Geagea A, Jurjus A, Bou Assi T, Messina M, Carini F. Nutrition, oxidative stress and intestinal dysbiosis: Influence of diet on gut microbiota in inflammatory bowel diseases. Biomed Pap Med Fac Univ Palacky Olomouc Czech Repub. 2016 Dec;160(4):461-466. doi: 10.5507/bp.2016.052. Epub 2016 Oct 26. PMID: 27812084.

Treatments for Constipation: A Review of Systematic Reviews [Internet]. Ottawa (ON): Canadian Agency for Drugs and Technologies in Health; 2014 Nov 17. PMID: 25535635.

Tuomilehto J, Lindstrom J, Eriksson JG, et al. Prevention of type 2 diabetes mellitus by changes in lifestyle among subjects with impaired glucose tolerance.N Engl J Med 2001;344:1343–50.

Turner RE, Langkamp-Henken B, Littell RC, Lukowski MJ, Suarez MF. 2003. Comparing nutrient intake from food to the estimated average requirements shows middle- to upper-income pregnant women lack iron and possibly magnesium. J Am Diet Assoc 103(4):461-6.

U.S. Department of Agriculture and U.S. Department of Health and Human Services. *Dietary Guidelines for Americans, 2020-2025.* 9th Edition. December 2020. Available at DietaryGuidelines.gov.

Van Horn L. Journal of the American Dietetic Association; Growing Data on Plant-Based diets; Editor-in-Chief; Nov 2005, volume 105/number 11; Pg.1695

Ventura AK, Birch LL. Does parenting affect children's eating and weight status? Int J Behav Nutr Phys Act. 2008;5-15. Abstract available from: http://www.ncbi.nlm.nih.gov/pmc/articles/PMC2276506/

Viguiliouk E, Glenn AJ, Nishi SK, Chiavaroli L, Seider M, Khan T, Bonaccio M, Iacoviello L, Mejia SB, Jenkins DJA, Kendall CWC, Kahleová H, Rahelic D, Salas-Salvadó J, Sievenpiper . Associations between Dietary Pulses Alone or with Other Legumes and Cardiometabolic Disease Outcomes: An Umbrella Review and Updated Systematic Review and Meta-analysis of Prospective Cohort Studies. This trial was registered at clinicaltrials.gov as NCT03555734. AdvNutr2019;10:S308–S319.

Viguiliouk E, Kendall CW, Blanco Mejia S, et al. Effect of tree nuts on glycemic control in diabetes: A systematic reviewand meta-analysis of randomized controlled dietary trials. Endocrinol Metab Clin North Am 2014;9:e103376.

Wallace TC, Bailey RL, Blumberg JB, Burton-Freeman B, Chen CO, Crowe-White KM, Drewnowski A, Hooshmand S, Johnson E, Lewis R, Murray R, Shapses SA, Wang DD. Fruits, vegetables, and health: A comprehensive narrative, umbrella review of the science and recommendations for enhanced public policy to improve intake. Crit Rev Food Sci Nutr. 2020;60(13):2174-2211. doi: 10.1080/10408398.2019.1632258. Epub 2019 Jul 3. PMID: 31267783.

Walston JD. Sarcopenia in older adults. Curr Opin Rheumatol. 2012;24(6):623-627. doi:10.1097/BOR.0b013e328358d59b

Wanders AJ, van den Borne JJ, de Graaf C, Hulshof T, Jonathan MC, Kristensen M, Mars M, Schols HA, Feskens EJ. Effects of dietary fibre on subjective appetite, energy intake and body weight: a systematic review of randomized controlled trials. Obes Rev. 2011 Sep;12(9):724-39. doi: 10.1111/j.1467-789X.2011.00895.x. Epub 2011 Jun 16. PMID: 21676152.

Wang Z, Zhao Y. Gut microbiota derived metabolites in cardiovascular health and disease. Protein Cell. 2018 May;9(5):416-431. doi: 10.1007/s13238-018-0549-0. Epub 2018 May 3. PMID: 29725935; PMCID: PMC5960473.

Wang F, Zheng J, Yang B, et al. Effects of vegetarian diets on blood lipids: A systematic review and meta-analysis of randomized controlled trials. J Am Heart Assoc 2015;4:e002408.

Weaver CM, Proulx WR, Heaney R. Choices for achieving adequate dietary calcium with a vegetarian diet. Am J Clin Nutr 1999 Sep;70(3 Suppl):543S-8S. Available from: https://www.ncbi.nlm.nih.gov/pubmed/10479229

Wedlake L, Slack N, Andreyev HJ, Whelan K. Fiber in the treatment and maintenance of inflammatory bowel disease: a systematic review of randomized controlled trials. Inflamm Bowel Dis. 2014;20:576–586. [PubMed] [Google Scholar]

Weiss R, Fogelman Y, Bennett M. Severe vitamin B12 deficiency in an infant associated with a maternal deficiency and a strict vegetarian diet. J Pediatr Hematol Oncol. 2004 Apr ;26(4):270-1. Abstract available from: https://www.ncbi.nlm.nih.gov/pubmed/15087959

Winter G, Hart RA, Charlesworth RPG, Sharpley CF. Gut microbiome and depression: what we know and what we need to know. Rev Neurosci. 2018 Aug 28;29(6):629-643. doi: 10.1515/revneuro-2017-0072. PMID: 29397391.

World Health Organization (WHO). Top 10 causes of death. 2020, December 9. Available from: https://www.who.int/news-room/fact-sheets/detail/the-top-10-causes-of-death

Xue QL, Walston JD, Fried LP, Beamer BA. Prediction of risk of falling, physical disability, and frailty by rate of decline in grip strength: the women's health and aging study. Arch Intern Med. 2011;171:1119–1121. [PubMed] [Google Scholar]

Yazıcı D., Sezer H. Advances in Experimental Medicine and Biology. Volume 960. Springer; Cham, Switzerland: 2017. Insulin resistance, obesity and lipotoxicity; pp. 277–304. [PubMed] [Google Scholar]

Yokoyama Y, Barnard ND, Levin SM, Watanabe M. Vegetarian diets and glycemic control in diabetes: a systematic review and meta-analysis. Cardiovasc Diagn Ther. 2014;4:373–382. [PMC free article] [PubMed] [Google Scholar]

Yokoyama Y, Nishimura K, Barnard ND, Takegami M, Watanabe M, Sekikawa A, Okamura T, Miyamoto Y. Vegetarian diets and blood pressure: a meta-analysis. JAMA Intern Med. 2014;174:577–587. [PubMed] [Google Scholar]

Yu K, Ke MY, Li WH, Zhang SQ, Fang XC. The impact of soluble dietary fibre on gastric emptying, postprandial blood glucose and insulin in patients with type 2 diabetes. Asia Pac J Clin Nutr. 2014;23(2):210-8. doi: 10.6133/apjcn.2014.23.2.01. PMID: 24901089.

Zaman SA, Sarbini SR. The potential of resistant starch as a prebiotic. Crit Rev Biotechnol. 2016;36(3):578-84. doi: 10.3109/07388551.2014.993590. Epub 2015 Jan 13. PMID: 25582732.

Zhang YZ, Li YY. Inflammatory bowel disease: pathogenesis. World J Gastroenterol. 2014;20:91–99. [PMC free article] [PubMed] [Google Scholar]

Zhao L, Zhang F, Ding X, Wu G, Lam YY, Wang X, Fu H, Xue X, Lu C, Ma J, Yu L, Xu C, Ren Z, Xu Y, Xu S, Shen H, Zhu X, Shi Y, Shen Q, Dong W, Liu R, Ling Y, Zeng Y, Wang X, Zhang Q, Wang J, Wang L, Wu Y, Zeng B, Wei H, Zhang M, Peng Y, Zhang C. Gut bacteria selectively promoted by dietary fibers alleviate type 2 diabetes. Science. 2018 Mar 9;359(6380):1151-1156. doi: 10.1126/science.aao5774.

THE WESTERN-STYLE DIET

By Julia Hilbrands MS, MPH, RD

"A journey of a thousand miles begins with a single step."
Quote by Laozi

The typical American diet looks nothing like the dietary recommendations that promote health and prevent disease. It is a diet that comes with a host of risks ranging from obesity and diabetes to cancer and kidney diseases. Unfortunately, changing this eating pattern seems insurmountable for many individuals. The thought of getting **from here** — eating donuts for breakfast, a latté for mid-morning snack, fast food for lunch, candy in the midafternoon and fried chicken for dinner — **to there** — eating a diet full of fresh fruit and vegetables, whole grains, healthful fat and lean protein — is just too much to consider for many individuals.

Asking someone to eat a healthful diet is asking them to follow over 150 specific pieces of dietary advice. Pair that with the 220 decisions most people make regarding food choices in a single day and you have a confused, disheartened, and overwhelmed person who is not eager to try a new way of eating, or if they do try, they quickly give up. As health professionals, we often ask too much too quickly.

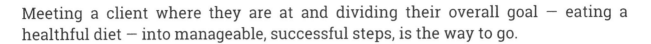

Meeting a client where they are at and dividing their overall goal — eating a healthful diet — into manageable, successful steps, is the way to go.

This chapter will explore the characteristics of a Western diet and discuss how this way of eating is strongly related to chronic disease. A step-by-step approach is described so that individuals can begin to shift their diets away from this unhealthful eating pattern without needing to adopt a new diet entirely.

SECTION 1: ORIGINS OF THE WESTERN-STYLE DIET

The origins of a Western-style diet, also referred to as the Standard American Diet or the meat-sweet diet, can be traced back more than 10,000 years to the Neolithic period where advances in agriculture and food processing made it possible for humans to eat more animal and grain products (Grotto and Zied 2010). As food production and processing have continued to evolve, the Western-style diet became a calorie-dense, nutrient-poor diet and is now blamed for the staggering rates of chronic disease we've seen in recent decades, including rates of obesity, type 2 diabetes, hypertension, and heart disease that continue to increase.

During the early parts of the twentieth century, one third of the U.S. population still lived on a farm, and approximately 40% of American workers were engaged in some type of agricultural activity (Hariharan, Vellanki, and Kramer 2015). During this time, the majority of the U.S. diet was vegetable-based, and meat came largely from animals raised on small family farms. Fast-forward several decades to the 21st century and you'll see that now less than 2% of the American workforce works on a farm, and meat now comes from large factory farms rather than from a pasture outside the kitchen window ("USDA ERS - Farming and Farm Income" 2020).

As the landscape of American farming has shifted, so has the landscape of the food that is typically available to the average American. Food of all types is now abundantly available, and high calorie convenience foods are now cheaper and more readily accessible than their healthful counterparts. For example, since 1983, the price of fresh fruit has increased by almost 200%, while the cost of sugar has increased by only 30% (Hariharan, Vellanki, and Kramer 2015). Accordingly, refined grains, fats, and sugars have contributed to the greatest intake in calories since the 1950s (Youfa Wang et al. 2010).

As we explore the components of a Western-style diet, keep in mind that the term "Western" largely refers to the culture and practices in countries that have been colonized by Europeans, such as Australia, New Zealand, the United States and

Canada (Hariharan, Vellanki, and Kramer 2015). However, these dietary patterns are also seen increasingly in countries throughout Europe and Asia as well as in the developing world.

SECTION 2: COMPONENTS OF A WESTERN-STYLE DIET

A Western diet, like many other dietary patterns, can take on different shapes and forms, but it typically has the same key elements: excess calorie consumption that includes a large amount of refined grains, red and processed meats, saturated fat, added sugar, alcohol and highly processed foods while being low in fruits, vegetables, and whole grains (Odermatt 2011; Lin et al. 2011).

EXCESS CALORIE CONSUMPTION & LARGE PORTION SIZES

If a Western-style diet had a signature component or a defining factor, it is arguably excess calorie consumption. Average individual caloric intake has increased from about 1,900 calories in the 1950s to 2,661 calories in 2008, representing a 761 calorie increase over almost six decades (USDA ERS 2020). **Much of the increase in calorie consumption can be attributed to an increase in portion size of foods eaten outside the home** (Piernas and Popkin 2011; Nielsen and Popkin 2003). The average caloric intake for a meal has increased by over 20% in the last half century (Hariharan, Vellanki, and Kramer 2015). An analysis of food and eating habits between 1977 and 1996 found that portion size and energy intake for many key food groups increased over a 19-year period; key food groups include salty snacks (93 calorie increase), soft drinks (49 calorie increase), hamburgers (97 calorie increase), French fries (68 calorie increase) and Mexican dishes (133 calorie increase) (Nielsen and Popkin 2003). As portion sizes increase, overall intake increases, as many studies have demonstrated that when people are served larger portions of food, they tend to eat more (Wansink and Kim 2005; Ello-Martin, Ledikwe, and Rolls 2005).

Eating patterns have also changed over the past several decades. Americans are spending more of their food budgets on dining out and thus eating substantially more high calorie foods than in the past (Grotto and Zied 2010). By eating outside the home more frequently, the average American is increasing the frequency at which they dine at, or get food from, fast-food restaurants. Fast food is notorious for large portions, low prices, and high palatability due to a high sugar, salt, and fat content, and there is good evidence among both teens and adults that frequent consumption of fast food contributes to overeating and subsequent weight gain (Duffey et al. 2007; Rosenheck 2008). Americans are also snacking more frequently than ever before, creating another realm in which calorie intake is increasing (Grotto and Zied 2010).

REFINED CARBOHYDRATES

Average intake of total grains within the United States and other Western countries is actually close to the recommendations laid out in the Dietary Guidelines for Americans (DGAs). However, **most individuals do not meet the recommended intake of whole grains while exceeding limits for refined grains** (Grotto and Zied 2010). A recent study found that while Americans consume an estimated 8.1 ounce equivalents of grains per day, 89% of those grains are refined grains (USDA and HHS 2015). As a reminder, the DGAs recommend that at least half of one's grain consumption come from whole grains.

Figure 1: Food Group Intake Versus Recommendations

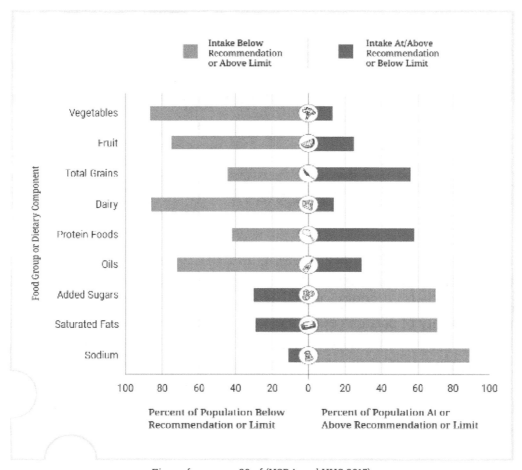

Figure from page 39 of (USDA and HHS 2015).

Almost half of all refined grain intake in the United States and other Western countries comes from mixed dishes, such as pizza, tacos, burgers, sandwiches and pasta dishes. Roughly 30% of refined grain intake is from separate food items such as cereals, breads, or rice. The remaining 20% of refined grains come from snacks and sweets such as cakes and cookies (USDA and HHS 2015).

There is an in-depth exploration of whole and refined grains in the Grains chapter. In short, whole grains products still contain dietary fiber and key vitamins and minerals, while refined grains are missing fiber and are often accompanied by a lot of added sugar.

RED AND PROCESSED MEATS

Western diets are not lacking in protein, and **the typical U.S. diet contains about twice the amount of protein** that is recommended by the DGAs (Moshfegh, Goldman, and Cleveland 2005). While the DGAs recommend that dietary protein come from a variety of sources such as meat, poultry, fish, nuts and legumes, much of the dietary protein in a Western diet comes from red and processed meats. Indeed, recent analyses show that average intakes of seafood are low for all age groups; average intakes of nuts, seeds, and soy products are low but closer to recommendations; intake of meats, poultry, and eggs is high; and intake of legumes is far below recommendations (USDA and HHS 2015).

A Western-style diet is characteristically high in red and processed meats, as mentioned above. Processed meats contain high levels of saturated fat, sodium, and nitrates (a preservative), all of which may promote atherosclerosis and vascular dysfunction and have been linked to poor health outcomes such as increased risk of cardiovascular disease and diabetes (Micha, Wallace, and Mozaffarian 2010). Nitrates and their byproducts have been shown to promote atherosclerosis and vascular dysfunction (Micha, Wallace, and Mozaffarian 2010).

SATURATED FATS

While the DGAs recommend that intake of saturated fat be less than 10% of one's total calorie intake and that more fats come from polyunsaturated fats (PUFAs) and monounsaturated fats (MUFAs), less than one-third of individuals in the United States are currently meeting this recommendation (USDA and HHS 2015). Current estimates for a Western diet are that the percentage of calories from MUFA, PUFA, and saturated fat is 12%, 7%, and 11% respectively (Grotto and Zied 2010).

The majority of saturated fats in the Western diet are found in mixed dishes, especially those containing meat or cheese. This includes burgers, sandwiches, pizza, tacos, pasta and grain dishes, and other meat, poultry, or seafood dishes. Dairy products such as cheese, whole milk, and dairy-based desserts are also significant contributors of saturated fat, as are snack and sweet foods such as fried white potatoes, potato chips, corn chips and grain-based desserts. Finally, salad dressings, mayonnaise, nuts and nut butters are also common contributors of saturated fat (USDA and HHS 2015).

ADDED SUGARS

There is a range of estimates of how much added sugar Americans are consuming on a daily basis, but all estimates show that it is a substantial amount. On average, Americans consume between 13% and 24% of their daily calories from added sugar, which amounts to up to 22 to 30 teaspoons of sugar in one day (USDA and HHS 2015; Grotto and Zied 2010). Sugar sweetened beverages (SSBs) account for almost half of all added sugars consumed, and about 37% of added sugars consumed come from sweetened carbonated beverages specifically (Bachman et al. 2008; Johnson et al. 2009). American adults typically consume 411 additional calories from beverages alone, and much of these additional calories is from added sugars (Popkin 2010).

Besides beverages, other sources of added sugar in a typical Western diet include cakes, pies, cookies, brownies, doughnuts, sweet rolls and pastries, as well as dairy desserts such as ice creams and puddings. Candies, jams, syrups and sweet toppings are also contributors (USDA and HHS 2015; Popkin 2010).

SODIUM

Sodium is naturally found in foods in very small amounts but is often added to foods and food products as a flavor enhancer, preservative, and antimicrobial. The recommendation for sodium intake is less than 2,300 mg per day to reduce the risk of hypertension, though few Americans are achieving this goal. A recent study of 765 participants found that less than 5% of participants were meeting the DGA recommendations for sodium intake (Whelton 2018). In fact, average daily sodium intake for adult men is 4,240 mg whereas for adult women it is 2,980 mg, 84% and 30% above recommendations, respectively (USDA and HHS 2015).

Sodium is found in foods from all food categories, and the highest amounts are found in foods that are processed and/or have been commercially prepared. Examples of such foods include burgers, sandwiches, tacos, rice and pasta dishes, pizza and soups (USDA and HHS 2015).

ALCOHOL

In a Western-style diet, alcohol is a large contributor to total calorie intake from beverages, second only to SSBs (Popkin 2010). As of 2011, 56% of adults ages 21 and up said they were current drinkers, meaning they had consumed some alcohol in the past month (USDA and HHS 2015). In the same report, two in three adult drinkers reported that there are times they do not limit alcohol to only moderate amounts (USDA and HHS 2015). The most common type of alcohol consumed in the United States is beer, followed by spirits and wine (Popkin 2010).

LOW IN FRUITS, VEGETABLES, WHOLE GRAINS AND FIBER

Vegetable consumption in the United States is below recommendations in all age groups for both men and women. It is lowest among boys ages nine to 13 and girls ages 14 to 18 (USDA and HHS 2015). On average, Americans consume only 1.7 cups of fresh and processed vegetables each day, which is only about 68% of the recommended intake (Grotto and Zied 2010). Similarly, fruit consumption is about half of the recommended intake for all age groups, except for children one to eight years old (USDA and HHS 2015). The trend continues when looking at whole grains: Americans of all ages are below recommendations. Low intake in all of these categories results in a low intake of dietary fiber, which is currently at about 54% of the recommended intake level, on average (Mobley, Kraemer, and Nicholls 2009).

While overall intake in each of these food groups is low, the food that is being consumed is not necessarily desirable either. Among vegetables, potatoes dominate the landscape and are the most commonly consumed vegetable, accounting for 21% of all vegetable consumption (USDA and HHS 2015). Tomato products are closely behind at 18% of all vegetable consumption. About one-third of fruit intake in the U.S. is from fruit juice (USDA and HHS 2015), and as discussed previously, 89% of grains consumed in the U.S. are refined grains rather than whole grains (Grotto and Zied 2010).

ULTRA-PROCESSED FOODS

Ultra-processed food is defined as "industrial formulations made entirely or mostly from substances extracted from foods (e.g. oils, fats, sugar, starch and proteins), derived from food constituents (e.g. hydrogenated fat and modified starch), or synthesized in laboratories from food substrates or other organic sources (e.g. flavor enhancers, colors, and several food additives used to make the product hyper-palatable)" (Zinöcker and Lindseth 2018). The main food groups falling into this category include sugary products and drinks, starchy foods and breakfast cereals, and ultra-processed fruits and vegetables (Fiolet et al. 2018).

The availability of these food products has been increasing in Western societies and is **positively associated with the prevalence of obesity** (Monteiro et al. 2018; Canella et al. 2014). In addition to the food types listed above, processed meats also fall into this category and have been associated with an increased risk of several health conditions (Larsson and Orsini 2014; Bouvard et al. 2015; Micha, Michas, and Mozaffarian 2012).

OTHER LIFESTYLE FACTORS

There are certain lifestyle factors common to most Western cultures that work in tandem with dietary habits to increase disease risk. In recent decades there has been **a decrease in home cooking** but an increase in time spent on food-related activities, such as dining out (Piernas and Popkin 2010). We have also seen an increase in eating alone, reduced physical activity, increased computer-based work, changes in common modes of transportation, shifts in leisure activities to include more technology, and more persuasive food marketing (Swinburn et al. 2011; Löffler et al. 2017).

SECTION 3: WESTERN-STYLE DIET AND HEALTH OUTCOMES

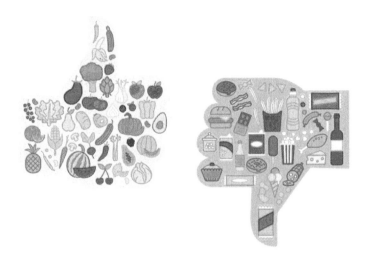

Of the top 10 leading causes of death in the United States, four have strong dietary etiologies: heart disease, several types of cancer, stroke and type 2 diabetes (Heidemann et al. 2008; Kant 2004). The dietary components to each of these conditions and a handful of others can be traced back to a Western-style diet that high in sugar, salt, fat and animal protein (Odermatt 2011).

OVERWEIGHT/OBESITY

The World Health Organization (WHO) defines obesity as excessive fat accumulation that impairs health, is diagnosed at a BMI above 30 kg/m2, and substantially increases the risk of many chronic diseases including type 2 diabetes, cardiovascular diseases, Alzheimer disease, depression and some types of cancer (Blüher 2019; Prospective Studies Collaboration 2009). While the etiology of obesity is complex and multifaceted, its fundamental cause is a long-term energy imbalance between too many calories consumed and too few calories expended (Blüher 2019). Obesity has increased by more than 20% in the past decade in the U.S., and more than one-half of U.S. adults are now overweight or obese (Must et al. 1999; Bar-Or et al. 1998). Similar trends are also observed in developed and developing countries worldwide.

Many aspects of diet and lifestyle contribute to this rise in obesity as a Western-style diet that typically include high amounts of red and processed meat, SSBs, sweets and refined grains have been linked to obesity in several large studies

(Schulze et al. 2006; Newby et al. 2004; Schulz et al. 2005; Newby et al. 2003). However, changes in lifestyle factors may play an even larger role than diet in the promotion of obesity. Lifestyle factors that have changed over the past several decades include a decrease in home cooking and increase in food eaten outside of the home, reduced physical activity, increased computer-based work, increased snacking and more persuasive food marketing (Swinburn et al. 2011; Löffler et al. 2017). In fact, one recent study that followed 3,000 young adults for 13 years found that those how had the highest fast food intake at the start of the study weighed an average of 13 pounds more than those who frequented fast-food restaurants the least (Duffey et al. 2009).

HEART DISEASE

Several elements of a Western-style diet work concurrently to increase the risk of heart disease, and one of the most studied elements is the consumption of red and processed meat. Processed meats in particular have received a lot of attention for their relationship to increased cardiovascular disease (CVD) risk (Bernstein et al. 2010). In a recent study among the European Prospective Investigation into Cancer (EPIC) cohort, **consumption of processed meat was associated with a 30% increased risk of CVD mortality** (Rohrmann et al. 2013). Similarly, a recent analysis of nine different studies found that each serving per day of processed meat was associated with a 42% higher risk of CHD (Micha, Wallace, and Mozaffarian 2010).

The relationship between unprocessed red meats and heart disease risk is less clear. Some studies have found an association between red meat consumption and an increased risk of coronary heart disease (Kelemen et al. 2005; Sinha et al. 2009; Bernstein et al. 2010), while other studies have found a null or nonsignificant relationship (Rohrmann et al. 2013; Micha, Wallace, and Mozaffarian 2010). One of the most notable differences between processed and unprocessed meats is the addition of preservatives, and processed meats contain about 400% more sodium and 50% more nitrates than unprocessed meats (Micha, Wallace, and Mozaffarian 2010). Excessive sodium intake has been associated with increased risk of CHD and hypertension — a relationship that will be explored in greater detail below (He and MacGregor 2010; C. A. M. Anderson et al. 2010). In fact, some speculate that much of the increased disease risk seen with processed meats is due to the hypertensive effects of the high sodium load (Micha, Michas, and Mozaffarian 2012).

While a high intake of red and processed meats may be contributing to increased heart disease risk, the increased risk is compounded by a low intake of fruits, vegetables, and whole grains within a Western-style diet. It has been observed that the consumption of vitamins A, C, and E (all antioxidants) as well as folate, vitamins B_6 and B_{12}, fiber and polyunsaturated fats — all of which are found in fruits, vegetables, and whole grains — is inversely associated with the risk of a circulatory disease (Lane et al. 2008).

HYPERTENSION

It is estimated that as many as nine out of 10 U.S. adults will develop hypertension, or high blood pressure, at some point in their lives, and much of this is due to the high sodium content of a Western-style diet (Vasan et al. 2002). Excessive sodium intake has been associated with prehypertension and hypertension, but also with stroke, renal disease, and coronary heart disease (He and MacGregor 2010; C. A. M. Anderson et al. 2010). The chapter on Sodium explores this relationship in great detail.

There is some evidence that other components of a Western diet may also contribute to hypertension risk. For example, in an eight-year cohort study of over 1,700 generally healthy middle-aged men, total and animal protein intake was positively associated with blood pressure, while intake of vegetable protein showed an inverse association with blood pressure (Stamler et al. 2002).

TYPE 2 DIABETES MELLITUS

Over the last century, the lifetime risk of type 2 diabetes increased from one in 30 during the early part of the 20th century to almost one in three today (Narayan et al. 2003). The increase in diabetes risk corresponds almost directly with the Westernization of diets both in North America and around the world. For example, in China between the years 1992-2002, the average proportion of energy from animal foods increased from 9.3% to 13.7%, and the proportion of energy from fat increased from 22% to 29.8% (Y. Wang et al. 2007). Similar patterns have been observed in India over the past several decades (Shetty 2002).

There are a few different mechanisms by which a Western-style diet increases the risk of type 2 diabetes risk. The first is through excessive calorie intake that leads to weight gain and obesity (Hu et al. 2001). In fact, in a prospective study of over 80,000 women in the Nurses' Health Study, overweight and obesity were the single most important and consistent predictor of diabetes risk (Hu et al. 2001). Both central obesity and a high proportion of body fat can lead to insulin resistance and subsequent type 2 diabetes (Yoon et al. 2006).

Another mechanism by which a Western-style diet leads to an increase in diabetes risk is through the high consumption of simple sugars and refined carbohydrates, particularly from SSBs and processed cereal grains (de Koning et al. 2011). The relationship between SSB intake and diabetes risk is well established, and a recent meta-analysis found that those in the highest quartile of SSB intake (at least one to two servings per day) had a 26% greater chance of developing type 2 diabetes than individuals in the lowest quartile of intake (Malik et al. 2010). Large amounts of easily absorbable sugars, such as those found in SSBs, result in a higher glycemic load that leads to rapid increases in blood glucose and insulin levels following consumption. Over time, these frequent rapid increases can lead to beta-cell exhaustion and eventual type 2 diabetes (Vessby 2000). Fructose from high fructose corn syrup, a common sweetener used in processed food products, may also lead to eventual insulin resistance (Hu, van Dam, and Liu 2001).

In addition to a high sugar content, a Western-style diet may also **cause chronic low-grade inflammation** which can increase the risk of type 2 diabetes as well as other chronic conditions such as heart disease and cancer (Schulze et al. 2006). In a recent study, researchers found that a dietary pattern with a high intake of SSBs, refined grains, and red and processed meats and low in wine, coffee, cruciferous vegetables and yellow vegetables was strongly related to elevated inflammatory markers as well as an increased risk of diabetes (Schulze et al. 2006). Similarly, a recent meta-analysis found that each serving per day of total meat was associated with a 12% increase in diabetes risk, and each serving per day of processed meat in particular was associated with a 19% increase in diabetes risk (Micha, Wallace, and Mozaffarian 2010). Higher levels of trans fat, which are known to contribute to chronic inflammation, have also been associated with increased diabetes risk (Hu, van Dam, and Liu 2001).

RENAL DISEASE

A Western-style diet has been shown to cause diminishing renal vascular function, inflammation, and albuminuria, resulting in an overall decrease in kidney function (Odermatt 2011; Knight et al. 2003). One explanation for this relationship **may be the high amounts of animal protein** (and corresponding saturated fat intake) that is characteristic of this dietary pattern (Odermatt 2011).

One sign of diminished kidney function is hyperalbuminuria, or an increased amount of protein in the urine (Wahba and Mak 2007). Glomerular filtration rate (GFR) is another measure of kidney function, and a declining GFR indicates declining kidney function. Both hyperalbuminuria and a declining GFR have been associated with a Western-style diet in general and intake of animal protein specifically in a handful of observational studies (Lin et al. 2011). For example, a recent observational study of over 19,000 adults found an association between 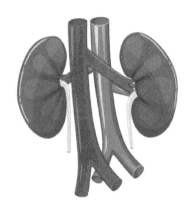 high saturated fat intake and hyperalbuminuria (Lin et al. 2011). In this same study, hyperalbuminuria was also observed among participants who had two or more servings of red meat per week. Among participants in the Nurses' Health Study, women in the highest quartile of a Western-style dietary pattern had twice the odds of having hyperalbuminuria and a rapid decline in GFR compared to women in the lowest quartile (Lin et al. 2011). In contrast, renal function decline has not been observed in diets with high amounts of plant protein (Odermatt 2011). The consumption of high amounts of animal protein has also been associated with the development of kidney stones (Reddy et al. 2002).

Another problematic element of a Western-style diet that wreaks havoc on the kidneys is **a high salt intake.** High salt intake is a risk factor for albuminuria and the subsequent development of kidney disease, and it has also been shown to accelerate disease progression in patients already diagnosed with chronic kidney disease (CKD) (du Cailar, Ribstein, and Mimran 2002; Verhave et al. 2004). It's also theorized that the combination of high amounts of saturated fat, added sugars, and salt common in a Western-style diet promotes dyslipidemia, hormonal disturbances, oxidative stress, inflammation and fibrosis that may contribute to impaired GFR (Odermatt 2011).

It's been established that a Western-style diet promotes obesity, and obesity may play a role in the progression of CKD. However, it is also thought that characteristics of a Western-style diet impact the incidence of kidney disease independent from obesity (Hariharan, Vellanki, and Kramer 2015). While portions sizes have increased over the past several decades concurrent with the prevalence of obesity, so, too, has the consumption of protein, sodium, and processed foods (Odermatt 2011).

CANCER

According to a recent combined report from the World Cancer Research Fund and the American Institute for Cancer Research, about **one-third of all cancers could be avoided by changing dietary habits** (World Cancer Research Fund/American Institute for Cancer Research 2018). There are many elements of a Western-style diet that may promote cancer risk, including a higher content of total fat, saturated fat, sugar, and salt combined with a lower intake of fiber, vitamins, and minerals (Fiolet et al. 2018). The regular consumption of ultra-processed foods, which are often high in fat, sugar, and salt, has been associated with an increased risk of certain cancers, and several studies throughout the developed world indicate that ultra-processed foods contribute to between 25%-50% of an average person's daily intake (Fiolet et al. 2018).

An excessive consumption of red meat has been associated with an increased risk of colon cancer (Giovannucci et al. 1994; Willett et al. 1990). In one study, daily intake of 100 grams of processed meats per day increased the risk of colorectal cancer by 18% (Chan et al. 2011). Cooking meats over high heat may also compound cancer risk, as methods such as pan frying or grilling result in the formation of heterocyclic amines and polycyclic aromatic hydrocarbons, both of which have been shown to cause cancer in animals (World Cancer Research Fund/American Institute for Cancer Research 2018). Additionally, there is probable evidence that **foods preserved with salt increase the risk of stomach cancer** (World Cancer Research Fund/American Institute for Cancer Research 2018).

The high amount of fat in a Western-style diet may also increase cancer risk, however more research is needed in this area. Most of the research to date has looked at the association between postmenopausal breast cancer and dietary fat, but further investigations are warranted as the results are unclear. It may be that certain types of fat increase breast cancer risk more than others (World Cancer Research Fund/American Institute for Cancer Research 2018).

There is also evidence that those with **low fruit and vegetable intake** — another characteristic of a Western-style diet — **experience about twice the cancer risk** as those with a high intake (Block, Patterson, and Subar 1992). In the same vein, it is well established that increased exposure to whole grains, foods containing dietary fiber, and non-starchy vegetables and fruits is protective against several different cancers, including colorectal cancer (World Cancer Research Fund/American Institute for Cancer Research 2018).

Overconsumption of all foods which is commonly seen in a Western-style diet can lead to overweight and obesity as described above. To take this a step further, **excess body weight can increase the risk of several types of cancers**, including cancers of the mouth, pharynx, larynx, esophagus, stomach, pancreas, gallbladder, liver, colon, breast, ovaries, prostate and kidneys (Fogli-Cawley et al. 2007; World Cancer Research Fund/American Institute for Cancer Research 2018). Overconsumption of **alcohol** in particular has been associated with an increased risk of cancers of the tongue, mouth, oropharynx, esophagus, larynx, breast and liver (Eckardt et al. 1981).

INFLAMMATORY BOWEL DISEASE

An emerging area of research is around the relationship between a Western-style diet and Inflammatory Bowel Disease (IBD). There are two main expressions of IBD, ulcerative colitis (UC) and Crohn's disease (CD), and the prevalence of both has been increasing over the past several decades (Laing, Lim, and Ferguson 2019).

A low consumption of fruit, vegetables, and fiber along with an increased intake of animal fat and refined sugars have been observed in individuals with IBD (Amre et al. 2007). Other studies have found that the risk of IBD is negatively associated with overall fiber intake, something that is often low in a Western diet (Persson, Ahlbom, and Hellers 1992; Kelly and Fleming 1995). Some researchers speculate that the increasing amount of fructose and other refined sugars in a Western diet may also contribute to IBD risk (Laing, Lim, and Ferguson 2019). In a recent study of over 300,000 European individuals, there was a positive association between sugar and soft drink intake and the risk of UC among individuals who also had a low vegetable intake (Racine et al. 2016). Others have suggested that the pro-inflammatory nature of a Western diet that is high in saturated fat and low in polyunsaturated fats may also promote the development of IBD (Patterson et al. 2012; Simopoulos 1991; Laing, Lim, and Ferguson 2019).

One flagship feature of IBD is gut dysbiosis, or a disruption of the normal diversity of the gut microbiome (Laing, Lim, and Ferguson 2019). There are several elements of a Western diet that may lead to gut dysbiosis, including the increased use of refined sugars, artificial sweeteners, and other additives (Mattes and Popkin 2009). The relationship between a Western diet and the gut microbiome will be explored further in the next section.

SECTION 4: THE WESTERN-STYLE DIET AND THE MICROBIOME

The gut microbiome refers to the collection of bacteria, fungi, archaea and viruses found in the gastrointestinal tract and together comprises over **one trillion cells that collectively carry more than 100 times more genes than their human host** (Bäckhed et al. 2005; Savage 1977; Sender, Fuchs, and Milo 2016). While the gut microbiome is a relatively new area of research, it is now well established that the diversity and functionalities of these microscopic communities have a significant impact on many different body systems, including digestion and absorption, immunity, and disease risk (Martinez, Leone, and Chang 2017).

The diversity and activity of the microbiome is heavily influenced by diet. Gut bacteria adjust their metabolism according to what is available in their nutrient supply (e.g. what the human host is eating), and the microbiome can change rapidly following dietary changes (Stecher, Maier, and Hardt 2013; David et al. 2014). A poor diet can lead to dysbiosis, which is characterized by decreased microbial diversity and changes in the relative abundance of certain microbes (Ley et al. 2005). Emerging research is showing that **dysbiosis may be induced by a typical Western diet that is rich in fat and sugar but low in fiber** (Martinez, Leone, and Chang 2017). Dysbiosis can lead to inflammation and metabolic disturbances, conditions which are also seen in several chronic conditions (Suez et al. 2014; Chassaing et al. 2015; Turnbaugh et al. 2008).

Results from both animal and human studies illustrate this complex relationship between diet, the gut microbiome, and health outcomes, and it has been shown that the gut microbiome of individuals with certain chronic conditions are different than those of healthy individuals. Research supports the hypothesis that a Western-style diet is causing changes in the gut microbiota that may be associated with obesity and metabolic disease (Martinez et al). For example, it has been shown that the microbiota in the small intestine differ between normal weight and obese individuals, and that transplanting gut microbiota from lean individuals to those with metabolic syndrome improves insulin sensitivity (Angelakis et al. 2015; Martinez, Leone, and Chang 2017).

There are several theories as to why and how a Western diet may impact the gut microbiota and subsequently health effects – a high fat/high sugar diet, food additives, ultra-processing, and others.

HIGH FAT, HIGH SUGAR DIETS

Western diets with a high amount of fat from animal-based foods such as meat and cheese have been shown to induce changes in the gut microbiota of humans, even when human factors such as genetics are accounted for (David et al. 2014; Carmody et al. 2015). In fact, changes in the gut microbiome were observed after just one day of eating a Western-style high fat diet, though the functional importance of these changes is unknown (Carmody et al. 2015). Research is beginning to show that microbiota in the gut behave differently when exposed to primarily plant-based versus animal-based diets, and dietary fat elicits changes in both the structure and function of the gut microbiome in as little as two days (David et al. 2014; Martinez, Leone, and Chang 2017).

In addition to fat content, the sugar content of a Western diet may also play a role in the composition and function of the gut microbiota. Foods high in sugar, especially fructose, may exceed the carbohydrate absorptive capacity of the small intestine and travel to the colon, providing an excess of nutrients for the gut bacteria residing there (I. H. Anderson, Levine, and Levitt 1981; Jang et al. 2018). Diets high in simple sugars result in a loss of bacterial diversity that may even have a compounding generational effect (Martinez, Leone, and Chang 2017).

FOOD ADDITIVES

Several recent studies have suggested that additives commonly found in processed foods can have an adverse effect on gut microbiota. Most of the research has focused on emulsifiers, which are added in food production to enhance texture and flavor, especially in low-fat foods. Common emulsifiers include **soy lecithin,**

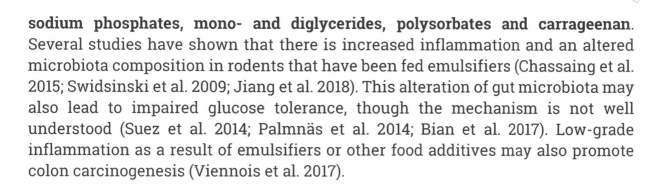

sodium phosphates, mono- and diglycerides, polysorbates and carrageenan.
Several studies have shown that there is increased inflammation and an altered
microbiota composition in rodents that have been fed emulsifiers (Chassaing et al.
2015; Swidsinski et al. 2009; Jiang et al. 2018). This alteration of gut microbiota may
also lead to impaired glucose tolerance, though the mechanism is not well
understood (Suez et al. 2014; Palmnäs et al. 2014; Bian et al. 2017). Low-grade
inflammation as a result of emulsifiers or other food additives may also promote
colon carcinogenesis (Viennois et al. 2017).

ULTRA-PROCESSING

While the content or composition of food in the diet has an impact on gut
microbiota, **the way the food is processed may also be impactful**, down to a cellular
level. During food processing, many cell walls within the food product rupture,
making their contents more easily available for uptake by the small intestine or by
gut microbiota (Zinöcker and Lindseth 2018). These nutrients have been termed
acellular nutrients (Grundy et al. 2016). For example, a whole grain of wheat
contains all of its nutrients in the cell, and the cell wall must be broken down by
bacteria in the gut before those nutrients are available. However, when grains are
milled into flour, many of those cells have been broken before ingestion, making
the nutrients inside readily available. This same effect can happen in the
processing or mincing of animal foods (Pennings et al. 2013).

Nutrients in intact cells (e.g. whole grains) will reach the colon before becoming
available to bacteria that can break down the tough fiber of the cell wall and access
the nutrients (Zinöcker and Lindseth 2018). When foodstuff enters the colon in an
intact state, it promotes the growth of bacteria that degrade fiber and produce
certain beneficial metabolites, such as short chain fatty acids (Zinöcker and
Lindseth 2018). However, when nutrients are consumed in their acellular form, they
are absorbed in the intestine before reaching colonic bacteria, and the change in
available substrate may disrupt bacterial diversity and functionality.

There is not much known about this phenomenon or the exact impact it has the
composition and function of the gut microbiota, but it is a theory that is worth
considering. Increased amounts of accessible nutrients may facilitate increased
growth of unwanted bacteria or an altered composition (Zinöcker and Lindseth
2018).

OTHER COMPONENTS

The relationship between diet, a human host, and the gut microbiota is multifaceted and complex, and there are obviously other factors at play in this relationship. Inflammation may be induced by a diet high in fats and certain additives, and it may be exacerbated by a diet that lacks plant-derived nutrients, such as fiber and phytochemicals (Zinöcker and Lindseth 2018). A Western diet that is high in fat and low in fiber may also lead to increased levels of endotoxin-producing bacteria in the gut, whereas dietary polyphenols derived from plants have been shown to restore gut barrier integrity (Ghosh et al. 2014).

SECTION 5: SHIFT TO A MORE HEALTHFUL DIET

While a Western-style diet is traditionally considered unhealthful and is associated with greater disease risk, there are small changes individuals and groups can begin to make to shift toward a more healthful eating pattern without needing to fully adopt a different diet or dietary pattern. Focus on making one healthful change at a time, achieve success, and then move on to the next change. The Dietary Guidelines for Americans suggests the following dietary shifts (USDA and HHS 2015):

CONSUME MORE VEGETABLES

For most individuals, the most significant dietary change they can make is to increase their consumption of vegetables from all subgroups, especially if vegetables are used to replace foods that are higher in calories, saturated fat, or sodium. Go to the Vegetable chapter for complete information.
- Increase the vegetable content of mixed dishes while simultaneously decreasing the amounts of other food components such as meats or refined grains

- Choose a vegetable dish as the main course of the meal rather than a meat dish
- Always include a green salad or vegetable side dish with each meal
- Choose a vegetable as a snack rather than something high in salt, fat, or sugar

CONSUME MORE FRUIT

Because of their natural sweetness, fruits can be used in place of desserts and foods with added sugar such as cakes, pies, cookies, doughnuts and ice cream. Go to the Fruit chapter for complete information.
- Try fresh fruit as a dessert rather than a baked good
- Choose a piece of fruit as a snack rather that something high in salt, fat, or sugar
- Add fruit to salads or serve as a side dish at meals

MAKE HALF OF ALL GRAINS, WHOLE GRAINS

Choosing more whole grain foods and less refined grain foods will help to bring more fiber and micronutrients into the diet. The DGAs recommend that at least half of total grain intake be from whole grains. Go to the Grain chapter for complete information.
- Choose brown rice instead of white rice or wheat pasta instead of regular pasta. If the taste or texture of the whole grain version is undesirable at first, try starting with a half-and-half mixture
- Experiment with a new whole grain, such as quinoa or farro, as a side dish at meals
- When purchasing processed grain foods such as bread, crackers, or breakfast cereal, look at the ingredient list to be sure the first ingredient is whole grain flour, and try to choose products without much added sugar or fat to ensure you are getting the most nutrient rich food product you can

SHIFT FROM SOLID FATS TO OILS

Using healthful oils rather than solids fats will decrease one's consumption of saturated fats and increase consumption of mono- and polyunsaturated fats. Go to the Fats and Oils chapter for complete information.
- Use a vegetable oil in place of solid fats (such as butter, margarine, shortening, lard or coconut oil) when cooking

- Increase intake of foods that naturally contain oils, such as seafood and nuts
- Read food labels to choose packaged foods that are lower in saturated fat and higher in unsaturated fats
- Choose salad dressings and spread made with oils instead of solid fats
- Add more vegetables and whole grains to mixed dishes while decreasing the amount of fatty meat and cheese in order to limit saturated fat intake

REDUCE ADDED SUGARS

- Choose beverages with no added sugars
- Reduce consumption of flavored dairy products such as chocolate milk, fruit-flavored yogurt, and ice cream
- Limit portion sizes of grain-based and dairy desserts as well as sweet snacks

Go to the Sugar chapter for complete information.

REDUCE SODIUM INTAKE

Use the food label to evaluate the sodium content of foods, and choose foods that are labeled low-sodium, reduced sodium, or no-added salt when available. Go to the Sodium chapter for complete information.

- Choose fresh, frozen (no sauce or seasoning), or no-salt-added canned vegetables as well as fresh rather than processed meat, poultry, and fish products
- Cook at home from scratch as often as possible, as prepared foods and foods eaten out of the home often contain high amounts of sodium
- Limit the use of sauces, mixes, and "instant" products including flavored rice, instant noodles, and ready-made pasta
- Flavor dishes with herbs and spices rather than salt

SUMMARY

The typical Western-style diet is laden with sugar and fat while fruits and vegetables rarely make an appearance — except for starchy fried potatoes. This way of eating is high in processed meats, refined grains, fatty foods, sugar sweetened beverages and overall calories while lacking in fruits, vegetables, and whole grains.

With high amounts for processed foods and few fruits and vegetables, it should come as no surprise that a Western-style diet is associated with many of the chronic conditions currently plaguing the Western world including obesity, type 2 diabetes, cancer, heart disease and chronic kidney disease to name a few. There is even emerging evidence that a Western-style diet elicits changes in gut bacteria which may further contribute to disease risk.

For those living in Western cultures that have become accustomed to the highly palatable processed foods that these places offer, all hope is not lost. There are always steps that can be taken — even if they're small — to begin to bring one's diet into closer alignment with dietary guidance that reduces disease risk and leads to a healthier lifestyle.

REFERENCES

Amre, Devendra K., Savio D'Souza, Kenneth Morgan, Gillian Seidman, Philippe Lambrette, Guy Grimard, David Israel, et al. 2007. "Imbalances in Dietary Consumption of Fatty Acids, Vegetables, and Fruits Are Associated with Risk for Crohn's Disease in Children." *The American Journal of Gastroenterology* 102 (9): 2016–25. https://doi.org/10.1111/j.1572-0241.2007.01411.x.

Anderson, Cheryl A. M., Lawrence J. Appel, Nagako Okuda, Ian J. Brown, Queenie Chan, Liancheng Zhao, Hirotsugu Ueshima, et al. 2010. "Dietary Sources of Sodium in China, Japan, the United Kingdom, and the United States, Women and Men Aged 40 to 59 Years: The INTERMAP Study." *Journal of the American Dietetic Association* 110 (5): 736–45. https://doi.org/10.1016/j.jada.2010.02.007.

Anderson, I. H., A. S. Levine, and M. D. Levitt. 1981. "Incomplete Absorption of the Carbohydrate in All-Purpose Wheat Flour." *The New England Journal of Medicine* 304 (15): 891–92. https://doi.org/10.1056/NEJM198104093041507.

Angelakis, Emmanouil, Fabrice Armougom, Frédéric Carrière, Dipankar Bachar, René Laugier, Jean-Christophe Lagier, Catherine Robert, Caroline Michelle, Bernard Henrissat, and Didier Raoult. 2015. "A Metagenomic Investigation of the Duodenal Microbiota Reveals Links with Obesity." *PloS One* 10 (9): e0137784. https://doi.org/10.1371/journal.pone.0137784.

Bachman, Jessica L., Jill Reedy, Amy F. Subar, and Susan M. Krebs-Smith. 2008. "Sources of Food Group Intakes among the US Population, 2001-2002." *Journal of the American Dietetic Association* 108 (5): 804–14. https://doi.org/10.1016/j.jada.2008.02.026.

Bäckhed, Fredrik, Ruth E. Ley, Justin L. Sonnenburg, Daniel A. Peterson, and Jeffrey I. Gordon. 2005. "Host-Bacterial Mutualism in the Human Intestine." *Science (New York, N.Y.)* 307 (5717): 1915–20. https://doi.org/10.1126/science.1104816.

Bar-Or, O., J. Foreyt, C. Bouchard, K. D. Brownell, W. H. Dietz, E. Ravussin, A. D. Salbe, S. Schwenger, S. St Jeor, and B. Torun. 1998. "Physical Activity, Genetic, and Nutritional Considerations in Childhood Weight Management." *Medicine and Science in Sports and Exercise* 30 (1): 2–10. https://doi.org/10.1097/00005768-199801000-00002.

Bernstein, Adam M., Qi Sun, Frank B. Hu, Meir J. Stampfer, JoAnn E. Manson, and Walter C. Willett. 2010. "Major Dietary Protein Sources and Risk of Coronary Heart Disease in Women." *Circulation* 122 (9): 876–83. https://doi.org/10.1161/CIRCULATIONAHA.109.915165.

Bian, Xiaoming, Liang Chi, Bei Gao, Pengcheng Tu, Hongyu Ru, and Kun Lu. 2017. "The Artificial Sweetener Acesulfame Potassium Affects the Gut Microbiome and Body Weight Gain in CD-1 Mice." *PloS One* 12 (6): e0178426. https://doi.org/10.1371/journal.pone.0178426.

Block, G., B. Patterson, and A. Subar. 1992. "Fruit, Vegetables, and Cancer Prevention: A Review of the Epidemiological Evidence." *Nutrition and Cancer* 18 (1): 1–29. https://doi.org/10.1080/01635589209514201.

Blüher, Matthias. 2019. "Obesity: Global Epidemiology and Pathogenesis." *Nature Reviews. Endocrinology* 15 (5): 288–98. https://doi.org/10.1038/s41574-019-0176-8.

Bouvard, Véronique, Dana Loomis, Kathryn Z. Guyton, Yann Grosse, Fatiha El Ghissassi, Lamia Benbrahim-Tallaa, Neela Guha, Heidi Mattock, Kurt Straif, and International Agency for Research on Cancer Monograph Working Group. 2015. "Carcinogenicity of Consumption of Red and Processed Meat." *The Lancet. Oncology* 16 (16): 1599–1600. https://doi.org/10.1016/S1470-2045(15)00444-1.

Cailar, Guilhem du, Jean Ribstein, and Albert Mimran. 2002. "Dietary Sodium and Target Organ Damage in Essential Hypertension." *American Journal of Hypertension* 15 (3): 222–29. https://doi.org/10.1016/s0895-7061(01)02287-7.

Canella, Daniela Silva, Renata Bertazzi Levy, Ana Paula Bortoletto Martins, Rafael Moreira Claro, Jean-Claude Moubarac, Larissa Galastri Baraldi, Geoffrey Cannon, and Carlos Augusto Monteiro. 2014. "Ultra-Processed Food Products and Obesity in Brazilian Households (2008-2009)." *PloS One* 9 (3): e92752. https://doi.org/10.1371/journal.pone.0092752.

Carmody, Rachel N., Georg K. Gerber, Jesus M. Luevano, Daniel M. Gatti, Lisa Somes, Karen L. Svenson, and Peter J. Turnbaugh. 2015. "Diet Dominates Host Genotype in Shaping the Murine Gut Microbiota." *Cell Host & Microbe* 17 (1): 72–84. https://doi.org/10.1016/j.chom.2014.11.010.

Chan, Doris S. M., Rosa Lau, Dagfinn Aune, Rui Vieira, Darren C. Greenwood, Ellen Kampman, and Teresa Norat. 2011. "Red and Processed Meat and Colorectal Cancer Incidence: Meta-Analysis of Prospective Studies." *PloS One* 6 (6): e20456. https://doi.org/10.1371/journal.pone.0020456.

Chassaing, Benoit, Omry Koren, Julia K. Goodrich, Angela C. Poole, Shanthi Srinivasan, Ruth E. Ley, and Andrew T. Gewirtz. 2015. "Dietary Emulsifiers Impact the Mouse Gut Microbiota Promoting Colitis and Metabolic Syndrome." *Nature* 519 (7541): 92–96. https://doi.org/10.1038/nature14232.

David, Lawrence A., Corinne F. Maurice, Rachel N. Carmody, David B. Gootenberg, Julie E. Button, Benjamin E. Wolfe, Alisha V. Ling, et al. 2014. "Diet Rapidly and Reproducibly Alters the Human Gut Microbiome." *Nature* 505 (7484): 559–63. https://doi.org/10.1038/nature12820.

Duffey, Kiyah J., Penny Gordon-Larsen, David R. Jacobs, O. Dale Williams, and Barry M. Popkin. 2007. "Differential Associations of Fast Food and Restaurant Food Consumption with 3-y Change in Body Mass Index: The Coronary Artery Risk Development in Young Adults Study." *The American Journal of Clinical Nutrition* 85 (1): 201–8. https://doi.org/10.1093/ajcn/85.1.201.

Duffey, Kiyah J., Penny Gordon-Larsen, Lyn M. Steffen, David R. Jacobs, and Barry M. Popkin. 2009. "Regular Consumption from Fast Food Establishments Relative to Other Restaurants Is Differentially Associated with Metabolic Outcomes in Young Adults." *The Journal of Nutrition* 139 (11): 2113–18. https://doi.org/10.3945/jn.109.109520.

Eckardt, M. J., T. C. Harford, C. T. Kaelber, E. S. Parker, L. S. Rosenthal, R. S. Ryback, G. C. Salmoiraghi, E. Vanderveen, and K. R. Warren. 1981. "Health Hazards Associated with Alcohol Consumption." *JAMA* 246 (6): 648–66.

Ello-Martin, Julia A., Jenny H. Ledikwe, and Barbara J. Rolls. 2005. "The Influence of Food Portion Size and Energy Density on Energy Intake: Implications for Weight Management." *The American Journal of Clinical Nutrition* 82 (1 Suppl): 236S-241S. https://doi.org/10.1093/ajcn/82.1.236S.

Fiolet, Thibault, Bernard Srour, Laury Sellem, Emmanuelle Kesse-Guyot, Benjamin Allès, Caroline Méjean, Mélanie Deschasaux, et al. 2018. "Consumption of Ultra-Processed Foods and Cancer Risk: Results from NutriNet-Santé Prospective Cohort." *BMJ (Clinical Research Ed.)* 360: k322. https://doi.org/10.1136/bmj.k322.

Fogli-Cawley, Jeanene J., Johanna T. Dwyer, Edward Saltzman, Marjorie L. McCullough, Lisa M. Troy, James B. Meigs, and Paul F. Jacques. 2007. "The 2005 Dietary Guidelines for Americans and Insulin Resistance in the Framingham Offspring Cohort." *Diabetes Care* 30 (4): 817–22. https://doi.org/10.2337/dc06-1927.

Ghosh, Siddhartha S., Jinghua Bie, Jing Wang, and Shobha Ghosh. 2014. "Oral Supplementation with Non-Absorbable Antibiotics or Curcumin Attenuates Western Diet-Induced Atherosclerosis and Glucose Intolerance in LDLR-/-Mice--Role of Intestinal Permeability and Macrophage Activation." *PloS One* 9 (9): e108577. https://doi.org/10.1371/journal.pone.0108577.

Giovannucci, E., E. B. Rimm, M. J. Stampfer, G. A. Colditz, A. Ascherio, and W. C. Willett. 1994. "Intake of Fat, Meat, and Fiber in Relation to Risk of Colon Cancer in Men." *Cancer Research* 54 (9): 2390–97.

Grotto, David, and Elisa Zied. 2010. "The Standard American Diet and Its Relationship to the Health Status of Americans." *Nutrition in Clinical Practice* 25 (6): 603–12. https://doi.org/10.1177/0884533610386234.

Grundy, Myriam M.-L., Cathrina H. Edwards, Alan R. Mackie, Michael J. Gidley, Peter J. Butterworth, and Peter R. Ellis. 2016. "Re-Evaluation of the Mechanisms of Dietary Fibre and Implications for Macronutrient Bioaccessibility, Digestion and Postprandial Metabolism." *The British Journal of Nutrition* 116 (5): 816–33. https://doi.org/10.1017/S0007114516002610.

Hariharan, Divya, Kavitha Vellanki, and Holly Kramer. 2015. "The Western Diet and Chronic Kidney Disease." *Current Hypertension Reports* 17 (3): 16. https://doi.org/10.1007/s11906-014-0529-6.

He, Feng J., and Graham A. MacGregor. 2010. "Reducing Population Salt Intake Worldwide: From Evidence to Implementation." *Progress in Cardiovascular Diseases* 52 (5): 363–82. https://doi.org/10.1016/j.pcad.2009.12.006.

Heidemann, Christin, Matthias B. Schulze, Oscar H. Franco, Rob M. van Dam, Christos S. Mantzoros, and Frank B. Hu. 2008. "Dietary Patterns and Risk of Mortality from Cardiovascular Disease, Cancer, and All Causes in a Prospective Cohort of Women." *Circulation* 118 (3): 230–37. https://doi.org/10.1161/CIRCULATIONAHA.108.771881.

Hu, F. B., R. M. van Dam, and S. Liu. 2001. "Diet and Risk of Type II Diabetes: The Role of Types of Fat and Carbohydrate." *Diabetologia* 44 (7): 805–17. https://doi.org/10.1007/s001250100547.

Hu, F. B., J. E. Manson, M. J. Stampfer, G. Colditz, S. Liu, C. G. Solomon, and W. C. Willett. 2001. "Diet, Lifestyle, and the Risk of Type 2 Diabetes Mellitus in Women." *The New England Journal of Medicine* 345 (11): 790–97. https://doi.org/10.1056/NEJMoa010492.

Jang, Cholsoon, Sheng Hui, Wenyun Lu, Alexis J. Cowan, Raphael J. Morscher, Gina Lee, Wei Liu, Gregory J. Tesz, Morris J. Birnbaum, and Joshua D. Rabinowitz. 2018. "The Small Intestine Converts Dietary Fructose into Glucose and Organic Acids." *Cell Metabolism* 27 (2): 351-361.e3. https://doi.org/10.1016/j.cmet.2017.12.016.

Jiang, Zengliang, Minjie Zhao, Hui Zhang, Yang Li, Mengyun Liu, and Fengqin Feng. 2018. "Antimicrobial Emulsifier-Glycerol Monolaurate Induces Metabolic Syndrome, Gut Microbiota Dysbiosis, and Systemic Low-Grade Inflammation in Low-Fat Diet Fed Mice." *Molecular Nutrition & Food Research* 62 (3). https://doi.org/10.1002/mnfr.201700547.

Johnson, Rachel K., Lawrence J. Appel, Michael Brands, Barbara V. Howard, Michael Lefevre, Robert H. Lustig, Frank Sacks, Lyn M. Steffen, Judith Wylie-Rosett, and American Heart Association Nutrition Committee of the Council on Nutrition, Physical Activity, and Metabolism and the Council on Epidemiology and Prevention. 2009. "Dietary Sugars Intake and Cardiovascular Health: A Scientific Statement from the American Heart

Association." *Circulation* 120 (11): 1011–20.
https://doi.org/10.1161/CIRCULATIONAHA.109.192627.

Kant, Ashima K. 2004. "Dietary Patterns and Health Outcomes." *Journal of the American Dietetic Association* 104 (4): 615–35.
https://doi.org/10.1016/j.jada.2004.01.010.

Kelemen, Linda E., Lawrence H. Kushi, David R. Jacobs, and James R. Cerhan. 2005. "Associations of Dietary Protein with Disease and Mortality in a Prospective Study of Postmenopausal Women." *American Journal of Epidemiology* 161 (3): 239–49. https://doi.org/10.1093/aje/kwi038.

Kelly, D. G., and C. R. Fleming. 1995. "Nutritional Considerations in Inflammatory Bowel Diseases." *Gastroenterology Clinics of North America* 24 (3): 597–611.

Knight, Eric L., Meir J. Stampfer, Susan E. Hankinson, Donna Spiegelman, and Gary C. Curhan. 2003. "The Impact of Protein Intake on Renal Function Decline in Women with Normal Renal Function or Mild Renal Insufficiency." *Annals of Internal Medicine* 138 (6): 460–67.
https://doi.org/10.7326/0003-4819-138-6-200303180-00009.

Koning, Lawrence de, Vasanti S. Malik, Eric B. Rimm, Walter C. Willett, and Frank B. Hu. 2011. "Sugar-Sweetened and Artificially Sweetened Beverage Consumption and Risk of Type 2 Diabetes in Men." *The American Journal of Clinical Nutrition* 93 (6): 1321–27. https://doi.org/10.3945/ajcn.110.007922.

Laing, Bobbi B., Anecita Gigi Lim, and Lynnette R. Ferguson. 2019. "A Personalised Dietary Approach-A Way Forward to Manage Nutrient Deficiency, Effects of the Western Diet, and Food Intolerances in Inflammatory Bowel Disease." *Nutrients* 11 (7). https://doi.org/10.3390/nu11071532.

Lane, John S., Cheryl P. Magno, Karen T. Lane, Tyler Chan, David B. Hoyt, and Sheldon Greenfield. 2008. "Nutrition Impacts the Prevalence of Peripheral Arterial Disease in the United States." *Journal of Vascular Surgery* 48 (4): 897–904. https://doi.org/10.1016/j.jvs.2008.05.014.

Larsson, Susanna C., and Nicola Orsini. 2014. "Red Meat and Processed Meat Consumption and All-Cause Mortality: A Meta-Analysis." *American Journal of Epidemiology* 179 (3): 282–89. https://doi.org/10.1093/aje/kwt261.

Ley, Ruth E., Fredrik Bäckhed, Peter Turnbaugh, Catherine A. Lozupone, Robin D. Knight, and Jeffrey I. Gordon. 2005. "Obesity Alters Gut Microbial Ecology." *Proceedings of the National Academy of Sciences of the United States of America* 102 (31): 11070–75. https://doi.org/10.1073/pnas.0504978102.

Lin, Julie, Teresa T. Fung, Frank B. Hu, and Gary C. Curhan. 2011. "Association of Dietary Patterns With Albuminuria and Kidney Function Decline in Older White Women: A Subgroup Analysis From the Nurses' Health Study." *American Journal of Kidney Diseases : The Official Journal of the National Kidney Foundation* 57 (2): 245–54. https://doi.org/10.1053/j.ajkd.2010.09.027.

Lin, Julie, Suzanne Judd, Anh Le, Jamy Ard, Britt B. Newsome, George Howard, David G. Warnock, and William McClellan. 2010. "Associations of Dietary Fat with Albuminuria and Kidney Dysfunction." *The American Journal of Clinical Nutrition* 92 (4): 897–904. https://doi.org/10.3945/ajcn.2010.29479.

Löffler, Antje, Tobias Luck, Francisca S. Then, Claudia Luck-Sikorski, Alexander Pabst, Peter Kovacs, Yvonne Böttcher, et al. 2017. "Effects of Psychological Eating Behaviour Domains on the Association between Socio-Economic Status and BMI." *Public Health Nutrition* 20 (15): 2706–12. https://doi.org/10.1017/S1368980017001653.

Malik, Vasanti S., Barry M. Popkin, George A. Bray, Jean-Pierre Després, Walter C. Willett, and Frank B. Hu. 2010. "Sugar-Sweetened Beverages and Risk of Metabolic Syndrome and Type 2 Diabetes: A Meta-Analysis." *Diabetes Care* 33 (11): 2477–83. https://doi.org/10.2337/dc10-1079.

Martinez, Kristina B., Vanessa Leone, and Eugene B. Chang. 2017. "Western Diets, Gut Dysbiosis, and Metabolic Diseases: Are They Linked?" *Gut Microbes* 8 (2): 130–42. https://doi.org/10.1080/19490976.2016.1270811.

Mattes, Richard D., and Barry M. Popkin. 2009. "Nonnutritive Sweetener Consumption in Humans: Effects on Appetite and Food Intake and Their Putative Mechanisms." *The American Journal of Clinical Nutrition* 89 (1): 1–14. https://doi.org/10.3945/ajcn.2008.26792.

Micha, Renata, Georgios Michas, and Dariush Mozaffarian. 2012. "Unprocessed Red and Processed Meats and Risk of Coronary Artery Disease and Type 2 Diabetes--an Updated Review of the Evidence." *Current Atherosclerosis Reports* 14 (6): 515–24. https://doi.org/10.1007/s11883-012-0282-8.

Micha, Renata, Sarah K. Wallace, and Dariush Mozaffarian. 2010. "Red and Processed Meat Consumption and Risk of Incident Coronary Heart Disease, Stroke, and Diabetes: A Systematic Review and Meta-Analysis." *Circulation* 121 (21): 2271–83. https://doi.org/10.1161/CIRCULATIONAHA.109.924977.

Mobley, Amy R., Dan Kraemer, and Jill Nicholls. 2009. "Putting the Nutrient-Rich Foods Index into Practice." *Journal of the American College of Nutrition* 28 (4): 427S-435S. https://doi.org/10.1080/07315724.2009.10718107.

Monteiro, Carlos Augusto, Jean-Claude Moubarac, Renata Bertazzi Levy, Daniela Silva Canella, Maria Laura da Costa Louzada, and Geoffrey Cannon. 2018. "Household Availability of Ultra-Processed Foods and Obesity in Nineteen European Countries." *Public Health Nutrition* 21 (1): 18–26. https://doi.org/10.1017/S1368980017001379.

Moshfegh, Alanna, Joseph Goldman, and Linda Cleveland. 2005. "What We Eat in America, NHANES 2001-2002: Usual Nutrient Intakes from Food Compared to Dietary Reference Intakes." U.S. Department of Agriculture, Agricultural Research Service. 2005.

https://www.ars.usda.gov/ARSUserFiles/80400530/pdf/0102/usualintaketables2001-02.pdf.

Must, A., J. Spadano, E. H. Coakley, A. E. Field, G. Colditz, and W. H. Dietz. 1999. "The Disease Burden Associated with Overweight and Obesity." *JAMA* 282 (16): 1523–29. https://doi.org/10.1001/jama.282.16.1523.

Narayan, K. M. Venkat, James P. Boyle, Theodore J. Thompson, Stephen W. Sorensen, and David F. Williamson. 2003. "Lifetime Risk for Diabetes Mellitus in the United States." *JAMA* 290 (14): 1884–90. https://doi.org/10.1001/jama.290.14.1884.

Newby, P. K., Denis Muller, Judith Hallfrisch, Reubin Andres, and Katherine L. Tucker. 2004. "Food Patterns Measured by Factor Analysis and Anthropometric Changes in Adults." *The American Journal of Clinical Nutrition* 80 (2): 504–13. https://doi.org/10.1093/ajcn/80.2.504.

Newby, P. K., Denis Muller, Judith Hallfrisch, Ning Qiao, Reubin Andres, and Katherine L. Tucker. 2003. "Dietary Patterns and Changes in Body Mass Index and Waist Circumference in Adults." *The American Journal of Clinical Nutrition* 77 (6): 1417–25. https://doi.org/10.1093/ajcn/77.6.1417.

Nielsen, Samara Joy, and Barry M. Popkin. 2003. "Patterns and Trends in Food Portion Sizes, 1977-1998." *JAMA* 289 (4): 450–53. https://doi.org/10.1001/jama.289.4.450.

Odermatt, Alex. 2011. "The Western-Style Diet: A Major Risk Factor for Impaired Kidney Function and Chronic Kidney Disease." *American Journal of Physiology-Renal Physiology* 301 (5): F919–31. https://doi.org/10.1152/ajprenal.00068.2011.

Palmnäs, Marie S. A., Theresa E. Cowan, Marc R. Bomhof, Juliet Su, Raylene A. Reimer, Hans J. Vogel, Dustin S. Hittel, and Jane Shearer. 2014. "Low-Dose Aspartame Consumption Differentially Affects Gut Microbiota-Host Metabolic Interactions in the Diet-Induced Obese Rat." *PloS One* 9 (10): e109841. https://doi.org/10.1371/journal.pone.0109841.

Patterson, E., R. Wall, G. F. Fitzgerald, R. P. Ross, and C. Stanton. 2012. "Health Implications of High Dietary Omega-6 Polyunsaturated Fatty Acids." *Journal of Nutrition and Metabolism* 2012: 539426. https://doi.org/10.1155/2012/539426.

Pennings, Bart, Bart B. L. Groen, Jan-Willem van Dijk, Anneke de Lange, Alexandra Kiskini, Marjan Kuklinski, Joan M. G. Senden, and Luc J. C. van Loon. 2013. "Minced Beef Is More Rapidly Digested and Absorbed than Beef Steak, Resulting in Greater Postprandial Protein Retention in Older Men." *The American Journal of Clinical Nutrition* 98 (1): 121–28. https://doi.org/10.3945/ajcn.112.051201.

Persson, P. G., A. Ahlbom, and G. Hellers. 1992. "Diet and Inflammatory Bowel Disease: A Case-Control Study." *Epidemiology (Cambridge, Mass.)* 3 (1): 47–52. https://doi.org/10.1097/00001648-199201000-00009.

Piernas, Carmen, and Barry M. Popkin. 2010. "Snacking Increased among U.S. Adults between 1977 and 2006." *The Journal of Nutrition* 140 (2): 325–32. https://doi.org/10.3945/jn.109.112763.

———. 2011. "Food Portion Patterns and Trends among U.S. Children and the Relationship to Total Eating Occasion Size, 1977-2006." *The Journal of Nutrition* 141 (6): 1159–64. https://doi.org/10.3945/jn.111.138727.

Popkin, Barry M. 2010. "Patterns of Beverage Use across the Lifecycle." *Physiology & Behavior* 100 (1): 4–9. https://doi.org/10.1016/j.physbeh.2009.12.022.

Prospective Studies Collaboration. 2009. "Body-Mass Index and Cause-Specific Mortality in 900 000 Adults: Collaborative Analyses of 57 Prospective Studies." *The Lancet* 373 (9669): 1083–96. https://doi.org/10.1016/S0140-6736(09)60318-4.

Racine, Antoine, Franck Carbonnel, Simon S. M. Chan, Andrew R. Hart, H. Bas Bueno-de-Mesquita, Bas Oldenburg, Fiona D. M. van Schaik, et al. 2016. "Dietary Patterns and Risk of Inflammatory Bowel Disease in Europe: Results from the EPIC Study." *Inflammatory Bowel Diseases* 22 (2): 345–54. https://doi.org/10.1097/MIB.0000000000000638.

Reddy, Shalini T., Chia-Ying Wang, Khashayar Sakhaee, Linda Brinkley, and Charles Y. C. Pak. 2002. "Effect of Low-Carbohydrate High-Protein Diets on Acid-Base Balance, Stone-Forming Propensity, and Calcium Metabolism." *American Journal of Kidney Diseases: The Official Journal of the National Kidney Foundation* 40 (2): 265–74. https://doi.org/10.1053/ajkd.2002.34504.

Rohrmann, Sabine, Kim Overvad, H. Bas Bueno-de-Mesquita, Marianne U. Jakobsen, Rikke Egeberg, Anne Tjønneland, Laura Nailler, et al. 2013. "Meat Consumption and Mortality--Results from the European Prospective Investigation into Cancer and Nutrition." *BMC Medicine* 11 (March): 63. https://doi.org/10.1186/1741-7015-11-63.

Rosenheck, R. 2008. "Fast Food Consumption and Increased Caloric Intake: A Systematic Review of a Trajectory towards Weight Gain and Obesity Risk." *Obesity Reviews: An Official Journal of the International Association for the Study of Obesity* 9 (6): 535–47. https://doi.org/10.1111/j.1467-789X.2008.00477.x.

Savage, D. C. 1977. "Microbial Ecology of the Gastrointestinal Tract." *Annual Review of Microbiology* 31: 107–33. https://doi.org/10.1146/annurev.mi.31.100177.000543.

Schulz, Mandy, Ute Nöthlings, Kurt Hoffmann, Manuela M. Bergmann, and Heiner Boeing. 2005. "Identification of a Food Pattern Characterized by High-Fiber and Low-Fat Food Choices Associated with Low Prospective Weight Change in the EPIC-Potsdam Cohort." *The Journal of Nutrition* 135 (5): 1183–89. https://doi.org/10.1093/jn/135.5.1183.

Schulze, Matthias B., Teresa T. Fung, Joann E. Manson, Walter C. Willett, and Frank B. Hu. 2006. "Dietary Patterns and Changes in Body Weight in Women." *Obesity (Silver Spring, Md.)* 14 (8): 1444–53. https://doi.org/10.1038/oby.2006.164.

Sender, Ron, Shai Fuchs, and Ron Milo. 2016. "Revised Estimates for the Number of Human and Bacteria Cells in the Body." *PLoS Biology* 14 (8): e1002533. https://doi.org/10.1371/journal.pbio.1002533.

Shetty, Prakash S. 2002. "Nutrition Transition in India." *Public Health Nutrition* 5 (1A): 175–82. https://doi.org/10.1079/PHN2001291.

Simopoulos, A. P. 1991. "Omega-3 Fatty Acids in Health and Disease and in Growth and Development." *The American Journal of Clinical Nutrition* 54 (3): 438–63. https://doi.org/10.1093/ajcn/54.3.438.

Sinha, Rashmi, Amanda J. Cross, Barry I. Graubard, Michael F. Leitzmann, and Arthur Schatzkin. 2009. "Meat Intake and Mortality: A Prospective Study of over Half a Million People." *Archives of Internal Medicine* 169 (6): 562–71. https://doi.org/10.1001/archinternmed.2009.6.

Stamler, Jeremiah, Kiang Liu, Karen J. Ruth, Jane Pryer, and Philip Greenland. 2002. "Eight-Year Blood Pressure Change in Middle-Aged Men: Relationship to Multiple Nutrients." *Hypertension (Dallas, Tex.: 1979)* 39 (5): 1000–1006. https://doi.org/10.1161/01.hyp.0000016178.80811.d9.

Stecher, Bärbel, Lisa Maier, and Wolf-Dietrich Hardt. 2013. "'Blooming' in the Gut: How Dysbiosis Might Contribute to Pathogen Evolution." *Nature Reviews. Microbiology* 11 (4): 277–84. https://doi.org/10.1038/nrmicro2989.

Suez, Jotham, Tal Korem, David Zeevi, Gili Zilberman-Schapira, Christoph A. Thaiss, Ori Maza, David Israeli, et al. 2014. "Artificial Sweeteners Induce Glucose Intolerance by Altering the Gut Microbiota." *Nature* 514 (7521): 181–86. https://doi.org/10.1038/nature13793.

Swidsinski, Alexander, Victoria Ung, Beate C. Sydora, Vera Loening-Baucke, Yvonne Doerffel, Hans Verstraelen, and Richard N. Fedorak. 2009. "Bacterial Overgrowth and Inflammation of Small Intestine after Carboxymethylcellulose Ingestion in Genetically Susceptible Mice." *Inflammatory Bowel Diseases* 15 (3): 359–64. https://doi.org/10.1002/ibd.20763.

Swinburn, Boyd A., Gary Sacks, Kevin D. Hall, Klim McPherson, Diane T. Finegood, Marjory L. Moodie, and Steven L. Gortmaker. 2011. "The Global Obesity Pandemic: Shaped by Global Drivers and Local Environments." *Lancet*

(London, England) 378 (9793): 804–14. https://doi.org/10.1016/S0140-6736(11)60813-1.

Turnbaugh, Peter J., Fredrik Bäckhed, Lucinda Fulton, and Jeffrey I. Gordon. 2008. "Diet-Induced Obesity Is Linked to Marked but Reversible Alterations in the Mouse Distal Gut Microbiome." *Cell Host & Microbe* 3 (4): 213–23. https://doi.org/10.1016/j.chom.2008.02.015.

USDA ERS. 2020. "Food Availability (Per Capita) Data System." 2020. https://www.ers.usda.gov/data-products/food-availability-per-capita-data-system/.

"USDA ERS - Farming and Farm Income." n.d. Accessed May 9, 2020. https://www.ers.usda.gov/data-products/ag-and-food-statistics-charting-the-essentials/farming-and-farm-income/.

USDA, and HHS. 2015. "Dietary Guidelines for Americans 2015-2020." U.S. Department of Health and Human Services and U.S. Department of Agriculture. https://health.gov/dietaryguidelines/2015/guidelines/.

Vasan, Ramachandran S., Alexa Beiser, Sudha Seshadri, Martin G. Larson, William B. Kannel, Ralph B. D'Agostino, and Daniel Levy. 2002. "Residual Lifetime Risk for Developing Hypertension in Middle-Aged Women and Men: The Framingham Heart Study." *JAMA* 287 (8): 1003–10. https://doi.org/10.1001/jama.287.8.1003.

Verhave, J. C., H. L. Hillege, J. G. M. Burgerhof, W. M. T. Janssen, R. T. Gansevoort, G. J. Navis, D. de Zeeuw, P. E. de Jong, and PREVEND Study Group. 2004. "Sodium Intake Affects Urinary Albumin Excretion Especially in Overweight Subjects." *Journal of Internal Medicine* 256 (4): 324–30. https://doi.org/10.1111/j.1365-2796.2004.01390.x.

Vessby, B. 2000. "Dietary Fat and Insulin Action in Humans." *The British Journal of Nutrition* 83 Suppl 1 (March): S91-96. https://doi.org/10.1017/s000711450000101x.

Viennois, Emilie, Didier Merlin, Andrew T. Gewirtz, and Benoit Chassaing. 2017. "Dietary Emulsifier-Induced Low-Grade Inflammation Promotes Colon Carcinogenesis." *Cancer Research* 77 (1): 27–40. https://doi.org/10.1158/0008-5472.CAN-16-1359.

Wahba, Ihab M., and Robert H. Mak. 2007. "Obesity and Obesity-Initiated Metabolic Syndrome: Mechanistic Links to Chronic Kidney Disease." *Clinical Journal of the American Society of Nephrology: CJASN* 2 (3): 550–62. https://doi.org/10.2215/CJN.04071206.

Wang, Y., J. Mi, X.-Y. Shan, Q. J. Wang, and K.-Y. Ge. 2007. "Is China Facing an Obesity Epidemic and the Consequences? The Trends in Obesity and Chronic Disease in China." *International Journal of Obesity (2005)* 31 (1): 177–88. https://doi.org/10.1038/sj.ijo.0803354.

Wang, Youfa, May A. Beydoun, Benjamin Caballero, Tiffany L. Gary, and Robert Lawrence. 2010. "Trends and Correlates in Meat Consumption Patterns in the US Adult Population." *Public Health Nutrition* 13 (9): 1333–45. https://doi.org/10.1017/S1368980010000224.

Wansink, Brian, and Junyong Kim. 2005. "Bad Popcorn in Big Buckets: Portion Size Can Influence Intake as Much as Taste." *Journal of Nutrition Education and Behavior* 37 (5): 242–45. https://doi.org/10.1016/s1499-4046(06)60278-9.

Whelton, Paul K. 2018. "Sodium and Potassium Intake in US Adults." *Circulation* 137 (3): 247–49. https://doi.org/10.1161/CIRCULATIONAHA.117.031371.

Willett, W. C., M. J. Stampfer, G. A. Colditz, B. A. Rosner, and F. E. Speizer. 1990. "Relation of Meat, Fat, and Fiber Intake to the Risk of Colon Cancer in a Prospective Study among Women." *The New England Journal of Medicine* 323 (24): 1664–72. https://doi.org/10.1056/NEJM199012133232404.

World Cancer Research Fund/American Institute for Cancer Research. 2018. "Diet, Nutrition, Physical Activity and Cancer: A Global Perspective." Continuous Update Project Expert Report 2018. 2018. dietandcancerreport.org.

Yoon, Kun-Ho, Jin-Hee Lee, Ji-Won Kim, Jae Hyoung Cho, Yoon-Hee Choi, Seung-Hyun Ko, Paul Zimmet, and Ho-Young Son. 2006. "Epidemic Obesity and Type 2 Diabetes in Asia." *Lancet (London, England)* 368 (9548): 1681–88. https://doi.org/10.1016/S0140-6736(06)69703-1.

Zinöcker, Marit K., and Inge A. Lindseth. 2018. "The Western Diet-Microbiome-Host Interaction and Its Role in Metabolic Disease." *Nutrients* 10 (3). https://doi.org/10.3390/nu10030365.

OTHER BOOKS IN THE SERIES

The Culinary Medicine Textbook: A Modular Approach to Culinary Literacy

Part 1: The Basics

Part 2: The Food

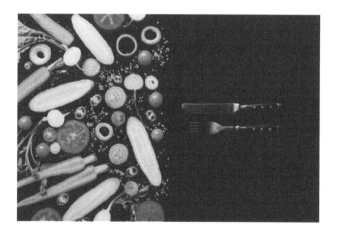

Part 4: The Kitchens

Part 5: The Specialties – Pregnancy, Lactation, Brain Health, Obesity, Heart Health, Seniors, Pediatrics, Athlete, Allergies/Intolerances, Diabetes, Intestinal Health, Immunity, Psychiatry, Cancer, and more

Made in the USA
Monee, IL
06 December 2024

72731627R00164